Moskitopanik!

Moskitopanik!

Mosquito fighters and fighter
bomber operations in the
Second World War

by

Martin W. Bowman

Pen & Sword
AVIATION

First published in Great Britain in 2004 by
Pen & Sword Aviation
an imprint of
Pen & Sword Books Ltd
47 Church Street
Barnsley
South Yorkshire
S70 2AS

ISBN 1 84415 025 9

A CIP catalogue record for this book is
available from the British Library

Typeset in 11/13 Sabon by
Phoenix Typesetting, Auldgirth, Dumfriesshire

Printed and bound in England by
CPI UK

For a complete list of Pen & Sword titles please contact
PEN & SWORD BOOKS LIMITED
47 Church Street, Barnsley, South Yorkshire, S70 2AS, England
E-mail: enquiries@pen-and-sword.co.uk
Website: www.pen-and-sword.co.uk

Contents

Acknowledgements

I am especially grateful to Eric Atkins DFC* KW; Chairman, the Mosquito Aircrew Association and all his members. Equally, I am indebted to Derek Carter in Denmark, who made available transcripts of the *Shellhaus* raid and associated material. The following people have also made it possible for me to include much diverse information and anecdotes on Mosquito operations: Michael Allen DFC; Don E. Aris; Norman Bacon; Squadron Leader R. K. Bailey; Tim Bates; John Beeching; David 'Taffy' Bellis DFC*; Gordon Bell-Irving; Theo Boiten; Lewis Brandon; Bob Bruce; Bob Collis; Hank Cooper DSO DFC; Patrick Corness; Ern Dunkley; Grenville Eaton; Al Gabitas; Revd. Nigel L. Gilson; Richard Goucher; Ken Greenwood; J. A. M. Haddon; Gottfried Hanneck; Lewis Heath; Vic Hester; Leslie 'Dutch' Holland; Bernard M. Job; R. E. 'Bob' Kirkpatrick; H. Mears; Paul Mellows; Dave McIntosh; Simon Parry, Air Research Publications; Graham Rice; Squadron Leader Derek Rothery; Walter Rowley DFC; Squadron Leader Philip Russell DFC; Mrs Edna Scholefield; Jerry Scutts; W. Knowle Shrimpton; Wilhelm Simonsohn; Ron Smith; Konrad 'Bob' Stembrowicz; Bob Symon; Jack Thompson; Les Turner; Harry Welham and Tim Woodman.

Glossary and RAF Slang
Terms in Common Everyday Use

10/10ths	Complete cloud cover
A 48	A 48-hour leave of absence
A Piece of Cake	Very Easy
A stooge	A boring flight
AA	Anti-Aircraft
AAA	Anti-Aircraft Artillery
Adj	Adjutant
ADLS	Air Delivery Letter Service
AF	Air Force
AFC	Air Force Cross
AI	Airborne Intercept
AM	Air Marshal
Anvil	Use of war-weary PB4Y-I Liberators as radio-controlled bombs
AOC	Air Officer Commanding
Aphrodite	Use of aged B-17s as radio-controlled bombs
ASH	AI.XV narrow-beam radar used for low-level operations
ASI	Air Speed Indicator
ASR	Air-Sea Rescue
AT	Airborne Interception (radar)
ATS	Air Training Squadron
AVM	Air Vice Marshal
Bang-on	Something very good or very accurate
Battle Bloomers	WAAF Issue Knickers – name originally given to them by the WAAFs themselves
BBC	British Broadcasting Corporation
Best Blue	Best uniform

BG	Bomb Group (USAAF)
Binding	Moaning, Complaining
Bird Sanctuary	WAAF quarters – usually well away from the rough airmen!
Blip	Radar echo or response
Blood Wagon	Ambulance
Bods	People, Bodies
Bogey	Unidentified aircraft
Bought it	Killed, failed to return
BS	Bomb Squadron (USAAF)
BSDU	Bomber Support Development Unit (RAF)
CCU	Combat Crew Unit
CH	Chain Home (early warning radar station)
Chaff	American Window
Cheese Cutter	Peaked Cap
Cheesed or Cheesed Off	Fed up, bored
CHEL	Chain Home Extra Low radar
Chiefy	Head of Aircraft Ground Crew – generally well respected
CHL	Chain Home Low
Clapped Out	Worn out, well past its best
CO	Commanding Officer
CoG	Centre of Gravity
Cookie	4,000lb Bomb
Crate	Aircraft
CRT	Cathode Ray Tube
C-scope	CRT showing frontal elevation of target
Day Ranger	Operation to engage air and ground targets within a wide but specified area, by day
DCM	Distinguished Conduct Medal
DFC	Distinguished Flying Cross
DFM	Distinguished Flying Medal
Dicey	Dangerous. A dicey do. An op when there was heavy opposition
Dicing (Dicing with death)	Mainly operational flying but sometimes, just flying. Are we dicing tonight? Are we on the Battle Order?
ditch	To land in the Drink
Diver	V1 flying bomb operation
Drem lighting	System of outer markers and runway approach lights
Drink	The sea
DSC	Distinguished Service Cross
DSO	Distinguished Service Order
Duff Gen	Bad information

Düppel	German code name for Window. Named after a town near the Danish border where RAF metal foil strips were first found
e/a	Enemy aircraft
Erks	Aircraftsmen – usually reserved for the lowest
ETA	Estimated Time of Arrival
Extracting the digit	Originally RAF slang term now in common use. In RAF it implied sitting on ones hands – politely
Fans	Propeller on aircraft. No fans – no engines.
FIDO	Fog Investigation and Dispersal Operation
Fire bash	100 Group Mosquito sorties using incendiaries/napalm against German airfields
Flensburg	German device to enable their night fighters to home in on *Monica* radar
Flieger	Airman (German)
Flight Offices	Usually occupied by the CO, Flight Commanders and their slaves
Flight	A Flight Sergeant
Flights	Where aircrew collected particularly on operational squadrons while waiting for the 'gen'. Cards and other games of chance were played here. More generally, any place around hangars where matters connected with flying took place.
Flying orifice	Observers Brevet – the polite versions
FNSF	Fast Night Striking Force
Freelance	Patrol with the object of picking up a chance contact or visual of the enemy
Fruit Salad	Lots of medal ribbons particularly on Americans.
Feldwebel	Sergeant (German)
GCI	Ground Control Interception (radar)
Gee	British medium-range navigational aid using ground transmitters and an airborne receiver
Get weaving	Get a move on – from aircraft taking avoiding action from fighters
Getting finger out	ditto
Going like the Clappers	Moving very fast indeed
Gone for a Burton	Killed, failed to return. It was never said that 'old so and so was killed last night'.
gong	Medal
Good Show	Done well
Got the chop	Killed, failed to return
Got the Gen	Have got the true information
GP	General Purpose bomb
Gruppe	German equivalent of RAF Wing
Gruppenkommandeur	Officer commanding a *Gruppe* (German)

H2S	British 10-cm experimental airborne radar navigational and target location aid
Had it	something coming to its end. For a person – 'He's had it' – he's died or is likely to
Hairy	Dangerous or very exciting
HE	High Explosive (bomb)
Heavies	RAF/USAAF four-engined bombers
HEI	High Explosive Incendiary
HMS	His Majesty's Ship
Hauptmann	Flight Lieutenant (German)
HRH	His Royal Highness
IAS	Indicated Air Speed
IFF	Identification Friend or Foe
Intruder	Offensive night operation to fixed point or specified target
IO	Intelligence Officer
JG	*Jagdgeschwader*: Fighter Group (German)
KG	*Kampfgeschwader*: Bomber Group (German)
Kite	Aircraft
KüFlGr	*Küstenfliegergruppe*: Coastal Flying Wing (German)
LAC	Leading Aircraftsman
Lichtenstein	First form of German AI radar
LMF	Lack of Moral Fibre
LNSF	Light Night Striking Force
LORAN	Long-Range Navigation
Leutnant	Pilot Officer (German)
Luftflotte	Air Fleet (German)
M/T	Motor Transport
Major	Squadron Leader (German)
Mandrel	100 Group airborne radar jamming device
MC	Medium Capacity bomb
MCU	Mosquito Conversion Unit
Meat Wagon	Ambulance
Met.	Meteorological
MG	*Maschinengewehr* Machine gun (German)
MO	Medical Officer
Monica	British tail warning radar device
MTU	Mosquito Training Unit
NCO	Non-Commissioned Officer
NFS	Night Fighter Squadron
Night Ranger	Operation to engage air and ground targets within a wide but specified area, by night
NJG	*Nachtjagdgeschwader*: Night Fighter Group (German)
Noball	Flying bomb (V1) or rocket (V2) site

OBE	Order of the British Empire
Obergefreiter	Corporal (German)
Oberleutnant	Flying Officer (German)
Oboe	Ground-controlled radar system of blind bombing in which one station indicated track to be followed and another the bomb release point
Oberst	Group Captain (German)
Oberfeldwebel	Flight Sergeant (German)
Oberfuehrer	Senior Colonel (German)
On a Fizzer	On a charge in front of senior
op	Operation
OSS	Office of Strategic Services. The US intelligence service activated during the Second World War and disbanded on 1 October 1945
OT	Operational Training
OTU	Operational Training Unit
Passion Bafflers	WAAF Issue Knickers – name originally given to them by the WAAFs themselves
Penguin	Non aircrew – often used for someone not popular
PFF	Pathfinder Force
Poor Show	Bad behaviour. Not done well
POW	Prisoner of War
PR	Photographic Reconnaissance
prang	a crash, usually of aircraft. To prang – to crash or to prang a target – to hit it well. A wizard prang – a good raid.
PRU	Photographic Reconnaissance Unit
Queen Bee	WAAF Commanding Officer
R/F	Radio Telephony
RAAF	Royal Australian Air Force
RAE	Royal Aircraft Establishment
RAFVR	Royal Air Force Volunteer Reserve
RCAF	Royal Canadian Air Force
RCM	Radio CounterMeasures
RN	Royal Navy
RNorAF	Royal Norwegian Air Force
RNVR	Royal Naval Volunteer Reserve
RP	Rocket Projectile
SASO	Senior Air Staff Officer
Scrambled Egg	Gold on caps of Senior Officers
SD	Special Duties
SEAC	South-East Asia Command
Second Dickie	Second Pilot
Serrate	British equipment designed to home in on *Lichtenstein* AI radar

Shaky Do	Near miss or lucky escape
Shoot a line	To brag, enlarge, blow ones own trumpet
SKG	*Schnelles Kampfgeschwader*: Fast Bomber Group (German)
Sky Pilot	padre
Snappers	Enemy Fighters
SOE	Special Operations Executive
Spot On	Something very good or very accurate
sprog crew	A new crew
Sprogs	New recruits
Staffel	German equivalent of RAF squadron
Staffelkapitän	Squadron Commander (German)
Stooge Around	Loiter. Hang around; fly around waiting for something to happen
Stores Basher	someone who worked in Stores
Suffering from the Twitch (particularly pilots)	To be avoided at all costs
TI	Target Indicator
TNT	TriNitro Toluene
'Torbeau'	Torpedo-carrying Beaufighter
Twitch	Nervy. Bags of twitch' – suffered when in danger particularly from fighters
UEA	Unidentified Enemy Aircraft
U/S	Unserviceable
Unteroffizier	Sergeant (German)
UHF	Ultra-High Frequency
USAAF	United States Army Air Force
VC	Victoria Cross
VHF	Very High Frequency
W/T	Wireless Telephony
WAAF	Women's Auxiliary Air Force
Waafery	WAAF quarters – usually well away from the rough airmen!
Wingco	Wing Commander usually Squadron Commanding Officer
Window	Metal foil strips dropped by bombers to confuse enemy radar
Wingless Wonder	Usually very unpopular non-aircrew
Y-Service	British organization monitoring German radio transmissions to and from aircraft
*	(medal) and Bar

Chapter One

Blunting the Blitz on Britain

By early 1942 RAF Bomber Command heavies were waging war on Germany while at home civilians continued to 'take it' from a number of night raids by the *Luftwaffe* on towns and cities in East Anglia. On 22 February Air Chief Marshal Sir Arthur Harris was appointed Bomber Command's new leader and for the rest of the war his name became synonymous with the attacks on German cities. A new directive calling for 'area bombing' of German cities had been sent to Bomber Command seven days before Harris' appointment. The Air Ministry decided that bombing the most densely built up areas of Germany's cities would produce such dislocation and breakdown in civilian morale that the German home front would collapse. With the new directive, bomber operations at night entered a new phase that was not restricted to one side of the divide. Following an attack by 234 RAF bombers on the old Hanseatic City of Lübeck on the night of 28–29 March Hitler ordered a series of *Terrorangriff* (terror attacks) mainly against English cities of historic or aesthetic importance, but little strategic value. In Britain they became known as the *Baedeker* raids, after the German guidebooks of the same name. Night after night terrified civilians were forced to cower in their cold and stinking Anderson shelters at the bottom of gardens in the weakly defended towns and cities in the west, south and east of the country while overhead the few RAF night fighters available struggled to blunt the terror attacks. Loss of life was heavy.

Though Britain's battered civilians did not know it, their only effective salvation from *Luftwaffe* attacks would be AI (Airborne Interception) radar equipped fighters such as the Beaufighter and the Mosquito. Radar equipped night fighters were desperately needed but in early 1942 both were in very short supply and were closely guarded secrets. Existence of the 'wooden wonder' would not be public knowledge until the night of 25 September 1942 when listeners to the BBC Home Service heard that this revolutionary new aircraft had made a daring roof-top raid on the *Gestapo* HQ in Oslo. Next day, the first photo of a Mosquito was published, along with a caption stating that 'armament may consist of four 20-mm cannon and four .303-in machine guns'. In fact, W4052, the Mosquito night fighter prototype, which was built to Specification F.21/40, had been the second of the de Havilland company prototypes to fly, on 15 May 1941. On 21 June the Air Ministry ordered five prototype Mosquitoes (one bomber, one PR and three fighter), nineteen PR models, and 176 fighters for RAF Fighter Command. 157 Squadron, which reformed at Debden, Essex, on 3 December 1941 under the command of Wing Commander Gordon Slade, became the first to operate the Mosquito night fighter. On 17 January 1942 157 took delivery of its first TIII at Castle Camps to begin work up on the new fighter but only fourteen NFIIs had arrived by the end of March. Six more were delivered in mid-April but three were not fitted with complete AI radar sets and only seven crews were trained to fly the aircraft.

At 20.15 hours on the night of 27–28 April 1942 twenty-eight German raiders were identified on radar heading for the historic city of Norwich and twenty Ju88s of *Kampfgeschwader (KG) 30* laid mines off the coast. Only three AI.V radar-equipped NFII Mosquitoes of 157 Squadron and nine Beaufighters and ten Spitfires were available to intercept and the city was not protected by enough anti-aircraft batteries. Though AI radar contacts were made none of the raiders were shot down. This was the first raid by *I/KG2* '*Holzhammer*' since converting to the Do217E. Together with *IV/KG30* and *II/KG40* from 23.40 hours to 00.45 hours they dropped forty-one tonnes of HE and four tonnes of incendiaries onto the Norfolk capital of over 126,000 inhabitants, killing 162 inhabitants, injuring 600 more and damaging thousands of buildings. Some reports said that the enemy bombers machine-gunned the streets. Anti-aircraft batteries were rushed to Norwich and gradually, more Mosquito IIs equipped with AI were sent to the squadrons.

Both attacks occurred out in the North Sea while the bombers headed for Great Yarmouth. On 30 May, another Do17 of *KG2* was almost certainly destroyed south of Dover by Squadron Leader G. Ashfield of 157 Squadron.

In July and August *III/KG2*, though heavily weakened, continued single daylight low-level bomber sorties or cloud cover 'pirate' raids on Britain. Several small-scale night raids also took place but 151 Squadron Mosquitoes destroyed four of the bombers. Off Spurn Head on 21–22 July Pilot Officer Fisher in W4090 accounted for Do217E-4 U5+IH of *I/KG2* flown by *Oberfeldwebel* Heinrich Wolpers. On 27–28 July Squadron Leader Pennington and Pilot Officer Field destroyed bombers flown by *Feldwebel* Richard Stumpf of *I/KG2* and *Leutnant* Hans-Joachim Mohring of *3./KG2*. Two nights later, on 29–30 July, when Birmingham was attacked, Do217E-4 U5+GV piloted by *Oberfeldwebel* Artur Hartwig of *II/KG2* was shot down by Flying Officer A. I. McRitchie and Flight Sergeant E. S. James.

On 22–23 August 157 Squadron was awarded its first confirmed victory when twenty miles from Castle Camps twenty-nine-year-old Wing Commander Gordon Slade, the CO, and his navigator Pilot Officer P. V. Truscott, shot down Do217E-4 U5+LP of *6./KG2*. Twenty-nine-year-old *Oberleutnant* Hans Walter Wolff, Deputy *Staffelkapitän*, and a pre-war *Lufthansa* pilot flew the enemy bomber.

In September 151 Squadron destroyed another two Dornier Do217E-4s. On 8–9 September when Bedford was attacked, Australian pilot Ian McRitchie destroyed F8+AP, on loan to *3./KG2* and flown by *Feldwebel* Alfred Witting. Then on 17 September during a raid on King's Lynn, Flight Lieutenant H. E. Bodien DFC downed U5+UR of *7./KG2* piloted by *Feldwebel* Franz Elias, which crashed at Fring where all four crew were made POWs. On 30 September 157 notched its first day combat victory when Wing Commander R. F. H. Clerke shot down Ju88A-4 off Holland. In October 157 Squadron scored three more victories over the *Luftwaffe*.

On 15–16 January 1943 during a German raid on Lincoln, Sergeants E. A. Knight RCAF and W. I. L. Roberts of 151 Squadron downed Do217E-4 U5+KR of *7./KG2* flown by *Leutnant* Günther Wolf, which crashed at Boothby Graffoe, killing everyone on board.

Over France on 17–18 January a Mosquito *Intruder* destroyed a Ju88A-14 of *I/KG6* (an experienced Pathfinder unit). Wing Commander C. M. Wight-Boycott, in a Beaufighter, destroyed a pair of Ju88s and a Do217 and damaged another Dornier. In October 1943 Wight-Boycott DSO took command of 25 Squadron equipped with the NFI at Church Fenton.

On 18–19 March *Fliegerkorps IX* attacked Norwich. Flight

Lieutenant D. Williams and Pilot Officer P. N. Dalton in a NFII shot down Do217 U5+AH (Werke No. 5523) of *I/KG2* flown by *Unteroffizier* Horst Toifel after the Dornier exploded in a huge ball of fire near Terrington St. Clement.

From 22.55 to 23.30 hours twenty bombers in *Fliegerkorps IX* dropped 18 tonnes of HE and 19.2 tonnes of incendiaries on Norwich with 3.3 tonnes falling on residential areas and factories. Meanwhile thirteen less experienced crews bombed Great Yarmouth on the coast. Flying Officer G. Deakin and Pilot Officer de Costa of 157 Squadron destroyed a Ju88, which crashed into the sea just off Southwold.

On 28–29 March 1943 *Fliegerkorps IX* again bombed Norwich. From 22.00 to 22.19 hours eighteen *Luftwaffe* machines scattered HE and incendiary bombs over Norfolk and Suffolk. Flying Officer J. R. Beckett of 157 Squadron shot down Dornier Do217E-4 U5+NM of *4./KG2* piloted by *Feldwebel* Paul Huth, which crashed into the sea just north of Yarmouth killing all the crew. The victory was shared with a 68 Squadron Beaufighter piloted by Flying Officer Vopalecky with Flight Sergeant Husar; both Czech.

On 14–15 April 1943 when the *Luftwaffe* raided Chelmsford, Squadron Leader W. P. Green and Flight Sergeant A. R. 'Grimmy' Grimstone of 85 Squadron destroyed Do217E-4 F8+AM of *4./KG40*. Off Clacton, Flight Lieutenant Geoff Howitt and Flying Officer George 'Red' Irving, shot down Do 217E-4 U5+DP of *6./KG2* piloted by *Unteroffizier* Franz Tannenberger. South-west of Colchester Flight Lieutenant James Gilles 'Ben' Benson DFC and Lewis Brandon DSO DFC of 157 Squadron brought down Dornier 217E-4 U5+KP of *6./KG2* piloted by *Unteroffizier* Walter Schmurr. The Dornier crashed at Layer Breton Heath near the town, after Schmurr and two of his crew had baled out.

On 16–17 April 1943 London was bombed. Focke Wulf 190A-4/U8 fighter-bombers of *Schnelles Kampfgeschwader (SKG) 10* each carrying a 250-kg or 500-kg bomb on its centreline, participated for the first time.

The main German bomber types raiding England were the Ju88 and Do217. On 24–25 April Flying Officer J. P. M. Lintott and Sergeant G. G. Gilling-Lax of 85 Squadron destroyed Ju88A-14 3E+HS of *8./KG6*, which fell in pieces at Bromley, Kent.

On 13–14 May 157 Squadron destroyed Do217E-4s of *KG2* flown by *Leutnant* Stefan Szamek and *Leutnant* Gerd Strufe. Sergeants R. L. Watts and J. Whewell of 157 Squadron destroyed Do217E-4 of

II/KG2 and it crashed near Colchester. A Do217K-1 of *4./KG2* piloted by *Unteroffizier* Erhard Corty was shot down near Norwich.

On 13 May 85 Squadron's Mosquitoes flew from Hunsdon to their new station at West Malling in Kent where they joined the Typhoons of 3 Squadron. They were replaced by 157 Squadron which moved from Bradwell Bay. During May 85 Squadron claimed eight enemy aircraft destroyed.

On the night of 16–17 May when Fw190A-4/U8 fighter-bombers of *I/SKG10* crossed the Straits of Dover the Typhoons were scrambled but the Mosquito crews were forced to wait for almost an hour before they could take off. Squadron Leader Peter Green and Flight Sergeant A. R. 'Grimmy' Grimstone shot down one of the Fw190s into the sea off Dover, after it had dropped his centreline bomb and was en route home to France. Geoff Howitt and 'Red' Irving destroyed a second Fw190 off Hastings.

Flight Lieutenant Bernard Thwaites and Pilot Officer Will Clemo pursued a Fw190 to the French coast before getting a recall signal but in mid-Channel they shot down a Fw190 and scored hits on another, claiming it as a 'probable'. Flying Officer I. D. Shaw and Pilot Officer A. C. Lowton flew through a 'friendly' searchlight area and destroyed a fifth Fw190 off Gravesend.

At West Malling celebrations continued until well into the early hours.

Soon there were more reasons for celebrations. On 19–20 May Flying Officer J. P M. Lintott and Sergeant G. G. Gilling-Lax, shot down a Fw190A of *2./SKG10*. Then, on 21–22 May Squadron Leader Edward Dixon Crew DFC* and Flying Officer Freddie French claimed a Fw190A over the sea twenty-five miles north-west of Hardelot.

On 29–30 May Lintott and Gilling-Lax destroyed Ju88S-1 3Z+SZ of *I/KG66* at Isfield, Sussex; the first Ju88S-1 lost over England. Just fifty of these speedy bombers were built; most examples, which first entered service with *I/KG66* at Chartres, being rebuilt versions of the A-4 with power-boosted BMW 801G-2 engines fitted with the GM-1 nitrous oxide injection system. Stripped of its ventral gondola and most of its armour and armament, with only a single MG13I machine gun, the Ju88S-1 was almost as fast as the Mosquito.

On 13–14 June Wing Commander John Cunningham DSO* DFC*, CO 85 Squadron, (with sixteen enemy aircraft shot down flying Beaufighters) and C. E Rawnsley scored their first victory in a

Mosquito when Fw190A-5 CO+LT of *3./SKG10* flown by *Leutnant* Ullrich was shot down, The Focke Wulf crashed at Nettlefold Farm, Borough Green near Wrotham; miraculously, Ullrich, who was hurled through the canopy survived and was taken prisoner. On 21–22 June Flight Lieutenant Bill Maguire and Flying Officer W. D. Jones of 85 Squadron shot down Fw190 GP+LA of *2./SKG 10*. On 9 July Lintott scored his fourth victory when he and Gilling-Lax destroyed Do217K-1 U5+FP of *6./KG2* flown by *Oberleutnant* Hermann Zink, which crashed at Detling killing all the crew. Lintott and Gilling-Lax were killed also when they were hit by the flying debris, the Mosquito crashing two miles from where the Dornier crashed.

On 13–14 July 1943 when *KG2* bombed Cambridge, Bunting and Freddie French destroyed Me410A-1 U5+KG of *16./KG2* crewed by *Feldwebel* Franz Zwißler and *Oberfeldwebel* Leo Raida. The *Hornisse* (Hornet), the first Me410 to be destroyed over Britain, fell into the sea five miles off Felixstowe.

Also on 13–14 July Do 217M-l U5+EL of *3./KG2* flown by *Unteroffizier* Willy Spielmanns was destroyed by a 410 (RCAF) Squadron Mosquito over the North Sea near the Humber Estuary. While flying an Intruder over Holland Flying Officer Smart of 605 Squadron shot down Do217M-1 U5+CK of *2./KG2* piloted by *Unteroffizier* Hauck, which was returning from a bombing raid on Hull and it crashed near Eindhoven. In all, *KG2* lost four Dorniers destroyed this night. On 15–16 July Flight Lieutenant Bernard Thwaites destroyed Me410 U5+CJ of *V/KG2* crewed by *Hauptmann* Friederich-Wilhelm Methner and *Unteroffizier* Hubert Grube off Dunkirk. Hull again was the target for the *Luftwaffe* on 25–26 July when Flying Officer Knowles of 605 Squadron destroyed Do217M-1 U5+KL of *3./KG2* piloted by *Leutnant* Manfred Lieddert. On 29–30 July when the *Luftwaffe*'s target was Brighton, twenty miles south of Beachy Head, Wing Commander Park of 256 Squadron destroyed Me410A-1 U5+BJ crewed by *Oberleutnant* Helmut Biermann and *Unteroffizier* Willi Kroger of *V/KG2*.

KG2 suffered one of its heaviest blows on 15–16 August when seven aircraft, six of them claimed by Mosquitoes, were lost during a raid on Portsmouth. Off Worthing Wing Commander Park destroyed two Do217M-ls flown by *Unteroffizier* Karl Morgenstern and *Unteroffizier* Franz Bundgens. He almost made it a hat trick on the night by claiming a Do217M-1, flown by *Unteroffizier* Walter

Kayser. Over France Flight Sergeant Brearley of 256 Squadron destroyed two Do217Ms flown by *Feldwebel* Theodor Esslinger, and *Leutnant* Franz Bosbach. Pilot Officer Rayne Dennis Schultz of 410 (RCAF) Squadron claimed Do217M-1 U5+GT of *9./KG2* flown by *Unteroffizier* Josef Schultes.

On 22–23 August Squadron Leader Geoff Howitt DFC and Pilot Officer J. C. O. Medworth of 85 Squadron destroyed Me410A-1, U5+AF of *15./KG2* crewed by *Feldwebel* Walter Hartmann and *Obergefreiter* Michael Meurer. The *Hornisse* crashed at Chemondiston. Meurer had baled out but Hartman's body was found in a field, his parachute unopened.

On the night of 24–25 August Captain Johan Räd and Captain Leif Lövestad of 85 Squadron in a NFXII claimed a Me410A-1 destroyed. One of two Hornets lost this night was U5+EG of *16./KG2* crewed by *Feldwebel* Werner Benner and *Unteroffizier* Hermann Reimers. This victory was officially shared with Wing Commander R. E. X. Mack DFC of 29 Squadron, which put in claims for two more enemy aircraft this night; the squadron's first Mosquito victories since converting from the Beaufighter.

On 6 and 8 September 85 Squadron brought down no less than five Fw190A-5s. Off Beachy Head on 15–16 September Flying Officer Jarris of 29 Squadron destroyed Me410A-1 U5+AF of *15./KG2* crewed by *Oberfeldwebel* Horst Muller and *Unteroffizier* Wolfgang Dose who raided Cambridge. South-east of Ramsgate Do217M-1 of *9./KG2* piloted by *Oberfeldwebel* Erich Mosler was destroyed by Flight Lieutenant Watts of 488 (RNZAF) Squadron, while Ju88A-14 3E+FP of *6./KG6* was shot down by Flying Officer Edward Hedgecoe and Pilot Officer J. R. Whitham of 85 Squadron. Their Mosquito was crippled by return fire and they baled out before the aircraft crashed at Tenterden, Kent. Flight Lieutenant Bunting destroyed a Ju88A-14 of *II/KG6*.

In October 85 Squadron's Norwegian pilots scored further victories. During a raid on the Humber Estuary on 2–3 October Pilot Officer Tarald Weisteen and Freddie French shot down two Do217Ks.

When the *Luftwaffe* raided London and Norwich on 7–8 October Flight Lieutenant Bill Maguire and Captain Leif Lövestad shot down a Me410A of *16./KG2*, crewed by *Feldwebel* Georg Slodczyk and *Unteroffizier* Fritz Westrich, the latter's body being buried at sea off Dungeness on 13 October.

Squadron Leader Bernard Thwaites and Will Clemo, who destroyed a Me410A of *14./KG2*, crewed by *Feldwebel* Wilhelm Sohn and *Unteroffizer* Günther Keiser, the *Hornisse* crashing at Ghent, saw Slodczyx and Westrich's 410 falling in flames into the sea and were able to confirm Maguire's victory. Off Clacton on 15–16 October Maguire and Flying Officer W. D. Jones destroyed Ju188 3E+RH of *1./KG6*. They also destroyed Ju188 3E+BL, also *1./KG6*, which crashed at Hemley, Suffolk, and was the first Ju188 brought down on UK soil.

On 8–9 October the first Ju88S-1 to be claimed by 85 Squadron occurred when ten intruders crossed the North Sea from Holland. Off Foulness Flying Officer S. V. Holloway and Warrant Officer Stanton destroyed 3E+US of *8./KG6* and ten miles south of Dover Flight Lieutenant Edward Bunting downed Ju88S-1 3E+NR of *7./KG6*. *Feldwebel* W. Kaltwasser, *Obergefreiter* J. Jakobsen and *Unteroffizier* J. Bartmuss all perished. On the night of 17–18 October Bunting and Flying Officer Freddie French claimed Me410 U5+LF of *15./KG2*.

The *Luftwaffe* attacked Chelmsford on the night of 10–11 December, with three of the four Do217Ms of *KG2* lost on the raid being credited to Flying Officer Rayne D. Schultz.

By 20–21 February 1944 Mosquito night fighters had, since the start of 1943, claimed just over 100 *Luftwaffe* bombers shot down. The *Luftwaffe* now became seriously depleted and new types such as the Heinkel He177 *Greif* (Griffon) were introduced to night operations. A few of these machines had operated in 1942 and some were flown on a night raid on London on 21–22 January 1944 when ninety-two enemy aircraft headed for the capital in the first of a series of revenge raids on Britain code-named Operation *Steinbock*. After take off the He177 crews usually climbed to height while still over their own airspace before penetrating the British defences in a shallow dive at about 400 mph. Even Mosquito crews found it difficult dealing with this type of approach. After attacking the *Grief*s would fly home at low-level.

The bombers, including fifteen He177A-3s of *I/KG100* were led by Pathfinders to London and *Düppel* (Window) was dropped in profusion by the raiders in an effort to confuse British radar. He177A-5 Werk No. 15747 of *I/KG40* became the first *Grief* destroyed over Britain when it was shot down by Flying Officer H. K. Kemp and Flight Sergeant J. R. Maidment of 151 Squadron, crashing at

Whitmore Vale, near Hindhead, Surrey. Flying Officer Nowell and Flight Sergeant Randall of 85 Squadron claimed a He177 of *2./KG40*. The first *Steinbock* raid cost the *Luftwaffe* twenty-one machines.

Units were rested until 28–29 January when sixteen Me410s and ten Fw190 fighter-bombers hit East Anglia, Kent and Sussex. An Me410 was shot down by a Mosquito but a defending fighter was also destroyed. The next night He177s of *3./KG100* and *I/KG40* formed part of the German raiding force of 285 enemy aircraft, which dropped their bombs right across Hampshire, the Thames Estuary and Suffolk. An AI.VIII radar equipped Mosquito of 410 (RCAF) Squadron, crewed by Lieutenant R. P. Cross RNVR and Sub Lieutenant L. A. Wilde RNVR fired at a Ju88A of *3./KG54* which might have been the same aircraft which crashed at Barham, Suffolk about this time was credited to the crew of a 68 Squadron Beaufighter.

On 3–4 February 240 German aircraft were abroad over London and south-eastern England but only seventeen reached London and fourteen failed to return thanks largely to six squadrons of Mosquitoes.

Flying Officer H. B. Thomas and Warrant Officer C. B. Hamilton of 85 Squadron in a NFXIII destroyed a Do217. The fourth victory this night was credited to Flight Sergeant C. J. Vlotman, a Dutchman and Sergeant J. L. Wood of 488 (RNZAF) Squadron who destroyed a Dornier over the North Sea, forty miles off Foulness Point, Essex.

The fourth significant *Steinbock* raid occurred on 13–14 February and Mosquitoes again returned victorious.

On 20–21 February ninety-five *Luftwaffe* bombers infiltrated the English coast between Hythe and Harwich and headed for London.

On 24–25 March Ju188E-1 U5+AN of *5./KG2* flown by *Unteroffizier* Martin Hanf was shot down forty-five miles south-east of Lowestoft by Flight Lieutenant V. P. Luinthune DFC and Flying Officer A. B. Cumbers DFC of 25 Squadron in a NFXVII. Hanf and his four crew were killed. In all ten German aircraft were claimed shot down by Mosquitoes this night. From 23 to 28 March 1944 Mosquitoes destroyed nine German bombers during attacks mainly on London and Bristol.

Rising losses forced *KG2* to begin using several other types even though *Oberst* Dietrich Peltz, 'Attack Leader England' favoured re-equipping *KG2* with the Ju88. Peltz disliked the Do217, considering it wholly unsuitable for night bombing and more suitable as a day bomber on the Eastern Front.

The last week of March was quieter, with only one large 100 aircraft enemy raid. April and May were less strenuous than February and March had been. In 410 'Cougar' Squadron for instance, the number of sorties, which had risen to over 130 for the earlier period, fell off to ninety-six for April and 109 for May. The number of enemy aircraft destroyed or damaged fell likewise. Only two aircraft were claimed as being destroyed and one damaged in the ten weeks preceding D-Day. The Canadians had Mosquitoes up on patrol or scrambled almost every night, but there were few contacts in the Cougar's area. There were only four contacts in April. Twice the raiders were too fast, although the Mosquitoes continued to chase them right up to the enemy held coastline. By contrast, the other two encounters were almost on the squadron's doorstep. On the night of 18–19 April, when the last 'Baby Blitz' raid was made on London about fifty *Luftwaffe* aircraft came over in a scattered raid, and eight victims were claimed by the Mosquito night fighters. Flight Lieutenants R. M. Carr and Saunderson of 25 Squadron at Coltishall shot down Ju188E-1, U5+DM, flown by *Hauptmann* Helmuth Eichbaum, a 4./KG2 off Southwold. A 5./KG2 Ju188E-1, U5+KN, piloted by *Feldwebel* Helmuth Richter, was shot down near Dymchurch by the CO 85 Squadron, Wing Commander Charles M. Miller DFC** and his radar operator, Captain L. Lövestad RNWAF.

On 18–19 April also two Ju88s were destroyed, by Pilot Officer Allen and Squadron Leader Green DFC of 96 Squadron. (On 11 August 1944 promoted to Wing Commander, Green took command of 219 Squadron in 2nd TAF where he and his radar operator Flight Lieutenant Douglas Oxby shot down nine enemy aircraft including three Ju87 *Stukas* in one night, 2–3 October 1944. On 1 March 1945, while testing a Mosquito Wilfrith Green DSO crashed near Amiens and was killed. Oxby, who was awarded a DSO at the end of the war to add to his DFC and DFM was the top-scoring radar operator having been involved in twenty-one successful AI interceptions in the Mediterranean and on the continent of Europe). The new CO, Wing Commander Edward D. Crew DFC*, shot down a Me410A-1 of 1./KG51 over Brighton. Flight Lieutenant J. A. Hall and Warrant Officer R. F. D. Bourke of 488 (RNZAF) Squadron each claimed a Ju88. Several of the raiders flew right over the Castle Camps sector with the result that 410 Squadron had an active night. Flying Officer R. J. Snowdon and Flight Sergeant A. McLeod got a contact a few minutes after they had been scrambled and held it through streams of

10

Düppel until the Mosquito had climbed to the raider's altitude. At 19,000 feet they caught sight of a Ju88 which, after some mild evasive jinking, was caught flying straight and level. A 100-round burst of 20-mm cannon fire knocked fragments from the cockpit and starboard wing, whereupon the Junkers turned over on its back and disappeared below. Some seconds later the crew noticed a large explosion and fire on the ground, about twelve miles from base, but it was not their Hun and they had to be content with credit for a damaged aircraft. They patrolled for ninety minutes without any further luck.

The explosion which Flying Officer Snowdon observed may have been the crash of He177 of *3./KG100* flown by *Feldwebel* Heinz Reis, which Flying Officer S. B. Huppert and Pilot Officer J. S. Christie shot down in flames at just about this moment near Castle Camps. They had taken off somewhat earlier on a searchlight cooperation exercise, which developed into the real thing when 'trade' appeared. Aided by a good searchlight intersection, they picked up a target, closed to a visual contact on a He177 heading for the London area, and let it have a long burst at 300 feet range. Debris from Reis' port engine struck the Mosquito, which received further damage in the starboard wing and aileron from an accurate burst fired by the Heinkel's rear gunner. For a moment Huppert lost sight of the big bomber as it peeled off, but he found it again thanks to the glow of a fire beginning to spread from the aircraft. He fired three more bursts, which smashed into the Heinkel as it began to go down. Then it burst into flames, stalled and went into a spin, exploding and blazing as it crashed near Saffron Walden. Another chase had to be broken off when the raider was engaged by the heavy ack-ack batteries of the London defences. These combats were the last made by the squadron from Castle Camps, as on 28 April it moved back to Hunsdon where it had been previously stationed for about two months in late 1943. The Cougars spent seven weeks there during the pre-invasion build up and two weeks of the Normandy campaign.

During 20–30 April Mosquitoes claimed sixteen enemy raiders destroyed as *Steinbock* raids were made on Hull, Bristol, Portsmouth and Plymouth by He177s, Ju188s and Do217s. Mosquitoes shot down nine raiders on 14–15 May when over 100 *Luftwaffe* raiders attacked Bristol. A 264 Squadron detachment was sent to West Malling for experience and in April the squadron moved under canvas. On 20 April forty miles ENE of Spurn Head Flying Officers

Corre and C. A. Bines shot down the Squadron's first Heinkel 177. May brought the expected and hoped for move on the 6th to Hartford Bridge. 264 Squadron lost no time in commemorating its lucky month for on 14–15 May Flight Lieutenant C. M. Ramsay DFC and Flying Officer J. A. Edgar DFM destroyed a Ju188 near Alton but they had to abandon their aircraft and Edgar was killed. On the 15–16th a Me110 was destroyed over the Channel by Squadron Leader P. B. Elwell and Flying Officer F. Ferguson. Mosquito fighters shot down a Ju188 and three Ju88s on 22 May when Portsmouth was again the target. On 28–29 May Wing Commander Cathcart M. Wight-Boycott DSO, CO 25 Squadron and Flight Lieutenant D. W. Reid destroyed Me410 9K+KP of *KG51* flown by *Feldwebel* Dietrich and *Unteroffizier* Schaknies. The *Hornisse* fell into the sea fifty miles off Cromer and the wreckage could be seen burning on the water from twenty miles away. It was the last day of the *'Baby Blitz'*. However, the respite from German attacks was brief.

In the summer of 1944 *V1* flying bombs began falling on London and the south of England. Incredible as it now seems, RAF Mosquito interceptor crews were not apprised of the coming *V1* threat even though the impending rocket blitz had been known about for over a year. It was on 12 June 1943, when Flight Lieutenant R. A. Lenton in a Mosquito took photos of a rocket lying horizontally on a trailer at Peenemünde, that the attention of RAF intelligence at Medmenham was aroused. On 23 June Flight Sergeant Peek brought back more photos of rockets on road vehicles for Medmenham so clear that news was relayed immediately to Prime Minister Winston Churchill. In August 1943 the RAF bombed Peenemünde but trials continued and by mid-June 1944 VIs were ready to launch against an unsuspecting London and southern England.

The first *V1* destroyed by a Mosquito was launched on 14–15 June 1944 and fell to Flying Officer Schultz of 605 Squadron from Manston, who was on a freelance sortie over the sea when he was passed by a 'queer aircraft' flying in the opposite direction. Schultz turned and gave chase, going through the 'gate' as he did so, and shot it down. He flew straight into the debris and returned to Manston with little skin left on his Mosquito. Over the coming weeks Tempests, Spitfires and Mosquitoes chased the 300–420 mph pilot-less bombs in the sky. Tempests of the Newchurch Wing destroyed 580 'Doodlebugs', as they were dubbed by the press or Divers as they were code-named, while Spitfire XIVs brought down a further 185.

NFXIIIs of 96 Squadron based at Ford shot down 174, and Mosquitoes of 418 Squadron, stationed at Holmsley South, Hurn and Middle Wallop, destroyed a further ninety. Ground batteries in the 'Diver Box' accounted for the rest.

Flight Lieutenant Vic Hester, a Mosquito pilot with 138 Wing at Lasham, recalls:

Word came down from Group HQ that the Prime Minister wanted a close-up cine film of a buzz bomb to show on Cinema newsreels, in an endeavour to reassure the public that this new German weapon did not baffle us. The fastest aircraft that could carry a trained cameraman equipped with a 35-mm cine camera was the Mosquito. DZ383 a modified B.IV Series II, which had an all-perspex nose, was occupied by a cine cameraman from Pinewood studios. The modified nose allowed the cameraman to squat and shoot his films at any angle. We also fixed up a 400ft-reel camera, fixed to shoot straight ahead. We rigged up a simple gun sight for the pilot so that he could operate this particular camera. Our task was to take 35-mm cine footage of selected raids by any squadron in 2 Group. This unusual Mosquito could carry either 4x500lb bombs in the fuselage or extra fuel tanks extending the range by some 300 miles. In fact these extra fuel tanks, when new, carried 80 gallons of Courage's Best Bitter to our colleagues stationed on B 5 landing strip near Bayeaux, France, in August 1944. I've continued to be amazed how short a time it took for the British Army & Air Force to consume over 600 pints of beer! We were not on the strength of any of the three squadrons that made up 138 Wing, so we could not use any known squadron letters on our aircraft, so a question mark was painted in place of a letter. The first attempt, by a Polish airman went wrong, as he got the question mark the wrong way round on one side!

Between 18 June and 3 July 1944 I piloted Flying Officer Oakley on sixteen flights in DZ383 and DZ414, flying mostly out of Biggin Hill, trying to get some good close-ups of these flying bombs. (We used two different Mosquitoes because our high speed dives were stripping off some of the fabric wing covering and the first aircraft had to go to Lasham for the airframe fitters to get to work with new fabric and the dope brush). Buzz bombs, or rather their launching pads were not new to us. We had been bombing them since the previous year. The main building of these launching pads was about the size of a small haystack plus the take-off ramp. There were perhaps over one hundred of these sites known in the RAF and US 8th & 9th Air force as Noball Sites. Over 90% were destroyed by allied airforces. Remembering the damage done in the south of England by the remaining 10% one cannot help thinking of the effect upon our war effort had the whole 100% been available to the Germans. 20% of these rocket sites were destroyed by Mosquito attacks. The German Ack-Ack defences of these rocket sites increased as the construction advanced until they became very heavily defended when they approached operational ability.

The buzz bomb was a liquid fuelled rocket and by the time they were crossing into southern England they would be flying at about 2 or 3,000 ft. and at a speed of about 350-mph. They were small and black and did not stand out as well as an aircraft. If you wanted to spot them easily you needed to be slightly lower than they were, so to catch them against the skyline; however if you followed such a procedure you had insufficient speed to catch them. How most flights ended up was that Spitfires would dive from about 5,000 ft. and if they spotted a target they would pull out of the dive when in line with the target, alert the Tempests, that were faster and they started from 7,000 ft and using the line of the Spitfire would dive to the attack. Our photographic Mosquito started diving from 10,000 ft and if we spotted a target would pull out of the dive at the last moment in an endeavour to maintain enough speed to keep up with the target for a short while. The 'G' forces experienced whilst pulling out of the dive made it almost impossible for the Cameraman to hold and sight the heavy 35 mm camera of the period. We took many pictures of the ground, with the occasional frame or two of a buzz bomb.

After about five days Oakley thought he might have got something worth processing, so after landing at Biggin Hill amongst all the balloons that were also trying to catch the buzz bombs, we rushed up to Shepherds Bush Film Studios to get our films processed. Whilst waiting, Oakley took me off to a local pub that he used regularly before the war. The landlord welcomed Oakley with considerable gusto and asked what he was doing in Shepherds Bush. Oakley told him that we had been trying to get a close up of a buzz bomb for some days. The landlord looked at his watch and then said that if we would accompany him to the roof of his five

14

storey building, in about ten minutes, there would be one passing over. We did in fact accept the offer and sure enough got the best shot so far achieved.

We did in the end, get a good air-to-air shot of a buzz bomb being shot down.

Bannock continues,

418 Squadron had been engaged in Night Intruding against enemy airfields as well as conducting low level Day Rangers against airfields when operating in pairs. On the night of 16 June 1944 we were departing on a Night Intruder sortie and while over Beachy Head at about 2,000ft we spotted what we thought was a burning aircraft flying at high speed below us and going inland. We called sector ops to alert them of the aircraft in distress but they replied that we were witnessing Hitler's new secret weapon, the V1 flying bomb. When we returned from our Intruder sortie there was great excitement in the op. room as several V1s had been dispatched towards London and 418 were assigned to patrol a sector of the English Channel from dusk until dawn starting the following night. We were to put up two aircraft for two-hour patrols. This was up to about 60% of the squadron strength for the next month.

There was V1 activity two nights later but as we were patrolling at 2–3,000ft and the V1s were travelling at about 400 mph between 500–1,000ft we were unable to catch up before the V1s crossed the coast. Our Mk VI Mosquitoes could only attain about 380 mph at full power. The following day Flight Lieutenant Don MacFadyen and I worked out some tactics of patrolling at 10,000ft and when we saw V1s being launched from their launching platforms on the French coast (there was a big flash when it was launched and then it streamed a flame approximately 15ft long). We headed for an intercept course over the Channel and turned our heading towards London until the V1 caught up directly below. We then dove on the V1 achieving a speed of approx. 430-mph, which gave us 20–30 seconds within gun range, before we decelerated and the V1 would pull away.

Bob Bruce and I vividly recall the occasion when we came up behind the first V1 that we intercepted from directly behind. Its pulsejet engine streaming a long flame reminded us of looking straight into a blast furnace. After picking up some small debris

15

from the first V1, we learned to attack from an angle-off of about 30 degrees. Each one that we destroyed exploded with a vivid white flash, which would temporarily blind us until we pulled away from the explosion. There was always a secondary explosion when the V1 hit the sea, which led us to conclude that only the fuel tanks exploded when hit with canon and mg. fire and the warhead exploded when it hit the sea. On one occasion we had an amusing experience when we only fired our 4 x .303 mg. (we were out of cannon ammo) and we only seemed to damage the autopilot. The V1 did a 180-degree turn, then the auto pilot righted it and we watched it continue southward and crash on the French coast.

As the V1s often came in salvos of 10 to 20 there was a general free for all with two or three aircraft diving on the same V1. There were four Mosquito squadrons on patrol so there were at least eight aircraft around at any time. Fearing collision we agreed that we would turn on our Nav lights when we were in a dive. Although there was a tremendous barrage of anti-aircraft fire along the south English coast we never saw a V1 shot down by anti-aircraft artillery although we saw several fly through the barrage. I learned after the war that the anti-aircraft had little success until they obtained the proximity fuse towards the end of the V1 threat from the French coast. 418 continued on V1 patrols until the launching sites were over run by the advancing 21st Army in August.

Bob Bruce adds,

Our first V1 destroyed was on 20 June. By 28 August we had destroyed 18 over the sea, and one whose speed was much reduced by our fire before we ran out of ammo. We were frustrated to watch it limp over the English coast before it exploded on the ground. As navigator, I had little to do but record the time and position of the kills, and recover those parts of my body, which had dropped into my boots as we pulled out of the dive. I was a victim of airsickness. It hit me on my first pre-training trip in a DH Dragon, pursued me through Nav training intermittently, and lasted into ops. I never found the cause; it was sometimes the aerobatics of the camera-gun practice, but I survived the strains of diving on V1s. It developed in straight and level flight, and blew away in the first whiff of action at Parow at sunrise. A real agony of psychology which reality banished in an instant. I always thought it an example of the highest toleration that Russ put up with my failings.

Everyone who flew in Mossies will know the benefit to crew co-operation of that close cockpit. Russ tells a story, which I am sure (I hope), is apocryphal, of a dive he was making on a ground target, when a left hand appeared to help him pull out! I can only speak for my own case, but crew co-operation was so close that Russ has consistently included me even in actions where my role was simply passive, and I am duly gratified.

Altogether, Mosquitoes accounted for 471 V1s with 418 Squadron flying 402 sorties and destroying eighty-three V1s; all but seven of them being shot down over the sea. This was fourteen per cent of the total V1's shot down. From July to 21 August, based variously at Hurn, Middle Wallop and Hunsdon, 418 Squadron, during the anti-Diver offensive, had destroyed no fewer than 123 V1 pilotless bombs.

VIs however continued to pose a big threat for some time to come. It had been intended that V1 flying bombs would rain down on Britain as part of the *Steinbock* offensive but, fortunately for the civilian population of this island, problems delayed the anticipated 'rocket blitz' until 13 June 1944. On this day ten V1s were catapult-launched at the capital from sites in north-eastern France. The *Vergeltungs-waffe 1* (Revenge Weapon No. 1), or Fieseler Fi103 *Kirschkern* (Cherry Stone), was a small pilotless aircraft with a 1,870-lb high explosive warhead, which detonated on impact. By the end of June 1944 605 Squadron had shot down thirty-six Doodlebugs and in July, the squadron destroyed a further twenty-nine. August started well for 264 Squadron with six VIs and a probable by the 10th of the month. Flight Lieutenants Beverley and Sturley had to bale out after being shot up by Allied flak during their successful chase of a VI. The former was injured as a result. By September the Allied advance had overrun launching sites in the Pas de Calais but the *Luftwaffe* mounted a new terror blitz by air-launching Doodlebugs from aircraft over the North Sea. By August, 410 VIs had been air-launched against London, Southampton and Gloucester, all of them being fired from Heinkel He111s of *III/KG3* based at Venlo and Gilze Rijen in Holland. In September 1944 the Allied advance forced *III/KG3* to abandon its bases in Holland and move to airfields in Germany. Only the radar-equipped Mosquito and Tempest V night fighter were able to counter the new threat. On 25 September Mosquitoes downed their first He111H22s over the North Sea, the 'kills' being credited to 'Mossies' of 409 and 25 Squadrons. Despite rising losses, during October *I/KG53 (III/KG3* redesignated) was joined by *II/KG53* and *III/KG53* for further air-launching of V1s. Of fifty Fi103s, which were air-launched from Heinkel He111s against Manchester on 24 December 1944, thirty crossed the coast, but only one actually exploded in the city. On the night of 6 January 1945 a Mosquito of 68 Squadron claimed the last shooting down of a Heinkel He111H-22. Altogether, about 1,200 *V1s* were air-launched against Britain, although of these only 638 approached the coast. *KG53* ceased operations having lost seventy-seven Heinkels, sixteen of them claimed by Mosquitoes.

Chapter Two

The Lone Rangers

Blenheim squadrons had pioneered offensive night fighting in June 1940, in much the same vein as 151 Squadron, operating Sopwith Camels had done in the First World War. In November 1939, 600 Squadron had become one of the first squadrons to use AI (Airborne Interception) radar (604 followed suit in July 1940). When the *Luftwaffe* began operating at night from France in 1940 the opportunity of attacking German aircraft on French airfields arose but the only suitable aircraft available were Hurricanes and Blenheims, and later Havocs and Bostons. By 1942 RAF bombers had begun to suffer increasing losses due to *Luftwaffe* night fighter interceptions and it was decided that RAF intruder aircraft roving over enemy airfields in France and the Low Countries could alleviate some of the attacks on the bomber streams. The first major support of bombers by night fighter squadrons was on the night of 30–31 May 1942 during the 1,000-bomber raid on Cologne when Blenheims, Havocs and Boston IIIs of 23 and 418 (City of Edmonton) Squadron RCAF, intruded over Holland. (In February 1943 418 converted to the Mosquito). No radar-equipped aircraft were used as its operation over enemy territory was still banned.

Mosquitoes were ideal for Intruder operations and the FBVI would eventually (in 1943), make possible Intruder sorties to as far afield as Austria and Czechoslovakia, but in 1942, squadrons re-equipping from other types had to soldier on with converted NFIIs with increased fuel capacity and bereft of their MkIV radar. There were few NFIIs that could be spared and any Mosquitoes that were available were welcome, whatever their pedigree. Starting in March 1943, C Flight in 85 Squadron at Hunsdon were presented with five NFXV high-altitude fighters, which had been pressed into service in response to the threat posed by the Ju86 high altitude bomber. The prototype (MP469) was the first Mosquito with a pressurized cabin, and first flew on 8 August 1942, later being fitted with AI.Mk.VIII radar, as were the four NFXVs built – all modified BIVs with two-stage 1,680hp Merlin 72/73 or 1,710hp 76/77 engines driving three or four-bladed air screws. The NFXV, which was capable of reaching heights of 43,000 feet, was armed with four .303-in machine guns in under-belly pack. In August the NFXVs were re-allocated to Farnborough for use in pressure cabin research. That same month 85 Squadron finally began Intruder patrols with the NFII. However, they would have to wait until October that year before getting their first scent of a kill, a Ju88 damaged and a Do217 probably destroyed.

The same state of affairs concerning conversion to the NFII persisted at Colerne where, in May, 264 (Madras Presidency) Squadron began their conversion. On 30–31 May Squadron Leader C. A. Cook and Pilot Officer R. E. MacPherson scored the squadron's first Mosquito victory when they shot down a Ju88A-4 of *KüFlGr 106* at North Malvern Wells. In December 1942 what few NFIIs were available carried out Night Rangers to airfields in France from Trebelzue, Cornwall. Rangers were low level operations on moonlit nights, mainly against railway rolling stock and road transport, although one could shoot down enemy aircraft if they were en-countered. Nightly 264 Squadron patrolled in the West Country and by day they operated in the Bay of Biscay and the Western Approaches. On 21 March, during a Bay of Biscay patrol, two Ju88s were destroyed, the second of which being the squadron's 100th German aircraft destroyed. On 29 March a He111 was probably destroyed during an Intruder patrol. April added nothing to the score but many locomotives and ground targets were damaged and destroyed. May saw the squadron at Predannack for Bay of Biscay patrols and Day Rangers (concentrating on Laon and Juvincourt), with fair success. June was excellent over the Bay. On the 13th a Fw190 was damaged after an encounter with three of the single-engined fighters. On the 20th a Ju88 was probably destroyed, and on the night of the 20th–21st 'a real picnic was enjoyed' as the squadron diarist wrote, by Wing Commander Allington when three Blohm und Voss seaplanes were sighted. A BV138 was destroyed in the air and two six-engined BV222s were destroyed in the sea with another BV138 destroyed on the water. Another BV222 was damaged and a minesweeper and hangars left in flames. Wing Commander Allington was awarded a bar to his DFC for leading the sortie. On 27–28 June a Do217 was claimed as 'damaged' and on the 28–29th, Flying Officer A.J. Hodgkinson forced down *Unteroffizier* Rudolf Blankenburg of *KG2* over Creil as he made for home in a Do217E-2 after a raid on Weston-Super-Mare.

July 1943 saw no combats. The first patrols of August 1943 included a successful attack on armed trawlers, one being destroyed. On the 7th 264 Squadron left for Fairwood Common, where they carried out Night Rangers and ASR cover patrols and on the 18th 264 dropped its first bombs on Laon airfield. Bomber support patrols were carried out from Castle Camps. During September detachments were sent there and to Bradwell Bay and for raids on enemy airfields, Coltishall and Ford were sometimes used. In November 264 operations largely meant liaison with the Navy at Swansea and a move to Exeter for Day Rangers; several trains were successfully attacked. On 17 November 264 Squadron moved again, this time to Coleby Grange in Lincolnshire and Coltishall was used as a forward base for bomber patrols. In mid-December 1943 264 moved to Church Fenton to re-equip with MkX AI equipment which it retained until after the end of the war.

Meanwhile in July 1942, 23 Squadron, which had received a TIII for training on 7 June, began conversion to the NFII at Ford but these aircraft were at a premium because of the need to equip home defence squadrons. Eventually, twenty-five of the modified NFIIs would be issued to 23 Squadron but for a time the only one available for intruding was 00670/S-*Sugar*. Appropriately, the squadron's first NFII Intruder sortie was flown in this aircraft on 5–6 July by the CO, the inimitable Wing Commander Bertie Rex O'Bryen Hoare DSO DFC*, and Pilot Officer Cornes. 'Sammy,' who sported a large handlebar moustache, 'six inches, wingtip to wingtip,' was one of the leading Intruder pilots of his generation having flown first Blenheims then Havocs on intruder sorties over the Low Countries. He succinctly described Intruder operations thus: 'I should like to tell you not to measure the value of this night fighter work over German aerodromes by the number of enemy aircraft destroyed. This is considerable, but our mere presence over the enemy's bases has caused the loss of German bombers without a shot being fired at them.'

Sammy Hoare's first NFII sortie however, proved somewhat

21

uneventful in that no sightings were made, but the night following, 6–7 July, he and Pilot Officer Cornes dispatched a Dornier Do217 sixteen miles east of Chartres with three short bursts of cannon fire. On 8–9 July Squadron Leader K. H. Salisbury-Hughes used *S-Sugar* to destroy a Do217 over Etampes and a He111 at Evreux. On 30–31 July Sammy Hoare in *S-Sugar* destroyed an unidentified enemy aircraft at Orleans. Intruding was dangerous work and as Sammy Hoare has written,

Night-fighter pilots chosen for intruder work were generally of a different type to the ordinary fighter pilot. They must like night-fighting to begin with, which is not everybody's meat. They must also have the technique for blind flying, and when it comes to fighting, must use their own initiative and judgement, since they are cut off from all communications with their base and are left as freelances entirely to their own resources. Personally I love it. Once up, setting a course in the dark for enemy-occupied country, one gets a tremendous feeling of detachment from the world. And when the enemy's air base is reached there is no thrill — even in big game shooting – quite the same. On goes the flare path, a bomber comes low — making a circuit of the landing field – lights on and throttle shut. A mile or two away, in our stalking Havoc, we feel our hearts dance. The throttle is banged open, the stick thrust forward, and the Havoc is tearing down in an irresistible rush. One short burst from the guns is usually sufficient. The bomber's glide turns to a dive – the last dive it is likely to make. Whether you get the Hun or miss him, he frequently piles up on the ground through making his landing in fright.

Sammy Hoare's first successful intruder in a Havoc, was on the night of 3–4 May when he got a He111 for sure and a Ju88 as a probable.

It was the night of the last big raid on London, and the Huns were streaming back to their bases in swarms. I got a crack at the Ju, as with navigation lights on, it came down to land [at Le Bourget]. The bullets appeared to enter the starboard engine and fuselage of the bomber. My onward rush carried us over the Ju, some 10ft above it, and as we passed my rear gunner poured a longish burst into the port engine. The bomber went into an almost vertical dive. She was only 800ft up, and it is practically impossible that the pilot could have pulled out of the dive, apart from the fact that both his engines were damaged. But we only claimed the Ju as a probable.

After this, all the aerodrome lights were turned off. We climbed away and the lights came on again. So we bombed the aerodrome, and large fires resulted. The aerodrome lights were again put out. But there were numerous bombers still trying to land. We came down to 1,000ft again and met a He 111. I opened fire close in. The bullets entered one engine and the fuselage. After a second burst smoke poured from both engines, and it went into a steep, sideslipping turn. As we passed beneath her, the gunner put in another burst.

On 8–9 September three Mosquitoes were lost on Intruder sorties over the Continent. Then, on 10–11 September, Sammy Hoare and J. F. Potter, flying *B-Bertie*, destroyed another UEA twelve miles south of Enschede. On occasion, 157 Squadron at Castle Camps flew NFII sorties over the Continent, and on 30 September Wing Commander R. F. H. Clerke, in DD607, destroyed a Ju88A-4 thirty miles off the Dutch coast. In December 1942 23 Squadron was posted to Malta for Intruder operations against the Axis. Sammy Hoare left 23 Squadron prior to its departure overseas to set up a specialized Intruder training school at No. 51 OTU at Cranfield, Bedfordshire.

In February 1943 605 Squadron at Bradwell Bay began replacing its Bostons and Havocs with the NFII. On 16 February 151 Squadron, which had equipped with the NFII at Wittering in April 1942, began Night Intruder operations over France flying Mosquitoes fitted with Monica, a tail warning device. 151 continued to fly Night Ranger operations over the Continent, from May to 1943–April 1944 using NFXIIs, attacking all targets. Also during February NFIIs of 410 Squadron RCAF, the third Canadian night fighter squadron to be formed, had moved south from Acklington to Coleby Grange for Night *and* Day Rangers.

The moon period of March came and went while the Night Rangers cursed the weather, which made it impossible for them to operate. Nine Day Ranger sorties were dispatched on the 26th, 27th and 30th but eight were aborted at the Dutch coast because of unsuitable weather. The danger appertaining to these operations was borne out on 6 April, when Flight Lieutenant C. D. McCloskey, one of the Squadron's original members, and Pilot Officer J. G. Sullivan, were shot down and taken prisoner of war. Four days later Flying Officer

J. E. Leach and Flying Officer R. M. Bull were killed in action over Friesland. Ranger operations began again when the moon period arrived in mid-April, and on the night of the 15th, the CO, Wing Commander Frank W. Hillock, headed for the Ruhr. The weather was poor and, as the Mosquito skipped along at 300 feet over Holland, Hillock suddenly saw the eight radio masts of Apeldoorn station rushing towards him. There was no time to climb, and no room to fly between them, so he threw the Mosquito on its side and ripped through the antennae, tearing away several wires. On return to Coleby Grange it was found that one wing tip had been sliced off, and the other wing had been cut through to the main spar before the wire had broken; about 300 feet of well-made ¼-in copper cable was trailing behind the Mosquito! Despite this shaking experience, Hillock had coolly flown to his target before coming home. (Hillock completed his tour on 20 May and was succeeded by Wing Commander G. H. Elms).

Over the next four nights crews located a convoy off the Dutch coast suitable for a naval attack, strafed barges in Holland and a factory in Rees, and strafed rail yards at Cleve. On 20 April Flight Sergeant W. J. Reddie and Sergeant Evans went missing. There then followed a week of poor weather, which made it unsuitable for Rangers. Operations resumed again on the 30th and during the moon period in May 410 Squadron extended its sphere of operations to include France and Belgium. Taking off at 14.15 hrs on the afternoon of 27 April, Pilot Officer W. A. Cybulski and his navigator, Pilot Officer H. H. Ladbrook, struck across the North Sea to Vlieland. They turned south-east past Stavoren to Mepple where they altered course eastwards and, hedge-hopping across northern Holland, reached Meppen, just across the German border. Here they flew down to the Ems canal to Papenburg and then turned westward for home where they landed at 17.27 hrs after covering more than 600 miles. Flying down the canal and railway lines between Meppen and Papenburg, the Mosquito attacked five targets. First Cybulski damaged a tug and two barges, from which debris flew into the air, and then he riddled a locomotive and raked a line of six freight cars. Two military buses were shot up and, to end the strafe, pieces were shot off another locomotive which was left wreathed in clouds of steam. Newspapers heralded the record flight but the pilot's name had to be suppressed lest it bring reprisals upon his relatives in Poland. Cybulski's home was in Renfrew, Ontario, but his grandparents were Polish.

24

On 7–8 May 1943 418 Squadron RCAF, still predominantly equipped with Bostons and Havocs, flew its first Mosquito sortie, when Pilot Officer Tony Croft claimed a Ju88 destroyed in the Melun-Britigny area. In May the Canadian squadron took delivery of its first FBVI and on 27–28 June Squadron Leader C. C. Moran claimed a Ju88 and a He111 destroyed at Avord. Moran also blasted a train and bombed a radio mast. By the end of the summer Moran had earned something of a deserved reputation as a train-buster, his technique usually consisting of a strafing run to stop the locomotive and then finishing off the stopped train with bombs. Between 14–29 May Cougar Squadron flew ten Night Intruder and fourteen Night Ranger sorties. Enemy airfields were patrolled in support of Bomber Command operations, though these proved to be uneventful. Seven of the Ranger crews found targets to attack, mainly locomotives and their wagons. Fourteen locomotives, eleven freight cars, and several barges were claimed as destroyed, Butch Bouchard and Fyfe, a very good team, who were on their sortie to the Dummer Lake area on 15 May, made a spectacular haul of five locomotives and eleven freight cars.

Meanwhile in April, 604 Squadron at Scorton converted to the NFXIII and 256 Squadron began equipping with the NFXII. They were followed, in May, by 29 Squadron who did likewise. 456 Squadron RAAF, which was largely equipped with Beaufighter VIfs, in February-March began to include some NFII Ranger operations in addition to their day fighting role, first from Middle Wallop and then from Colerne. From late May they were successfully employed on Intruder sorties over France attacking railway rolling stock and intruding on French airfields. In May 1943, 60 OTU at High Ercall was expanded and made responsible for all Intruder training. Flight Lieutenant Tim Woodman, who flew Beaufighters and Mosquitoes on Intruder operations, recalls,

> Individually in the moonlight we crossed the Channel into France. The French Resistance informed us that the midnight passenger train out of Paris to Rouen was normally packed with German troops returning from leave. Shooting up the engines resulted in the first passenger coaches also being hit. The Resistance then informed us that, because of this, the rear coaches were reserved for officers, so we shot up the engine (steam would sprout out like hosepipes and the engines would be put out of action and the lines

blocked for some time), then came round again and shot up the rear coaches. The cine film had large trees silhouetted against the moonlight.

Predannack was also used by a detachment of 25 Squadron NFIIs detached to 264 Squadron. (25 Squadron had received NFIIs in October 1942 and had started freelance Ranger sweeps over the continent).

In June Mosquitoes of 456 RAAF and 605 Squadrons began successful, albeit small scale, Bomber Support 'Flower' attacks on German night fighter airfields during raids by main force bombers. Flowers supported bombers by disrupting enemy Flying Control organizations. Long range Intruder aircraft fitted with limited radar equipment were used, and these proceeded to the target at high altitude, diving down whenever they saw airfields illuminated. This type of operation if correctly timed, prevented the enemy Night Fighters who were already short of petrol from landing at their bases.

One of the Mosquito crews rapidly making a name for themselves on offensive night fighting patrols at this time was that of Flight Lieutenant James Gillies Benson DFC and Flight Lieutenant Lewis Brandon DSO DFC of 157 Squadron. On the night of 3–4 July 1943, using OO739, a NFII, they shot down a Do217 over St Trond. On 13–14 July Flying Officer Smart of 605 Squadron, flying a NFII, destroyed a Do217M-1 near Eindhoven. In July 456 and 605 Squadrons re-equipped with the FBVI for Intruding and 418 Squadron flew the last of its Boston sorties and concentrated on Flower operations using the FBVI.

For 410 Squadron June 1943 was a rather quiet and uneventful period as far as scrambles and Rangers were concerned. Coastal Command anti-submarine operations in the Bay of Biscay were being hampered by enemy counter air activity and 410 Squadron was requested to supply fighter support. (Another 410 Intruder detachment was temporarily established at Hunsdon). Four crews were detached to Predannack for Instep patrols in company with Polish crews from 307 Polish Squadron, who began flying Night Rangers, and 456 Squadron RAAF. The Cougar crews remained at Preddanack for a month and flew twenty patrols lasting between four-five hours' duration. On the afternoon of the 13th Pilot Officer R. B. Harris and Sergeant E. H. Skeel were accompanied by three other Mosquitoes on patrol, when SW of Brest the formation intercepted four Ju88s.

Fw190s then arrived on the scene and three aircraft, including the 410 Squadron crew, were shot down. The next morning, Pilot Officer's J. Watt and E. H. Collis, with three Polish crews, sighted five U-boats in the bay. When the Mosquitoes were sighted they drew into a tight defensive circle. Two of the Mosquitoes attacked the U-boats, which sent up a considerable amount of flak. Strikes were made on the conning towers of the U-boats, and one Mosquito was damaged by flak. All the aircraft returned safely to Predannack.

On the 19th on another patrol with 307 Squadron Flying Officer's E. A. Murray and P. R. Littlewood of 410 Squadron encountered a Bv138 flying boat as they zig-zagged at low level over the Bay of Biscay. The Mosquitoes made two line astern attacks on the Bv138, which attempted to climb into cloud cover. On the first attack one engine was hit and began to smoke; the aircraft being unable to gain height nosed down towards the sea. On the second attack the starboard engine was hit and caught fire. The aircraft then crashed into the sea. Three crew emerged and scrambled into a dinghy. The last action occurred on 21 June when Pilot Officer C. F. Green and Sergeant E. G. White were members of a patrol which attacked two small armed merchant vessels or trawlers, both of which were damaged.

July 1943 was a month of high activity, thanks in considerable measure to enemy activity. On the 12–13th, four Mosquitoes of 410 Squadron were scrambled from Coleby Grange to intercept an enemy raid on Hull and Grimsby. Squadron Leader A. G. Lawrence DFC and Flight Sergeant H. J. Wilmer intercepted a Do217 over the mouth of the Humber, but after taking violent evasive action it got away after the crew had fired only one short burst at it. Flares, ack ack and searchlight activity made it impossible to continue the chase. The crew was then vectored onto another Do217 and following an AI contact and visual identification, the enemy aircraft was given a short burst of cannon fire. This had no effect and a second burst was given. This caused a huge flash in the Dornier's starboard engine, followed by clouds of smoke. In a diving turn with the engine glowing brightly, the bomber went down, hitting the sea with a great splash. The enemy gunners had returned fire but the streaks of red and white tracer passed under the Mossies' starboard wing. On the following night six crews were scrambled but no contacts were made.

Early in July, 410 Squadron received six FBVI bombers for use on Intruders and Ranger operations. Flight Lieutenant Murray took charge of a special section formed to carry out these activities, the first sortie being made on the 15th. On a Night Ranger to France from Ford, on the 18th, Pilot Officer L. A. Wood and Flying Officer D. J. Slaughter, failed to return. Poor weather prevented any further ops until the night of the 25th, when two crews went on Flower sorties (Bomber Command support), to Deelen airfield, in Holland. The first crew, Norman and Hunt, saw visual *Lorenz* lit three times during their patrol and noticed bombs fall on or near the aerodrome, starting fires. An hour later they were relieved by Murray and Littlewood. Approaching Deelen, after orbiting a dummy aerodrome for a few moments, the crew saw an aircraft come in and land. Thirty minutes later a second Hun appeared, flicking his navigation lights on and off. The crew came in behind a Do217 and fired a three second burst at the aircraft. Searchlights coned the Mosquito while the flak guns opened up. The port engine of the Dornier caught fire, and lit up by five searchlights, it veered to the left, crashed and exploded in flames on the airfield boundary. As the crew continued to circle the airfield, a third aircraft made a hurried landing and on reaching the end of the runway the navigation lights were turned on. Murray came down in a sharp diving turn and fired a long burst at the aircraft, damaging it. The navigation lights were quickly doused, and the enemy ground defences immediately came into action again.

Patrols were made on three nights between 28–30 July to Schleswig/Jegel, Gilze-Rijen and Venlo airfields, all without success. The Cougars suffered a severe blow on the 30th when Flight Lieutenant E. A. Murray and Flying Officer P. R. Littlewood were killed at Honiley, Warwickshire when flying an Oxford on a navigation flight. Murray, a native of Stelleraton, Nova Scotia was deputy flight commander of B Flight whilst Littlewood came from Saanichton, Vancouver Island, BC.

In August 1943 when it was realized that the *Luftwaffe* were operating radar equipped night fighters against the 'heavies' of Bomber Command, some AI equipped Beaufighters and Mosquito night fighters were released over enemy territory on Mahmoud operations as bait for enemy night fighters in their known assembly areas. With centimetre AI being used in Mosquitoes it was necessary to fit Monica tail warning devices, as the later marks of AI did not scan to the rear. Mosquitoes pretending to be bombers were not successful as the enemy soon recognized their speed difference. Nevertheless, on 15–16

August Flight Sergeant Brearley of 256 Squadron, flying a NFXII, destroyed two Do217M-1s over France.

On 15 August two Rangers were made from Castle Camps to St Dizier airfield. Lawrence and Wilmer dropped two 250lb bombs on the runway and, on the return flight, attacked a train near Paris. Pilot Officer Rayne Dennis Schultz and Flying Officer A. A. Williams in FBVI HP849 did not reach St Dizier. Instead they attacked three loco-motives between Clermont and Poix and they bombed a bridge. On their way home some twenty miles off Beachy Head they spotted another aircraft, and on closing, found it to be a Do217M-1. The Do217 under gunner opened accurate fire on the FBVI and the enemy pilot tried to shake off the Mosquito. A long pursuit followed. Schultz's second burst hit the cockpit where fires broke out and debris fell away. Three, perhaps four, of the crew were seen to bale out; then the Dornier turned for France in a shallow controlled dive. Schultz fired again, the starboard wing and engine broke away and, completely enveloped in flames, the bomber hit the sea where it continued to burn brightly. After taking some cine films of the scene and reporting the position of the crew, Schultz headed for home to report their first victory. Ranger sorties were flown on the 16th, 17th, 18th, 23rd, 27th and 29th (daylight); Flying Officer's G. B. MacLean and H. Plant were lost on the 18th over Germany. There were also a number of scrambles, the most significant being on the 31st when five crews were dispatched – only one contact was made. Flying Officer F. W. Foster and Pilot Officer J. H. Grantham were hit by enemy cannon and machine-gun fire shortly after becoming airborne. Foster took immediate evasive action by climbing to 10,000 feet, and the contact was lost.

On 17–18 August Flight Lieutenant D. H. Blomely of 605 Squadron in a FBVI destroyed a Bf109 east of Schleswig and on 22–23 August a 29 Squadron NFXII crew in HK164 destroyed a Me410A-1 north of Knocke. Blomely was credited with another victory on 21 September, when he destroyed two Ju88s west of the Skaggerak.

For 410 Squadron at least the first three weeks of September were somewhat quieter than August. Ranger sorties were cancelled, but Flower ops continued. Fifteen sorties were made between 3rd and 16th, attacks were made on St Michel, and Laon airfields and against railways targets. Pilot Officer J. E. Fisher and Sergeant D. Ridgeway failed to return from Melun on the 16th. This was the last night of FBVI ops, which were transferred. Ranger and Flower ops ceased and in their place Mahmoud, or offensive patrols over specific points in search of enemy aircraft were made. Two specially equipped Mk II's were used for these activities. During the period 17–23 September only a number of fruitless scrambles were undertaken and on the 24th 410 Squadron started Mahmoud operations, but these were not successful until the night of 27–28 September. Flight Lieutenant M. A. Cybulski and Flying Officer H. H. Ladbrook, flying NFII D7757, made a Mahmoud patrol of the Zeider Zee and Meppen area from Coleby Grange. The ninety minute patrol was unsuccessful but on the way home an AI contact was made on a Do217 which was then located flying east. The enemy pilot went into a steep climb with the Mosquito closing rapidly. A three-second burst was fired and the enemy aircraft immediately exploded with a terrific flash and descended enveloped in flames. Burning petrol and oil flew back onto the NFII, scorching the fuselage from nose to tail, the port wing inboard of the engine, the bottom of the starboard wing, the port tailplane and the rudder, from which the fabric was torn away. Pieces of the Dornier struck the port oil cooler, resulting in the loss of oil and making it necessary to shut down the engine. Cybulski was completely blinded and Ladbrook had to take control of the aircraft for about five minutes until the pilot regained normal vision. Course was set for base and the seriously damaged aircraft completed a hazardous 250-mile single engine return. The crew received immediate DFC awards. A further eight more Mahmouds were completed, all without incident, and between the 1st-19th, twenty-six scrambles were made. Coleby Grange was made unserviceable one night by enemy bombing activity. 410 Squadron moved from its base to West Malling having completed a total of 286 sorties of which 125 had been scrambles, seventy-eight Rangers, forty-nine Intruders and Flowers, twenty Insteps, and twelve Mahmouds; nine crews had been lost on operations and two in flying accidents. 410 Squadron moved again, to Hunsdon, October 1943, then Castle Camps where regular patrols were flown in defence of southern England.

By September 605 Squadron were flying Intruder sorties over Denmark and Germany. That same month Sammy Hoare assumed command of the Squadron and he returned to combat operations on 27–28 September whereupon he promptly dispatched a Do217 at Dedelsdorf; his seventh confirmed air to air victory. (On 10–11 January 1944 Sammy Hoare scored the County of Warwick Squadron's 100th victory when he and Flying Officer Robert C. Muir in an FBVI shot down a Ju188 four miles east of Chievres. Sammy claimed a probable and damaged three aircraft in 1944 and shot down his ninth and final aircraft in March that year).

Intruder victories were now hard to find, and in fact none were recorded until Flight Lieutenant Blomely DFC destroyed a Bf110 twenty-five miles west of Aalborg on 9 November, and Wing Commander Roderick A. Chisholm DFC and Flight Lieutenant F. C. Clarke of the FIU, in NFII HJ705, destroyed a Bf110 at Mannheim on 18–19 November. In November 1943, a 307 Squadron detachment at Sumburgh, Scotland carried out raids over Norway, destroying two He177s and a Ju88. When they returned south they continued intruding and later flew Bomber Support operations until March 1945.

Chapter Three

The Hungry Hun Hunters
of 100 Group

In late 1942 and early 1943, whilst commanding 89 (Night Fighter) Squadron Detachment in Malta, we were intruding on North African Supply Routes at night, and also into Sicily and Southern Italy. Besides monitoring German aircraft take-offs and landings from the Sicilian airfields, we were beating up convoys on the North Africa German supply lines, and also the railway into Messina in South Italy. In May 1943 I was posted home to Fighter Command, to a newly created post of Fighter Operations 3(c), which was to organize Intruder Operations at night from England to the Continent. For this I had my own operations room next to the Main Operations Room at Fighter Command. Many Squadrons were involved in these operations, the main aerodromes used were Hunsdon and Ford.

During this period, Malvern came up with a new 'toy' – Serrate. This was a method of homing onto the German IFF, which was particularly useful at night. It was decided to equip three squadrons of Mosquitoes to undertake the job of protecting night bomber forces in their raids. I asked the AOC-in-C if I could have one of them, and he agreed that I could have 239 Squadron and convert it from Mustangs to Mosquitoes. It was decided that the three Squadrons, 141, 169 and 239 should go to 100 Group in Bomber Command, as the job was so closely connected with Bomber Command Operations. We converted with 169 Squadron at Ayr in Scotland in October and did our training at Drem with a training Flight Commanded by Squadron Leader Vernon

Motion. When we were operational, 239 was posted to West Raynham to join 141 Squadron, which was already operating there and 169 went to Litttle Snoring also in Norfolk. It can be said that the total operation was very successful; we had many victories against the German Night Fighters. 239 was the most successful of the three squadrons and their scoreboard is now in the Bomber Command Museum at Hendon, in the corner reserved for 100 Group.

Night Intruder Operations by Wing Commander Paul Evans DFC, CO, 239 Squadron September 1943–September 1944

100 (Bomber Support) Group had been formed on 8 November 1943 under the command of Air Commodore (later AVM) E.B. Addison after it was obvious to all that the RAF needed a specialized bomber support force. The task of 100 Group, based in Norfolk, was two-fold; its heavy bomber squadrons being used on radio counter-measures (RCM) and 'spoofing' operations, while its Mosquito squadrons were used on loose escort duties for the main force as well as night intruder operations. Eventually, eight night fighter squadrons were wholly equipped, while 192 Squadron was equipped with Mosquito IV, Halifax and Wellington X aircraft for the ELINT (Electronic Intelligence) role (monitoring German radio and radar). Throughout 1944 and early 1945 192 Squadron crews listened in on enemy radio frequencies and jammed enemy VHF transmissions. They even afforded RAF control of German fighters.

First to join 100 Group was 141 Squadron which, in June 1943, had started using Beaufighter VIfs fitted with Gee, AI (Airborne Intercept) Mk.IV, and Serrate equipment. The latter enabled the crew to 'home in' on radar transmissions from German night fighters and was used in conjunction with AI Mk.IV. In September the Serrate apparatus was installed in 141 Squadron's first NFII aircraft and the squadron joined 100 Group at West Raynham on 4 December. Many of the NFIIs supplied to 100 Group were war-weary, many of whose engines often proved unreliable and maintenance and radar problems were many. On 10 December 239 Squadron, who also received NFIIs, joined them. Then 169 and 515 Squadrons transferred to 100 Group at Little Snoring. The first 100 Group operation was flown on the night of 16–17 December 1943 when two Beaufighters and two NFIIs of 141 Squadron supported the main force raiding Berlin.

The first Mosquito victories occurred on the night of 28–29 January 1944, when Flying Officer Harry White DFC and Flying Officer Mike Allen DFC shot down a Bf109 near Berlin and Flying Officer N. Munro and Flying Officer A. R. Hurley of 239 Squadron got a Bf110, also near Berlin. On 30–31 January Flight Lieutenant G. J. Rice and Flying Officer J. G. Rogerson of 141 Squadron destroyed a Bf110 and Squadron Leader Joe Cooper and Flight Lieutenant Ralph Connolly shot down a Bf110 in the Brandenburg area. 169 Squadron had flown its first operation on Mosquitoes on the night of 20 January 1944, supporting the main stream bombers attacking Berlin. In February 1944 four more enemy night fighters were shot down by 141, 169, and 239 Squadrons. One of the pilots in 239 Squadron was David 'Taffy' Bellis DFC*:

It was in January 1944 that I first heard of 100 Group. I was stationed at TRU Defford, nr Worcester, at the time and was on rest after completing a tour of ops at Malta with Denis Welfare. Defford was basically a research station at which new airborne electronic equipment was being tested and life was pleasant, but rather boring. I flew about 10 hours a month and there was plenty of time for bridge and sampling the beer and food at the local pubs – especially the 'White Lion' at Upton-on-Severn.

By the end of 1943 I longed for an operational squadron again, for the camaraderie that went with it and for the addictive excitement of flying over enemy territory. Thus it was with relief that I was told in January that my posting had arrived. I remember reading the signal from the Air Ministry – it read something like You are posted to 100 Group and you will report to O/C 239 Squadron at West Raynham as soon as possible. I had never heard of 100 Group before – nor had other aircrew at Defford. We all thought there was a mistake – there could not be 100 groups in the RAF! Jumbo Harkness, one of the flight commanders at Defford, said that 239 was a Special Duties Squadron and I had visions of flying VIPs or even dropping agents over occupied Europe.

Denis Welfare had received the same posting and we arrived at West Raynham, where we soon found what 100 Group was about. By the autumn of 1943, a large part of the *Luftwaffe* had been concentrated over Western Europe and its night fighters had developed tactics and electronic equipment that were causing serious losses to RAF bombers on their night operations over

Germany. Consequently, 100 Group was formed as a matter of urgency to counteract the *Luftwaffe* night fighters by jamming their ground control, organizing spoof raids and by attacking the night fighters at their bases and in the air.

When we arrived at West Raynham, 239 Squadron, which was previously on low level reconnaissance, was being reformed and re-equipped with Mosquito IVs for offensive night fighting. Like other crews joining 239 at the time, Denis and I had no experience of offensive night fighting. Our first squadron in 1942 was 141 at Tangmere and Acklington, flying Beaufighters on defensive night flying duties. This was followed by a tour with 272 Squadron in Malta, also flying Beaufighters, but this time on daylight operations against German and Italian supply lines between Italy and North Africa. Consequently, Denis and I spent the first few weeks at West Raynham on familiarization courses on Mosquitoes and the specialized electronic equipment that they were fitted with, i.e. AI (Airborne Interceptor), Serrate, and Gee navigational aid.

We had some experience of the Mk IV AI since our days on 141 Squadron. This airborne radar enabled us to pick up an echo from another aircraft and to home accurately on to it. The range of this radar was equal to our altitude – the echoes from the ground below drowned out everything else further away. Thus, successful defensive night fighting depended on ground control guiding us to within, say, 10,000 ft of an intruder. There was, of course, no such ground control to assist a Mosquito night fighter over Germany and the chances of a crew picking up a German fighter on AI was negligible. This is where Serrate came in. A radio receiver in the Mossie picked up Lichtenstein radar transmissions from a German night fighter and enabled the Mossie to home in on it – usually a Me 110 or a Ju 88 – until it came into AI range. The Serrate receiver had two screens – one giving the vertical and the other giving the horizontal direction of the source of the radar transmission. The Mosquito would home onto the transmitting aircraft until it came within AI range, when the Serrate was switched off. Gee was also new to me. It made navigation easy; in fact, the old-fashioned skills that I used over the sea and deserts of North Africa on my previous operational tour were now sadly obsolete.

Ground and air exercises followed thick and fast during February and we were operational by the middle of March. Operations were of two categories. The first was to patrol known

German night fighter beacons. These were locations where German night fighters were held in readiness until their Ground Control decided where the main bomber stream was going. Here we used AI alone and success obviously depended on our navigation being correct, on the *Luftwaffe* using a particular beacon on a given night, and on our luck – the sky is a big place and 10,000-ft range for our AI was not much. The second category of operation was to patrol in the vicinity of the bomber stream, using both AI and Serrate. Success was a matter of luck – a German fighter using his own radar at the right time and place. Our first op was on 19 March, when we patrolled Holland and France with no contacts. Similarly no luck with further patrols during the following weeks. Success came at last on the night of 31 May when we picked up a Serrate transmission North of Paris. Our first priority was to make sure that the transmission didn't come from a fighter homing on us from behind! We then manoeuvred our Mossie to get behind the transmitting aircraft. To our dismay, the transmission was switched off before we were in AI range. However, we kept on the same course and picked up an AI contact a minute or so later and convened this to a visual and the shooting down of a Me 110. Our next success was on the night of 5–6 June when we picked up an AI contact of a Me 110 circling a beacon near Aachen. The fighter was shot down a few minutes after midnight and could well have been the first German aircraft to be destroyed on D-Day.

Such was the pattern of operations by 239 and 141, its sister squadron, at West Raynham and other squadrons at nearby airfields. Between them, many German night fighters were destroyed. The net result of our efforts, together with those of other 100 Group squadrons involved in electronic jamming of *Luftwaffe* operations, intruding in fighter airfields, and in spoof and window operations, was a large decrease in Bomber Command losses. After July however, successes became few and far between. German fighters did not use radio beacons as before and Serrate contacts dried up – perhaps the frequency of their AI was changed. Also, and more importantly, we experienced massive radio interference on our AI and it was impossible to pick up a radar contact from more than a few hundred feet.

By October Denis and I had completed 50 sorties from West Raynham and we were posted to non-operational duties. We were lucky to have been in 239 Squadron at the right time – with fine aircraft and equipment and, most of all, to be part of the happiest squadron imaginable.

239 was a very happy squadron. Firstly, the aircrews, most of them experienced, joined a new squadron more or less together. The type of operations was new and we were 'all in the same boat' and the 'squadron spirit' built up quickly. I shall never forget those heady days of May, June and July. During those gloriously successful months all the Squadron personnel – the off duty crews, the CO, the Adjutant and ground crews congregated at the watch tower in the early hours, to greet the returning Mosquitoes and to cheer each time a plane signalled a success by 'beating up' the watch tower with its landing lights flashing. Looking back, I realize that the successes belonged to the Squadron as a whole and not to the individuals concerned. In this connection, it is too easy to forget that the dedication and expertise of the personnel who maintained the Mossies and the electronic equipment played a major role.

Another factor was West Raynham itself – it was a pre-1939 station with all the comforts that implied. Important too was the fact that most of the aircrews were flying Mosquitoes for the first time. Many, like us, had been flying Beaufighters before. Everyone respected a Beaufighter – it was sturdy, solid and tough. A Mosquito, on the other hand, was all this and much more. It had the grace, sleek lines, responsiveness and behaviour of a thoroughbred – it was an aeroplane that crews had a lifetime love affair with. In fact, our wives and sweethearts complained that they had to share our affections with the Mosquitoes! Lastly, there were the personnel themselves. Types such as the tolerant CO Paul Evans, the flight Commanders, the irrepressible 'Jackson' Booth and 'Golden' Neville Reeves with his navigator 'Mad' Mike O'Leary. Adj Hawley always had a ready smile and nothing was too much trouble for him. Then there was 'Buster' Reynolds – Buster was the Chief Intelligence Officer. He was a solicitor in civvy life and not only was he a thorough and relentless debriefer of crew returning from ops, but also he was the drinking and singing leader during the never-to-be-forgotten mess parties.

West Raynham holds one very special memory for me – it was during my tour of ops there that Gwyneth and I were married. She came to live in digs in King's Lynn. Living out during ops was frowned upon, but not forbidden. Because it was unofficial, I was not allowed petrol to travel and back and fore, nor food coupons. The petrol problem was overcome because I was able to borrow a motorcycle, but how Gwyneth managed to stretch her rations to feed me, I will never know. Fortunately, King's Lynn was within cycling distance of the 'Crown' at Gayton – the pub known to aircrews for miles around because of the quality of its beer and, more importantly, because bacon and eggs seemed to be always available. Those days must, of course, have been worrying for Gwyneth. When I left her in the morning, I could never say 'see you tonight'. If I appeared late afternoon, I would be stood down; if not, I was on ops. Then Gwyneth at dusk would listen to the drone of the heavy bombers heading to Germany and, a little later, the hum of the Mosquitoes flying out after them. She would know I was in one of them. But when she heard them returning some hours later, she would not know if I was coming back until I appeared in the early hours. I shall not forget the night of 25 September, when we landed a Bradwell Bay because West Raynham was closed for fog, and I turned up some 12 hours 'late'. I was one of those who believed that 'it will never happen to me', but I know how worried Gwyneth was. Nevertheless, neither of us would have wanted our lives otherwise – at that time one always lived for today.

On 24–25 February Wing Commander 'Jumbo' Gracie, CO, 169 Squadron and his navigator, Flight Lieutenant Wylton Todd, were shot down in the Hanover area. Six weeks later news was received that Gracie had been killed. Todd was a POW in *Stalag Luft III*. (He later designed the memorial to the fifty airmen murdered by the Gestapo). 515 Squadron's Beaufighters and Blenheims were replaced by NFIIs, beginning on 29 February, for training on the type. The unit began operations in March, equipped with the FBVI. At first, 515 Squadron's Mosquitoes operated on detachment with 605 Squadron at Bradwell Bay. A He177 was destroyed by a 515 Squadron NFII flown by the CO, Wing Commander Freddie Lambert with Flight Lieutenant E. Morgan, in the first squadron sortie, on 5 March.

On 21 April 1944, the Special Duty Radar Development Unit, which had been formed at West Raynham on 10 April for trials and development work on radar and various apparatus carried by 100 Group aircraft, moved to Foulsham. On 1 May it became the BSDU (Bomber Support Development Unit). Apart from the B.IV and

B.XVI, the unit operated Beaufighters, Stirlings, and Halifaxes. In April also, 515 Squadron moved from Bradwell Bay to Little Snoring and flew its first operation from there on 7 April.

On 20–21 when the Main Force went to Cologne, Squadron Leader E.W. Kinchin and Flight Lieutenant O. Sellars of 239 Squadron, who had downed a Bf110 near Frankfurt a month earlier, were shot down and killed by *Oberleutnant* Fritz Krause of *1./NJG10* flying a Fw190A-5 over Berlin. On the credit side Flight Lieutenant Gordon Cremer and his navigator, Flying Officer R. O'Farrell had better luck during their Serrate patrol. They were airborne from Little Snoring at 01.10 hours and except for intense enemy activity over England their first patrol point was reached uneventfully. After patrolling a beacon for ten minutes without incident they headed towards Cologne along a line from the NW for five minutes, afterwards turning starboard to a westerly course. Cremer continues,

Shortly after making this turn at approx. 0234 hrs obtained an AI contact at maximum range . . . we closed to 9000 ft astern of (enemy) aircraft. He took evasive action consisting of climbing and diving turns to port and starboard. However, with good AI interception and full throttle the range was reduced rapidly and 7 minutes after original contact a visual was obtained ahead and above. Despite navigator's early warning to throttle back I was approaching much too fast. I saw the aircraft silhouetted slightly above against cirrus cloud and instantly recognized it as a Me 110 by its tail fins. To avoid overshooting I pulled up to port losing visual momentarily and then turned starboard and regained visual. As the (enemy) aircraft was diving away to starboard I closed astern and gave a short burst at about 100 to 50 yards range from slightly above. Strikes were seen instantaneously inboard of the port engine followed by a large flash of flame which clearly illuminated the cockpit, fuselage and tailplane. We then overshot, but in passing both my observer and I were easily able to recognize the enemy aircraft as a Me 110 in the glare of the flames. I turned first to port and then to starboard and my next visual of the aircraft was its vertical descent in flames. It disappeared through the clouds whose tips were at 10,000 ft and a few seconds later there was the reflection of an explosion, followed by a red glow on the clouds. No return fire experienced. When last seen the cockpit was enveloped in flames as the enemy aircraft dived vertically into cloud and this fact, coupled with the explosions and red glow seen immediately after this through cloud is taken as the basis for the claim of 1 Me 110 DESTROYED.

Cremer had fired just forty rounds of 20-mm to down the Bf110.

In April-May 1944, 85 and 157 Squadrons, equipped with NFXIIs and XVIIs, and XIXs, respectively, and fitted with the first AI Mk.X radar sets, left Fighter Command, joining 100 Group at Swannington. 85 and 157, and 23 Squadron, which would also join 100 Group, in June, after arriving from the Mediterranean where they had been blasting Rommel's supply lines, were expert in the Intruder role. 23 Squadron's FBVIs would operate from Little Snoring alongside 515, with 169 Squadron and 1692 Flight, moving to Great Massingham on 4 June.

During May 100 Group Mosquitoes claimed eighteen aircraft destroyed. The first was on 8–9 May. Squadron Leader R. G. Woodman and Flying Officer Pat Kemmis of 169 Squadron were aloft as the bombers hit targets in northern France and Belgium. Woodman recalls: 'We could clearly see the bombers, as many as ten at a time, but no sign of German night fighters. We sniffed around for 109s and 190s over the target area but saw none. I saw three Halifaxes weaving like dingbats, up at 0011. Below the leading bomber was a twin-engined aircraft climbing up to it.' The Bf110, flown by *Leutnant* Wolfgang Martstaller, and his radar-operator/air gunner, of I./NJG4, had taken off from Florennes at 03.00 hours. In a letter to his parents on 12 May, Martstaller wrote: 'The sky was fully lit, so we could easily see the Tommy. Our crew saw at least ten bombers. However we could only concentrate on one aircraft. When I was near him and fired (and my burst of fire bloody well blinded me!) the *Schweinhund* fired off a flare with a signal pistol, so that an enemy night fighter could post us.' Woodman fired a two-second burst and Martstaller dived into the darkness, Kemmis following him on Serrate. Marstaller soared up in a steep climb and Woodman fired from 800 yards. Woodman continues: 'This time he opted out and took us on a chase across the French countryside at treetop height, not seeing him as he flew away from the moon but following him on Serrate.' Martstaller wrote: 'I went into a steep dive to almost zero feet (at night!), but still we could not escape from the Mosquito's attention.' Woodman continues: 'He made the mistake of flying towards the moon and I saw the moonlight glint off his wings. I fired and got some strikes on his fuselage and wings as he flew across a wide-open space, which looked like an aerodrome. He went into a steep turn and firing 50 yards ahead of him to allow for deflection, I hit him again. White smoke poured from his port engine and closing to 150 yards I gave him another 2 seconds burst and hit him again.' Marstaller concludes: 'I was fortunate to spot a field in which to belly-land. We were slightly injured from shrapnel. When we found that we were OK, we then saw a large explosion two miles away from us. Next day this turned out to be my Viermot [four motor bomber], with seven crew members (Flight Lieutenant Chase and crew of Lancaster ND587 of 405 Squadron burned to death). 'We were so happy!' (Martstaller was killed in a crash on St Trond aerodrome in August 1944.)

On 10–11 May Bf110 740179 3C+E1, of *1./NJG4* piloted by *Oberleutnant* Heinrich Schulenberg, was intercepted and shot down near Ellezelles, Belgium by Flying Officer Viv Bridges DFC and Flight Sergeant Donald G. 'Spider' Webb DFM of 239 Squadron at 00.10 hours. *Oberfeldwebel* Hermann Meyer, the radar operator, recalled: 'We were shot down with one engine on fire. We could save ourselves by bailing out, and came down near Elobeg. I was wounded on the skull and was badly concussed. I spent three weeks in hospital at Brussels and then had four weeks leave at home.'

On 11–12 May two German night fighters fell to 141 Squadron when six Serrate Mosquitoes were dispatched to Bourg Hasselt Louvain in Belgium. Flight Lieutenant Harry White DFC and Flight Lieutenant Mike Allen DFC registered their tenth victory when they shot down a Ju88, while a Ju88 of *6./NJG2*, flown by Wilhelm Simonsohn, fell to the guns of the remarkable forty-six year old, bespectacled Belgian pilot, Flight Lieutenant Lucien J. G. LeBoutte, whose radar operator was Flying Officer Ron Mallett. Wilhelm Simonsohn recalled:

We started around 22.00 in Raum Brussels and flew at a height of 6,500 metres (20,000ft) towards the Channel coast. At times, we saw flak shells exploding. However, compared to the large attacks on the German cities and the huge fires there, this was a quiet area. We were about 1½ hours in the air and now patrolled at a height of around 6,000 metres (18000ft). There were some clouds above us when suddenly a chain of tracer bullets struck our port engine, coming in from the left side. I immediately did a steep dive, hoping that the enemy would break off his attack. The flames from the engine blinded our eyes, which were used to the darkness. I yelled through my microphone at my throat, 'Bail Out!'

Franz kneeled at the escape hatch, pulled the red handle and flew out of the plane together with the hatch. Günther, who was sitting with his back towards me, dived towards the hatch and also disappeared. Meanwhile, I loosened my straps, but our aircraft was in a high-speed dive by now. I tried to pull the stick towards me in an effort to reduce the speed. I think that during this manoeuvre the left wing broke off, probably as a result from the attack. The aircraft, or what was left of it, was out of control.

I broke through the cockpit canopy and catapulted myself into the night air. I waited for about 5 seconds before I pulled the ripcord, then I pulled (I did that so hard that I had the ripcord in my hand!) and there followed a huge jolt. I will never forget that feeling, while I was hanging under that chute and listening to the air flowing through the silk. Far away from me, I saw burning pieces of my aircraft falling towards the earth.

Below me in the light of a white signal flare, I saw another parachute. I pulled my own signal pistol to respond, but it fell out of my hand, which had become stiff in the descent. The landing was without any problem. I landed in the yard of a farm near Mechlen, north east of Brussels. My chute fell down – there was no wind – and I heard the raid sirens wailing. Next morning I met up with my crew. We were together again, slightly shocked, but happy and we were then transported to Brussels.

On 12–13 May, Viv Bridges and 'Spider' Webb DFM of 239 Squadron were again successful, shooting down at Hoogcruts near Maastricht, Ju88C-6, 750922 05+2 of 5./NJG3, crewed by pilot *Unteroffizier* Josef Polzer (KIA), *Obergefreiter* Hans Kluender, radar operator (KIA), and *Gefreiter* Hans Becker, air gunner (WIA).

New crews arrived at the 100 Group stations to fly Mosquito intruder operations. One of these, in early May 1944, was Warrant Officer Les Turner and Flight Sergeant Frank Francis, who were posted to 169 Squadron after crewing up at 51 OTU. Frank recalls:

Although we had little in common on the ground, he was an excellent radar screen 'reader' and our successes were in no small part due to his expertise. Until going onto ops in the Mosquito, until then I thought the best fighter was the Beaufighter. Seated

42

centrally between those two great radial engines gave a sense of power, which had to be experienced to be believed. 169 Squadron was then equipped with rather ageing NFIIs with forward and rearward looking Al Mk.IV radar and armed with four 20mm Hispano-Suiza cannon. Serviceability was a continuing problem until, at the end of June 1944, we would get FBVIs.

As well as radar we also had Serrate. This was a homing device, which was supposed to lock on to German night fighter radar transmissions. It could not give range or altitude, merely direction, and while it worked after a fashion in practice (we did a two week course on it on Beaufighters before going to the squadron) my log-book records only one instance where we got Serrate indications, and these proved abortive. However, after about a fortnight's practice both day and night, we set out on our Freshman op, on 19 May. We had in fact been scheduled for 15 May but it was thought that the penetration was too deep for an inexperienced crew. (The crew that replaced us, Pilot Officer W. H. 'Andy' Miller and Pilot Officer Freddie Bone, had a field day that night – two Ju 88s and a Bf 110 – an unbroken squadron record). The 'Freshman' was to Dieppe and Amiens and was totally uneventful over enemy territory but I frightened the life out of myself as we were climbing over southern England to our patrol. There were a number of 'cu-nimbs' – storm clouds – around us and as we reached 12,000 ft, there was an enormous flash of lightning away to starboard. At that moment, the Auto-gear change of the supercharger operated with its usual 'thump'. Such was the state of my nerves, I was sure that we had been struck by lightning until rational reason returned a few seconds later! Trip No. 2 was to Amiens and Metz and was again uneventful.

On 22–23 May another *NJG3* machine was shot down by a Mosquito when Bf110G-4 720050 05+2 of *3./NJG3,* was shot down by Wing Commander N. B. R. Bromley OBE and Flight Lieutenant Philip V. Truscott of 169 Squadron. *Feldwebel* Franz Muellebner, pilot, *Unteroffizier* Alfons Josten, radar operator and *Gefreiter* Karl Rademacher, air gunner, were all wounded in action and baled out successfully. The Junkers crashed at Hoogeveen, south of Groningen.

On 24–25 May two more Bf110s were shot down by 239 Squadron crews. Raby and Flint and Hughes and Perks each shot down Bf110G-4s of *7./NJG6.* Wrk Nr. 730105 27+AR crashed at 02.30 hours in forest between Zweifall and Mulartshuette, SE of Aachen and *Oberleutnant* Helmut Schulte, pilot, and *Unteroffizier* Hans Fischer, air gunner, both baled out. *Unteroffizier* Georg Sandvoss, radar operator, was killed. The other Bf 110, flown by *Unteroffizier* Oskar Voekel, crashed five minutes later at the Wesertalsperre near Eupen, south of Aachen. Voelkel, *Unteroffizier* Karl Hautzenberger, radar operator, *Unteroffizier* Gunther Boehme, air gunner, all baled out safely.

On the night of 27–28 May a 515 Squadron Mosquito flown by Flying Officer David Kay Foster with his radar operator, twenty-year old Flying Officer Robert Stanley Ling, which took off from Little Snoring at 01.55 hours, and was detailed to patrol Leeuwarden, failed to return. They were shot down by airfield defence flak and crashed into a hangar on the airfield. Both are buried in Leeuwarden Northern General Cemetery. Flight Lieutenant Harry White DFC* and Mike Allen DFC* of 141 Squadron destroyed a Bf109. At West Raynham meanwhile, six Mosquito night fighter crews in 239 Squadron were detailed to arrive at Leeuwarden airfield north Holland at a precise time. Squadron Leader Reeves and Pilot Officer O'Leary shot down Bf110 140032 G9+CR of 7./NJG1. The 110 crashed at Spannum in Friesland province in Holland at 01.15 hours. *Unteroffizier* Joachim Tank, the twenty-six year old pilot, was slightly wounded; *Unteroffizier* Gunther Schröder, the nineteen-year old radar operator, and *Unteroffizier* Heinz Elwers, the twenty-four-year old air gunner, were both killed. Squadron Leader R. K. Bailey and his navigator failed to return, as Bailey recounts:

Intelligence had declared Leeuwarden to be the main reaction base of the German night fighter force for operations that night. We were detailed to arrive at Leeuwarden when the German fighters would be reacting to the radar indication of the approach of the main force of bombers (we crossed the North Sea at sea level to avoid detection). The plan of operations worked for no sooner had we reached the Leeuwarden area than the navigator called 'Serrate contact'. We followed this target in a climbing orbit to 11,000ft where in conditions of high haze and resultant poor visibility I sighted a Me 110 directly ahead and at very close range. Two bursts from the four 20mm cannon resulted in an explosion and showers of debris into which we flew. The navigator called out another Serrate contact, which I had to ignore being engaged in feathering the propeller of the starboard engine, which had overheated and stopped. Assessing the situation the navigator said he would give a course for our base in Norfolk. I asked him instead for a course to Calais and thence to Manston, Kent, to avoid a North Sea crossing in a damaged aircraft, the extent of which was unknown. Ten minutes later the port engine failed and I ordered bail out. Within seconds the navigator was gone and I made to follow diving head first across the cockpit to the escape hatch. I had trimmed the rudder for asymmetric flying when the starboard engine failed but I omitted to neutralize trim when the port engine failed. The result was a steep spiral dive. Meanwhile I was trapped having caught the top section of the hatch. I was head and shoulders out in the slipstream with my legs and torso in the aircraft. I was almost reconciled to this situation when a stupid thought crossed my mind that when the aircraft struck the ground I would be sheared in two! This possibility brought about a frenzied new effort. Suddenly I was free from the whistling slipstream and falling in space. I pulled the ripcord and the parachute opened; I said a prayer of thanks. Some seconds later I made contact heavily with the ground.

Bailey was taken in by the Dutch Underground but his immediate concern was for his wife Jean who was eight months pregnant on 29 May and how she would react to the news that he was 'missing'. Bailey spent three months with the Dutch Underground – even taking part in a raid on a post office to augment supplies of ration cards and money – before being sent down the escape lines to Belgium in August 1944. Unfortunately the line had been infiltrated. Bailey, an American Fortress pilot by the name of Bill Lalley from Lowell, Michigan and Viv Connell, a RAAF Lancaster navigator from Broken Hill, NSW, were taken prisoner by the Germans.

On the night of 5–6 June – D-Day eve – 1944, the Mk 10 radar equipped Mosquitoes of 85 Squadron and 157 Squadron at Swannington flew their first operations in 100 Group while twenty-one Serrate Mosquitoes were dispatched to northern France. 85 Squadron dispatched twelve Mosquitoes over the Normandy invasion beaches and four Mosquitoes of 157 (and ten of 515 Squadron) made Intruder raids on Belgian and Dutch airfields. 'On 5 June 1944' recalls Flying Officer Bob Symon of 85 Squadron, 'Wing Commander Michael Miller and myself were transferred to Colerne, arriving at 1pm. There was quite an uproar when nobody was allowed to leave the airfield, no phone calls to wives to say they would not be home for dinner. We flew patrols 75 miles inland over the beachhead. We had four Mossies making a line covering the territory on the British and Canadian landings. Michael and I were the first on patrol, Pavilly-Bernay. This was the beginning of an invasion and there was nothing in our part of the sky. One searchlight groped around for less than a minute and then went out. The real sight was on our way back to Colerne after our relief had taken over. On the return to base looking north over the water we could see for miles the tugs and gliders making their way over the Channel: a fabulous sight.'

100 Group claimed two victories, and 239 Squadron crews scored both. Ju88G-1 710454 of *5./NJG3*, was shot down by Flying Officer W. R. Breithaupt DFC and Flying Officer J. A. Kennedy DFC of 239 Squadron. It crashed twenty kilometres north of Spiekeroog killing *Unteroffizier* Willi Hammerschmitt, pilot, *Unteroffizier* Friedrich Becker, radar operator and *Feldwebel* Johannes Kuhrt, air gunner. Flight Lieutenant Dennis Welfare DFC* and Flying Officer D. B. 'Taffy' Bellis DFC* of 239 Squadron, also claimed a Bf110 north of Aachen. Bf110 440272 G9+NS of *8./NJG1* crashed at 00.54 hours on the northern beach of Schiermonnikoog. *Unteroffizier* Adolf Stuermer, the twenty-two year old pilot, *Unteroffizier* Ludwig Serwein, the twenty-one year old radar operator, and *Gefreiter* Otto Morath, the twenty-three year old air gunner, were killed.

There was plenty of night fighter activity in June 1944, with thirty-three victories in all being claimed by 100 Group Mosquito crews. Warrant Officer Les Turner and Flight Sergeant Freddie Francis of 169 Squadron were one of the crews who patrolled the beach head area in Normandy. They saw fires on the ground, presumably Caen, and seemed to be 'in and out of cloud all the time.' Their fourth trip, two days later, on 8–9 June, made up for the lack of incident as Les Turner recalls:

While somewhat south of Cherbourg I noticed that the glycol coolant temperature was rising 'off the clock'. I assumed the worst – a pump failure, possible seizure and maybe a fire, and feathered the engine. We set a rough course for the UK – 'steer north and you are bound to hit something' – and when we were within radio range of Tangmere got them to give us a course. We then settled down to what turned out to be one hour 50 minutes of single engine flying at the recommended 170 mph (IAS) at 12,000-ft. We had picked what turned out to be one of the worst nights of the year, from the point of view of weather. One of the crews of a neighbouring squadron baled out when they were unable to get in and were nearly out of fuel. Tangmere kept hold of us all the way. We transmitted for radio fixes every few minutes and eventually, I was instructed to commence a controlled descent of say, 300ft a minute until instructed further. I had a marked reluctance to lose height with only one engine and in cloud, and when we reached, I believe, 1,400ft, I asked urgently if further descent was safe. I was assured that it was and we broke cloud at 600ft over Dante's Inferno, actually the paraffin flares of FIDO at Hartford Bridge.

We were given permission to land immediately and executed a very tight circuit to hold the (literally) flare path in view. We had to lower the undercarriage by pump and this took so long that we didn't have time to get the flaps down! We touched down reasonably well but at 150 mph. Another pilot in the tower said later that it looked like a take off! When, after about two thirds of the runway had gone past, the tail wheel touched down, I locked the brakes on but the runway ended and we careered on what seemed like ploughed land for another 100 yards or so when we hit the drainage ditch, slewed to port a bit and stopped. I still remember the tremendous silence after the noise of the landing, broken only by the 'chufferty-chuff' of the one Merlin, which was still ticking over. The crash crew arrived almost at once and we clambered down, relieved, somewhat breathless, but unhurt. The Mossie suffered a damaged undercarriage and in view of its years was, I believe, subsequently written off.

On the night of 11–12 June 1944 Wing Commanderdr. C. M. Miller, DFC** and Flying Officer Bob Symon of 85 Squadron took off from Swannington in a Mosquito XIX fitted with AI X at 22.15 on an Intruder patrol to Bretigny and Melun. While they were orbiting the town of Melun at 3,000 feet, Miller passed over the airfield and their Mosquito was momentarily lit up by searchlights. Shortly afterwards, another aircraft was engaged by the searchlights and fired a recognition signal – a number of white stars. Miller turned towards this aircraft, which was at the same level and two miles range. Symon continues:

We were at 3,000ft looking around Melun and Bretigny airfields when my pilot said 'searchlights and white stars were on for a moment.' As he began to turn in that direction, I saw the blip on my tube and I had us in position in two and a half minutes behind. We made a very simple interception. Michael insisted that I keep my eyes on the tube even when he had a visual, well that is quite proper, but when I protested that we had closed inside minimum range and there was nothing to look at he relented and said I could look out. So I looked out and saw a completely empty sky. He pointed upwards with one finger and there it was – a Bf 110: I felt that I could have stood up and autographed its under-side.

Miller said in his report:

Gave chase, the enemy aircraft firing further recognition signals and from 600 ft got a visual of the enemy aircraft silhouette. Closing in to about 50 ft and immediately below, he recognised a Me 110, small fins and rudders, long nose, square wing-tips, and drop-tanks. No exhausts were visible from below but a stream of small sparks was seen. We dropped back to about 150 yards, height now about 2,000 ft and pulled up behind, but the silhouette having become rather indistinct, we fired in anticipation of its position. No strikes were seen at first, but by raising the airing point strikes became visible and the aim was steadied. A fire started in the port engine, which spread over the fuselage. Large pieces of flaming wreckage flew back, and enemy aircraft dived vertically down-wards, exploding on impact with the ground, about 10 miles N. E. of Melun A/F at 0035 hours. No return fire was experienced.

Symon concludes, 'When we got back to Swannington we found that we had opened the scoring, which I thought was a right and proper thing for the CO of 85 to do! (I regret that 108 days from this event my pilot was compelled to retire due to illness.)'

On 12–13 June Flight Lieutenant James G. Benson of 157 Squadron shot down a Ju188 at Compiêgne. The night following, on 13–14 June Warrant Officer Les Turner and Flight Sergeant Freddie Francis of 169 Squadron took off from Great Massingham at 23.20 hours in their Mk VI still looking for their first victory. Turner reported:

Took off on 13–6–44 in Mosquito P. Set course at 5,000 ft over base at 2331. In good visibility obtained visual of English coast and subsequently of Enemy coast, which we crossed at 0005 at 15,000 ft. Tuned on to Southerly course and during this leg we observed no sign of activity. We then turned West and lost height down to 5,000 ft in the hope of finding some joy. The lights of Paris were observed 3 miles port of track so we climbed to 9,000 ft and orbited lights on the off chance of arousing some re-action. This was however unavailing so we climbed on a Westerly course to 12,000 ft where an AI contact was obtained 8,000 ft in front at 0112 hours. We turned towards aircraft, which was travelling in a Northerly direction at approximately 250-mph. A contact was showing considerably below, we lost height down to 8,000 ft from which point aircraft began to weave violently tuning alternately port and starboard through 180° at speed approximately 350 mph and losing height to 5,000 ft at 12lbs boost and 2800 rpm. We closed to 2,000 ft after approximately six minutes. Then enemy aircraft flew into a patch of cloud and as range closed rapidly, I throttled back obtaining visual at 1300 ft of enemy aircraft above and to port, positively identifying plan view as a Ju 88. We over-shot slightly so I let enemy aircraft come ahead and followed portly visually through wispy cloud. When this was cleared I closed to 300–400 yards and opened fire on port engine, which immediately burst into flames. Enemy aircraft turned port and in avoiding enemy aircraft, which was now burning fiercely, I turned port and on to my back, thus upsetting gyro instruments. I regained control on natural horizon and saw enemy aircraft hit the ground and explode. We then set course towards northerly sky and when instruments had settled down, set course of 350 degrees for coast, which we crossed 3 miles West of Dunkirk at 0200 hours. No Serrate indications were observed throughout the trip.

They flew on home and crossed the coast five miles west of Dunkirk at 02.00 hours, satisfied with their night's work but reaching the shores of England they were warned that there were German intruders about. With a pessimism, which is probably part of his character, Turner was convinced that they would not make it back to report the combat! They did though.

On 15–16 June Squadron Leader E. S. Gonsalves and Flight Lieutenant B. Duckett of 85 Squadron shot down Bf110 5664 G9+IZ of 12./NJG1, and it crashed nine kilometres west of Tongres, between St Trond and Maastricht. *Unteroffizier* Heinz Baerwolf, pilot, who was injured, and *Unteroffizier* Fischer, radar operator, baled out.

Obergefreiter Edmund Kirsch, the twenty-three year old air gunner, was killed. The following night, 16–17 June, Ju88 710590 of *l./NJG2* crashed in the Pas de Cancale, possibly shot down by Flying Officer Andy Miller DFC and Flying Officer Freddie Bone of 169 Squadron. All three crew were killed. On 17–18 June, a Bf110 of *NJG1* was shot down at 02.30 hours by Flying Officer P.S. Kendall DFC* and Flight Lieutenant C. R. Hill, and crashed at Soesterberg airfield. Muller, the pilot, and two others were killed. Also this night Flight Lieutenant G. E. Poulton and Flying Officer John Neville of 239 Squadron came across some Ju88s orbiting a beacon and fired at two of them. Neville recalls:

> We claimed one destroyed after it plunged earthwards thoroughly on fire, and the second likewise plunged down with one engine on fire which fairly soon went out. This we claimed as damaged and both were credited to us. (The first was Ju 88 G-1 710866 of 8./NJG2. It crashed at Volkel airfield killing two of the crew and wounding the third).

On 21 June 1944 Bf110G 440076 G9+NS of *8./NJG1*, was shot down at 15.19 hours by Squadron Leader Paul Rabone DFC and Flying Officer E. C. H. Johns. It crashed on the northern side of Eelde airfield killing *Unteroffizier* Herbert Beyer, the twenty-one-year-old pilot, *Unteroffizier* Hans Petersmann, the twenty-one-year-old radar operator and *Obergefreiter* Franz Riedel, the twenty-year-old air gunner. On 25 June some Mosquitoes from 85 and 157 Squadrons were detached to West Malling for anti-Diver patrols.

On the night of 27–28 June a 515 Squadron crew destroyed a Ju88 at Eindhoven. Warrant Officer Harry Welham and Warrant Officer E. Hollis, and Squadron Leader Graham Rice and Flying Officer Jimmy Rogerson of 141 Squadron each claimed a Ju88. Rogerson recalls:

> It was now approaching half-way house, with unlucky number thirteen of the thirty operations making up the full tour behind us. Action was just around the corner. On 27 June we were given another of the one-hour beacon patrols, taking in two of them in Northern France code-named Emil and Goldhammer. We took off just after the last of midsummer's long daylight had faded and a bright full moon was rising into a cloudless sky, made our way across the North Sea to Flushing, and began our stipulated patrol

soon after midnight. The skies were crystal clear, brilliant from the harsh illumination of an un-obscured moon, but otherwise apparently empty. After some twenty minutes of stooging calmly up and down, quite unexpectedly a sudden burst of four red stars, exactly like one of Standard Fireworks better rockets, exploded in the air away to our right, followed almost immediately by four more of the same, now slightly closer. Not our own chosen colour combination for the night. My driver promptly turned towards this pretty display of pyrotechnics to investigate, myself with eyes glued to the radar screens searching for non-existent Serrate indications. Half a minute later, I had it. A good clean blip, racing out of the ground response and down the time base so rapidly that we were obviously meeting whatever it was head on.

Waiting until the range had closed to 4000 ft, I gave instructions to haul round to starboard through 180 degrees, so that if all went according to plan we would finish up directly behind our customer and in a position to chase and intercept. Which is exactly what happened. The Mosquito completed its turn to show me my contact directly ahead at a distance of two miles but well below our own altitude of 15,000 ft. On this occasion I was really going to have to apply myself. The target ahead was weaving steadily about to right and left, added to which it was a question of reducing our height whilst trying to follow spasmodic twists and turns and close the distance respectfully between us. After ten minutes, during which time we found that we had descended some 4,000 ft, Graham obtained a visual thanks to the clean brilliance of the white moon on an aircraft flying at least 1,500 ft ahead of us.

At that precise moment, our target took a gentle turn to port and finally steadied to fly directly into the full blinding glare. There was no doubt whatsoever about its identity. The marked dihedral of the longer than average wing-span and the engines close-set to the fuselage shouted Ju 88. But any hopes of closing to a position where my driver could see properly to open fire would have to be deferred. It was back to the radar screens and follow the blip for very nearly quarter of an hour, and that I can tell you was an irritatingly long time.

Finally, it turned once more, this time out of the glare altogether, and we were able to close without more ado right in to firing range. Seizing the opportunity whilst we had it, we opened fire at once in two short bursts. Large pieces flew off-and passed uncomfortably

51

close above our heads just as they had with the 110 up at Hamburg and this time both engines burst into flames simultaneously. The sequence of events, which followed, is yet another that is burnished into my memory like a roll of cine-film. So well alight was the Ju 88 that the black crosses on its wings were clearly visible as it went down beneath us in a steep dive to port, where it disappeared into the only bank of cloud anywhere in sight, almost as though it were seeking refuge.

Just as we thought we would not see it again and so be unable to vouch positively for its destruction, it suddenly re-appeared out of the cloud in a zooming vertical climb, ablaze from end to end, described a perfect loop directly above, and then came down straight at us, as though by some will of its own it was bent upon revenge by taking us with it in a mid-air collision. Its fiery downward path surged desperately close behind our port wing, and for one awful moment I was absolutely convinced that it would hit us! The whole astonishing performance seemed to last for ever as we sat there watching its progress in open mouthed amazement, yet in the event I suppose it cannot have taken more than a couple of minutes before it all ended with a huge explosion as it hit the deck in the Cambrai area of Northern France.

Flight Lieutenant D. Welfare DFC* and Flying Officer D. B. Bellis DFC* of 239 Squadron shot down a Me410 east of Paris and a Fw190 was destroyed by their CO, Wing Commander Paul M. J. Evans flying with navigator Flying Officer R. H. Perks DFC. Evans recalls:

I was returning from accompanying the bomber force to Stuttgart. Near the Channel on the French side we picked up an IFF contact which turned out to be a Fw 190. I shot it down from behind but unfortunately it exploded covering my aircraft with burning petrol. This burnt off a great deal of the doped control surfaces, which were not wood, and made the aircraft difficult to control. I made a very fast landing at Manston after numerous trials at height to determine at what speed I lost control.

A Ju88 was also claimed destroyed by Flight Lieutenant Donald R. 'Podge' Howard and Flying Officer Frank A. W. 'Sticky' Clay of 239 Squadron over France. Howard reported to Flight Lieutenant C. H. F. Reynolds the Intellegence officer:

Mosquito took off West Raynham 2311 hrs on a Serrate patrol in support of the bombers on Vitry le Francois, crossing in at St. Valery and contacting the bombers at 0106 hrs. After intercepting and obtaining a visual on a Lancaster at 0120 hrs well away from the bomber stream and at 14,500 ft (6,000 ft above the other bombers), Mosquito went on to Vitry le Francois. After patrolling there for 8 mins while the bombing was in progress, it was decided to set course for the French coast as the port engine was running very badly. At 0210 hrs when north of LAON at 16,000 ft, 0215 hrs, an AI contact at 6,000 ft ahead and to the East was picked up but it faded almost at once. When about 5 miles N of Cambrai, still at 16,000 ft, 0215 hrs, an AI contact was observed nearly head-on, 12,000 ft range, crossing gently port to starboard below an estimated course of 130°(T). Mosquito, which was on 320°(T) allowed contact to pass below and then turned round starboard, gradually losing height to 8,000 ft and then climbed to 12,000 ft. during this climb Mosquito found it was impossible to gain on contact which was doing 260 ASI but fortunately it turned port on to 050°(T), reduced height and eventually settled down straight and level at 9,500 ft. This enabled Mosquito to close in to 1,500 ft where a fleeting visual was obtained on the silhouette of an aircraft 20° above. At 1,000ft range a clear visual was obtained on what the pilot believed to be a Ju 88 but in order to be quite certain, Mosquito was brought in to within 50 ft and any doubt of the target's identity was removed. Dropping back to 75 yards dead astern and slightly below, a 1-sec burst of cannon caused strikes on the fuselage and E/A's port engine blew up. As E/A dropped away to port, Mosquito put its nose right down and with another 1 sec burst set E/A's starboard engine on fire. E/A then turned slowly to starboard, well on fire, and dived vertically into the ground where it exploded. No lights had been visible on E/A and no return fire was experienced. Claimed as a Ju 88 destroyed (Cat. A(i). E/A was shot down from 9,500' to 9,000 ft at 0230 hrs a few miles NE of Brussels.

The AI became u/s after the cannon had been fired and 3 mins later the starboard coolant temperature was seen to be 160°, flames started spurting along the starboard engine and fumes filled the cockpit. Pilot feathered the starboard propeller and turned on to 290°(T) climbing into cloud at 10,000 ft recrossing the enemy coast at Knocke at 0255 hrs. The port vacuum pump was u/s and gyro instruments would not perform. The starboard engine having been put out of action, all electric services had to be switched off to conserve the supply of electricity. Later the navigator tried to get a Gee fix, but could not get a normal picture and a fix was unobtainable. R/T was switched on and a Mayday call to Kinglsey was given on Channel 'D' with IFF on Stud 3, but after two transmissions and when Kingsley had given a vector to Manston, R/T became completely u/s. Mosquito was holding hard at 10,500 ft so an approximate course of 260°(T) was maintained until Sandrs lights were seen and the Manston pundit was identified. Mosquito fired the colours of the day several times and then made a perfect landing at Manston at 0330 hrs. A number of pieces of '88' and a handful of Window (broad) have been recovered from Mosquito's starboard engine.

On 30 June–1 July Flight Lieutenant D. J. Raby DFC and Flight Sergeant S. J. Flint DFM of 239 Squadron destroyed Ju88 711114 of 5./NJG2 over France. They stalked the Junkers and were fired at by the enemy air gunner but his tracer passed harmlessly over the top of the Mosquito, Raby fired a two-second burst from 450 feet and saw strikes all along the port fuselage and wing and the port engine burst into flames. He pumped another two-second burst into the doomed Junkers, which exploded, scattering debris into the path of the charging Mosquito. As it fell vertically to earth Raby continued to pepper the machine, finally breaking away just before another explosion tore the wings off the night fighter. It crashed south-east of Dieppe in a massive explosion.

'At the end of June,' recalls Bob Symon of 85 Squadron, 'we were sent back to West Malling to chase Flying Bombs. None of us liked the thought of going back to flying over Germany with our engines having been beaten hard trying to keep up with the bombs.' On 25 June 1944 85 and 157 Squadrons in 100 Group were switched to anti-Diver patrols. (By the start of 1945 85 Squadron were still using AI.VIII radar sets, but at least their Mosquitoes were made more powerful, with the injection of nitrous oxide, better known as 'laughing gas' with petrol, to give the added power needed to catch the V-1s). They operated against the Doodlebugs until 20 August when both squadrons resumed bomber support duties from Swannington.

Chapter Four

The Gestapo Hunters

Second Tactical Air Force had been formed on 1 June 1943 under AVM Basil Embry, whose eleven squadrons of Bostons, Venturas and Mitchells in 2 Group in Norfolk were to help prepare the way for the invasion of the continent planned for the summer of 1944. Embry, whose command began moving to Hampshire to be nearer the enemy coast, wanted FBVIs, which were ideal for 2nd TAF operations. While it retained the same armament as the fighter version the VI had the additional capability of being able to carry two 500lb bombs in the rear half of the bomb bay. The forward half was taken up with cannon breeches. Wing racks were fitted to carry two 50-gallon drop tanks or a further two 500lb bombs. Crews could carry out a round trip of 1,000 miles carrying 4,000 rounds of .303 ammunition, 1,000 rounds of cannon shells, and 2,000 lbs of bombs, while still being able to cruise at between 255–325 mph. However, the wooden wonder was in short supply so priority had been given to re-equipping the three Ventura squadrons – 21, 464 RAAF and 487 RNZAF in 140 Wing. On 3 October every bomber squadron in 2 Group was allocated a transformer station target between Paris and Brittany, which were to be attacked from low level. For the first time 464 and 487 Mosquito squadrons took part, 487 being led by the wing commander, Group Captain Percy 'Pick' Pickard, while 464 Squadron was led by Wing Commander H. J. Meakin. Pickard was a daring and revered leader and as a flight lieutenant he and Wellington *F-Freddie* had appeared in the British wartime film, *Target for Tonight*. Their targets were power stations at Pont Château and Mur de Bretagne and to reach them they had to fly to Exeter before crossing the Channel. The series of attacks caused maximum disruption to the

French electrical system and the railways, which were electrified, from Paris to Brittany.

On 15 October 138 Wing at Lasham near Alton, Hampshire, began re-equipping with the FBVI when 613 Squadron gave up its Mustangs. Then, on 18 November 305 Polish Squadron at Swanton Morley moved to Lasham after flying just five operations in Mitchell IIs and in November-December also converted to FBVIs. 613 Squadron flew its first Mosquito operation on 31 December 1943, with an attack on a *V-1* site in northern France. That same day, Nos. 21, 464 and 487 Squadrons took off from Sculthorpe for the last time, bombed Le Ploy, France, and landed at their new base at Hunsdon. On 1 February 1944 107 Squadron replaced its Bostons with FBVIs and moved to Lasham to complete the FBVI re-equipment of 138 Wing.

During January-February 1944 the targets of the Mosquito VIs of 2nd TAF were nominally the *V1* flying bomb sites in the Pas de Calais. Ron Smith, a pilot in 613 Squadron, remembers the Noball or Crossbow operations, as they were called:

> The method of attack was to fly out at low level to the target area in loose formation in boxes of four or five aircraft, pull up to 3,500 ft, peel off individually, and dive down steeply to 1,500 ft, releasing the 4x500 lb bombs and returning to base at low level. These aircraft carried no bombsights, so bombs were dropped at the crew's judgement. Most used the position of the target vis-a-vis the gunsight to decide when to release – taking into account the speed of the aircraft and the angle of the dive. It was a matter of practice and experience, and the end results were generally satisfactory. These targets were usually heavily defended by light ack-ack, and some damage to aircraft, and some losses, were experienced.

During March-April to simulate the type of tactical targets against which 2 Group would be employed in the run-up to D-Day, Boston, Mitchell and Mosquito crews arrived at 2 GSU (Group Support Unit) at Swanton Morley to take part in two-week training exercises in full field conditions. All crews lived under canvas and life was distinctly uncomfortable, while night interdictor training (bombing and strafing the enemy's communications by night), bombing of illuminated targets and convoys, and runs on a 'spoof' *V1* rocket site and a four-gun flak battery installation were carried out.

On average Mosquito squadrons destroyed one Crossbow site for each 39.8 tons of bombs dropped compared with an average of 165.4 tons for the B-17, 182 tons for the Mitchell and 219 tons for the Marauder. On occasion, 2nd TAF Mosquitoes were employed against Noball sites led by two PFF Mosquitoes fitted with Oboe, and escorted by Spitfires. However, this technique meant that they had to fly in tight formation, straight and level for ten minutes until bomb release, and a sitting target for the Flak gunners!

In April Mosquitoes of 2nd TAF were once again called upon to fly a very important low level strike mission, this time to Holland, when 613 Squadron, commanded by Wing Commander R. N. 'Bob' Bateson DFC, was directed to bomb the 'Huize Kleykamp' in the Hague. Before the war the five-storey, ninety-five feet high white building on Carnegie Square had been used for art exhibitions. Now occupied by the *Gestapo,* it housed the Dutch Central Population Registry and duplicates of all legally issued Dutch personal identity papers so that identity cards falsified by the Dutch Underground could be checked and recognized as false. Jaap van der Kamp and a few other Underground members had managed to infiltrate the Bureau staff in the building and sketches of the interior layout and its immediate surroundings were prepared. The *'Huize Kleykamp'* was strongly defended day and night and the ID card duplicates were stored in heavy metal cupboards so a raid by the Underground was just not possible. In mid-December 1943 London received word from Holland requesting that the building be destroyed from the air. It would be the most difficult job that a bomber squadron had ever had to face.

Light anti-aircraft weapons defended the *'Huize Kleykamp'* and it was tightly wedged among other houses in the Scheveningsweg, which made accuracy very difficult and heavy civilian casualties could be expected. By March 1944 there was no alternative; the building had to be destroyed. Planning for the raid, therefore, had to be meticulous. The attack would have to be carried out when the building was occupied on a working day so that the files would be open and the card indexes spread out on desks, otherwise they could not be destroyed by fire. The Dutch underground was not overly concerned with the deaths of the *Kleykamp* personnel as they were regarded as collaborators anyway. Finally, the time of the attack was scheduled for midday so that most civilians would be off the streets and having lunch. A scale model of the building, perfect in every detail right down to the thickness and the composition of the walls was built. Meanwhile, scientists developed a new bomb, a mixture of incendiary and high explosive, which was designed to have the maximum effect on the masses of *Gestapo* files and records. Bateson picked his crews carefully and put them through weeks of intensive training. Embry insisted that the mission could not go ahead until visibility of at least ten kilometres was available. At last, on Tuesday 11 April all was ready.

In the early morning Bateson led six Mosquitoes off from Lasham and set course very low over the North Sea to Holland with Spitfires for escort. The Mosquitoes climbed to 1,300 metres and flew a feint from the head of Goeree via Lehornhoven to the Reeuwijk Lakes near Gouda. No.2 in the second pair led by Squadron Leader Charles Newman and Flight Lieutenant F. G. Trevers, was Flight Lieutenant Ron Smith in HP927. 'I was completely occupied in flying the aircraft at very low level in formation and listening to Flying Officer John Hepworth, my navigator, on what landmark to expect next. The way in was deliberately made very roundabout in order to confuse the enemy of our objective and to achieve maximum surprise.'

As they approached the Dutch coast Bateson and his navigator, Flying Officer B. J. Standish noticed something strange. There were no recognizable landmarks; they found themselves flying over a vast expanse of water, dotted with islands where no islands should have been. Unknown to the aircrew, the Germans had opened the sluice gates on the River Scheldt inundating a large area of the flat Dutch countryside. There was relief all round, when, after flying on for a few more minutes, they finally got their bearings and learned that they were on track for the objective.

As they approached The Hague, the Mosquitoes split up into pairs, following in line astern, sweeping across the rooftops the narrow streets shuddering to the din of their engines. Bateson's and Flight Lieutenant Peter Cobley's, the first two FBVIs, lined up to attack while the other four circled Lake Gouda allowing the thirty-second 500lb delayed action bombs carried by the first two aircraft, to explode. The third and fourth aircraft carried incendiaries and the fifth and sixth aircraft, two HEs and two incendiaries. Rob Cohen, an ex-student at the Delft Technical University who had escaped to England by canoe, flew one of these Mosquitoes. Bateson's Mosquito streaked towards the target, bomb doors open, its port wing tip missing the tall spire on top of the Peace Palace diagonally opposite the '*Huize Kleykamp*' by inches. Cobley, following Bateson, saw the leader's bombs drop away. He had a hazy impression of a German sentry throwing away his rifle and running for his life, then he saw Bateson's three bombs quite literally skip through the front door and the large windows of the first floor of the building. A. Korthals Alter wrote later:

> Immediately after there were two large explosions. A streetcar about to turn into the Javastraat, stopped and the conductor, driver and passengers ran for cover. At the corner of Scheveningsweg and Laan Copes van Cattenburgh people lay flat on the ground. The only sound that followed after the explosions was that of broken glass and a dull rumbling noise resembling a distant thunderstorm. During the first few moments, people were so bewildered that no one uttered a sound. Only when the second Mosquito came rushing in and heavy explosions were again heard did people realize what was happening. 'They are bombing', they called out. A frightful noise then announced the second attack.

Cobley dropped his bombs in turn, pulling up sharply over the roof of the building. Two minutes later, with dense clouds of smoke already pouring from the shattered building, the second pair of Newman and Smith made their own attack. One of the Mosquito crews could barely see the target. After a further interval, the third pair, led by Flight Lieutenant Vic Hester and Flying Officer Ray Birkett, finished off the mission by dropping HE and incendiary bombs. By now little of the *Kleykamp* building remained and Hester's bombs flew the air and hit the Alexander barracks. Cohen, whose bomb drop failed, but who took photographs, was killed later that summer on a sortie over France. Flight Lieutenant Ron Smith's final recollection was of coming out over playing fields filled with footballers before crossing the coast north of the city to be escorted home by waiting Spitfires.

The *Gestapo* building had been completely destroyed and the majority of the identity papers destroyed. The card files lay buried under the burning wreckage or fluttered over the Scheveningsweg carried by the heat of the fire. The state police who rushed to the scene forced passers-by to pick up the file cards from the street and even made them search the wreckage, threatening them with their cudgels. Most realized why the raid had occurred and they slyly dropped file cards into the flames or destroyed the photos. Fire brigade personnel hosed people away from the devastated building instead of trying to save people in the *Kleykamp*. Among the dead lay Van der Kamp and some fellow Dutch Underground workers. Buildings that surrounded the *Kleykamp* had suffered only slight damage but sixty-one civilians were killed, twenty-four seriously injured and forty-three slightly injured. All six Mosquitoes got back safely, without a shot being fired at them. Five weeks later a report reached the RAF that the operation had been highly satisfactory. For his leadership of this operation Bateson was awarded the DSC and received the Dutch Flying Cross from Prince Bernhard of the Netherlands. An Air Ministry bulletin later described the raid as 'probably the most brilliant feat of low- level precision bombing of the war'.

During April-May FBVIs of 2nd TAF continued their bombing of German targets in France and the Low Countries in the build up to D-Day, 6 June. R. W. Smith, FBVI pilot, 613 'City of Manchester' Squadron, recalls:

Sometime before D-Day, the squadron was asked to provide two aircraft to fly on a mission which, except for the aircrew concerned, was kept completely secret. One aircraft had a pilot and navigator, and the other a pilot and a visiting passenger in the shape of an Australian wing commander. Subsequently, after D Day we learned that the passenger was General Browning in fact, and that the mission had been to fly over the airborne and parachute drop-ping grounds in Normandy. On the night of the D-Day landings and for many nights afterwards, the squadron's chief role was patrolling over and behind enemy lines, attacking troop move-ments and anything in the way of enemy activity on the ground. Our mode of entry and exit was via the sea corridor between Alderney and the Cherbourg Peninsula, entering France at Granville and then making our way to the 'Tennis Court' which was our patrol area. It did not always work out according to plan. On our first patrol, which was in the Caen-Vire area, we found ourselves in solid cloud between 2000 to 3000 ft as soon as we crossed the coast. We could not get below the cloud because in places the ground rises to almost 2000 ft. The Gee was being jammed so badly that the screen was covered with 'grass' and John [Flying Officer Jack Hepworth] was unable to verify our position. After stooging around our patrol area for the required time and seeing nothing, it was time to return home. We decided to fly so many minutes due west to bring us over the sea, then fly north for home. This we did, and after turning north we broke cloud into a lovely clear night immediately to be caught in a cone of searchlights when flying at a height of 4000 ft. At the same time all hell seemed to be let loose with tracer coming up from all sides. Instead of being over sea, we were approaching Cherbourg. We just put the nose down and went weaving and skidding in a dive, passing over the breakwater of Cherbourg at about 400-ft. We landed at Lasham unscathed.

During the period 5 June-11 July, John and I completed 17 operational sorties – all at night. In June these sorties were all in the Normandy area attacking roads, bridges, marshalling yards and any lights or movements seen. Sometimes we would rendezvous with Mitchells dropping flares for us to operate under in certain conditions. My chief recollections are of the fires, which seemed to be burning night after night at Caen and Vire. Lasham airfield is several hundred feet above sea level and, unless the cloud base was on the deck, we usually tried to return to base rather than to divert to Hartford Bridge; if we were diverted, we got less sleep and still had to get back to Lasham next morning. So, with low cloud over England, we tried to fly back under it and in so doing sometimes encountered the Navy. The Navy was quick on the draw and didn't seem to recognize the colours of the day. We would quickly disappear into cloud and settle for Hartford Bridge. From 6 July onwards we went further afield to places south of Paris, Chateauroux, Orleans, Nantes, La Rochelle, Le Mans, Tours, Rouen, Evreux and Dreux, still on the hunt for bridges, railways, trains and transport.

In night operations on 7–8 June 1944 seventy Mosquitoes of 107, 305 and 613 Squadrons operating to the west on rail targets at Argentan, Domfort and Lisieux, sealed approaches to the bridgehead in Normandy. The opportunity for breakout and the eventual invasion of Germany was now within reach, and 2nd TAF would go all the way with the ground forces. On 11 June six Mosquitoes of 464 and 487 Squadrons led by Wing Commander Bob Iredale and Flight Lieutenant McCaul attacked petrol tankers in a railway marshalling yard at Châtellerault at the request of the Army. Wing Commander Mike Pollard of 107 Squadron and his six Mosquitoes arrived at

22.44 hours to find fires burning in an area 300 x 200 yards with smoke rising to 4,000 feet. That night attacks continued on railway targets and fifty aircraft from 88, 98, 107, 180, 226 and 320 Squadrons bombed the railway junction at Le Haye, west of Carentan. Two nights later forty-two Mosquitoes of 107, 305, 464 and 613 Squadrons strafed and bombed troop movements between Tours and Angers-Vire, Dreux and Falaise, and Evreux and Lisieux. Until suitable airstrips could be made ready, the Mosquito wings flew operations from Thorney Island and Lasham. Some spectacular pinpoint daylight operations against specific buildings were flown. On 14 July, Bastille Day, the Mosquitoes of 2nd TAF were called upon for an important task in France, as Gordon Bell-Irving explains:

> AVM Basil Embry came to Thorney Island to brief us for a daylight low-level attack on a special target at Bonneuil Matours, near Poitiers. He was a formidable presence. We were told that the raid was on a Gestapo barracks and was to punish those responsible for the murder of some British prisoners of war who had been clubbed to death with rifle butts in a nearby village square.

In fact, the soldiers clubbed to death were a reconnaissance party of the SAS, code-named Bulbasket, who were dropped south-west of Châteauroux on 5 June to harass the 2nd SS Panzer Division on its move from Toulouse to Normandy. The main party was dropped on 11–12 June and joined up with the Maquis. On 3 July their main camp in the Forêt de Verrieres was attacked by German troops. Nine SAS members got away, but 31 SAS and Lieutenant Tom Stevens, a USAAF evader, who had joined them, were taken prisoner. One officer was wounded before capture and was tied to a tree and publicly beaten to death in Verrieres. Three SAS prisoners were also wounded and taken to hospital in Poitiers, where they were given lethal injections. The remainder, including the American and two other SAS captured previous to this engagement, were shot in the Foret de Saint Sauvant near the village of Rom. The German unit responsible for this atrocity was believed to be the 158th Security Regiment from Poitiers. The SAS survivors signalled the UK with the information of their disaster and that the unit responsible was billeted at Bonneuil Matours. The Mosquitoes' target was a collection of six buildings inside a rectrangle just 170 x 100 feet, close to the village, which had to be avoided.

Bell-Irving continues:

There was no model of the target for us – there hadn't been time to prepare one. Basil's final words before sending us on our way were, 'If you get shot down and taken prisoner don't shoot your mouth off about retaliation. You can't out-piss a skunk!' This struck me as being colourful but anatomically incorrect. I expect he'd heard it from a Texan.

The raid went quite smoothly. We took off in the late afternoon to hit the target at dusk, when the occupants of the barracks would be having dinner. There were 18 aircraft with crews from 21, 464 and 487 Squadrons led by Group Captain Peter Wykeham-Barnes DSO DFC* and Flying Officer Chaplin [Wing Commander R. H. Reynolds DSO DFC led the four FBVIs of 487 Squadron]. At about 2,000 ft we skirted the Cherbourg Peninsula, and on passing a little too close to the Channel Island of Alderney our tidy formation was fired on by a heavy shore battery. Considering our altitude and range this came as a surprise. We scattered in a relatively disciplined way and reformed as soon as we were out of range.

I think we made our landfall near St Malo and went down to about 50 ft from there until just short of the target, where we climbed to bombing height; our bombs were fused for a 25-second delay. Bert Holt, my navigator, and I were among the first to bomb, and as we dived on the target I noticed a 20-mm gun firing tracer rather wildly from the roof of the target building. Looking back after bombing there was a lot of smoke and no sign of tracer. We did not re-formate after bombing; it soon became dark and we returned to base independently. The rest of the trip was uneventful and all crews returned safely. Whoever was in the barracks, we were told that 150 had been killed in our raid. The Mosquitoes in shallow dives had dropped nine tons of bombs on the barracks while they were eating dinner. Three trains were attacked on the return flights for good measure.

On 30 July the SAS learned that 2,000–3,000 Germans were massing for an anti-Maquis/SAS sweep, and the majority were billeted in the Caserne des Dunes barracks at Poitiers. This resulted in a raid by twenty-four FBVIs of 487 and 21 Squadrons escorted by Mustangs on 1 August. Meanwhile, the SAS learned that the survivors of the 158th Regiment were now in the Château de Fou, an SS police HQ south of Châtellerault. This, and Château Maulny, a saboteur school, was attacked by twenty-three FBVIs of 107 and 305 Squadrons on

Sunday 2 August. It is estimated that eighty per cent of the regiment were killed, so that unit paid dearly for its actions. That same day, 613 Squadron attacked a château in Normandy, which was used as a rest home for German submariners. It appeared that Sunday was chosen because on Saturday nights the Germans had a dance, which went on rather late. The FBVIs attacked early in the morning, with rather devastating results. AVM Embry, under the alias 'Wing Commander Smith', and the Station Commander, Group Captain Bower, took part.

On 18 August at Lasham 613 Squadron crews, like those in 305 (Polish) and 107 Squadrons, had been granted a twenty-four-hour stand down by Group to celebrate 138 Wing's thousandth sortie since D-Day and no-one was expecting to fly again until the 19th. H. Mears, a navigator in 613 Squadron, recalls:

A station party was organized in the Airmen's Mess, together with the necessary bars. We had quite a heavy night, getting to bed about 2 am. About 1000 am, we were rudely awakened from our slumbers by a Tannoy announcement ordering all of Black Section (us) to report to the crew room. After a quick wash, we staggered into the daylight for a quick cuppa in the mess, then over to the crew room. The 'doc' was doing a good trade dispensing what he called 'Hangover pills'. Many chaps were missing; sleeping out with wives or whatever. My own driver [pilot] was missing so I flew out with Squadron Leader Bell-Syer, known as the 'Count', whose observer was missing.

Fifteen FBVI crews in 613 Squadron led by Squadron Leader Charles Newman were to carry out a daring low level attack on a school building at Egletons, fifty miles SE of Limoges, believed to be in use as an SS troops barracks. AVM Basil Embry and Group Captain Bower, as usual, went along. Mears continues:

We had drop tanks fitted to the aircraft, so we knew that it was going to be a long ride. However, we eventually started off in formation, low level, across the Channel and on the deck down to the target. The use of wing tanks necessitated emptying the outer tanks, going onto the inners then going back to outers when they were emptied, making a final change to inners.

Fourteen of the Mosquitoes located and bombed the target, scoring at least twenty direct hits and the target was almost completely destroyed. One Mosquito, crewed by Flight Lieutenant House and Flying Officer Savill, was hit in the starboard engine over the target area and failed to return but the crew survived and returned to the squadron just five days later.

The heavier components of 2nd TAF were expected to follow soon after the outbreak from the beaches, including 2 Group's Mosquito bomber and fighter wings. In the meantime they flew from airfields such as Thorney Island and Lasham. Most of 2 Group's flying, for the Mosquito anyway, took the form of night interdiction, while some of the 2 Group squadrons also interfered with German night flying. Mosquitoes from these squadrons would join the circuit of *Luftwaffe* airfields and shoot German aircraft down as they came in to land or just as they took off. In addition to these night expeditions, there were occasional daylight operations, which included spectacular pinpoint attacks on specific buildings.

On 25–26 August 138 Wing took part in all-out attacks on troop concentrations and vehicles in the Rouen area who were attempting to retreat across the Seine. Attacks continued on the night of 30 August against railways in the Saarburg and Strasbourg areas. On 31 August a huge petrol dump at Nomency near Nancy was destroyed and twelve FBVIs of 464 Squadron attacked a dozen petrol trains near Chagney from between 20 and 200 feet and caused widespread destruction.

Early in September the focus of the war changed dramtically. One of the first to hear about a new highly secret operation was Vic Hester, who had completed a tour as a pilot with 613 Squadron in June 1944 after thirty-one operations, and whose navigator, Ray Birkett, had left to do training duties. Hester recalls:

On 4 September my cameraman Ted Moore and I were detailed to attend a briefing at RAF Netheravon, which was filled to over capacity with tugs, gliders and their crews. Ted was very reserved, to a point of being thought unfriendly. Pre-war he was a cameraman with leading British film companies. He joined up and went to Canada for pilot training in 1942. He was pulled out just after qualifying to become part of a most extraordinary unit called the 'Pinewood Military Film Unit'. The men and ladies of this unit were all pre-war professionals at their trade/art, and who were now all in military service. The cameramen probably did more operations than most of us and spent more time over the target to get their pictures. Post war Ted became a Director of Photography who made at least four James Bond films, *Genevieve* and *A Man For All Seasons* – for which he got an Oscar.

We were briefed by most senior Army officers on operation Market Garden and thereafter confined to camp. After two days of bad weather we were allowed to return to our base on no more than normal wartime security, believing, at that time, the operation to be cancelled. Imagine our surprise when, roughly two weeks later, we were briefed locally for the same operation. The date was different; but the dropping zone was the same and the drop-time was similar. I still have doubts that our security was not jeopardized in those two weeks.

On 17 September Operation Market Garden, the airborne invasion in Holland, took place. Some thirty-two FBVIs of 107 and 613 Squadrons in 138 Wing were detailed to attack a German barracks at Arnhem, while 21 Squadron at Thorney Island bombed three school buildings in the centre of Nijmegen which were being used by the German garrison. Both raids were to eliminate the opposition before the airborne forces of Market Garden went in later that day.

Flying Officer Nigel L. Gilson, a navigator in 107 Squadron, had been spending a day's leave in Winchester and was all set for an enjoyable evening to round it off at a dance hall in Basingstoke, when a friend gave him the news that he had to return to Lasham immediately – they had been looking all day for him as the squadron was confined to barracks overnight.

We were met by the usual expectant rumours, but could still learn nothing definite except that we were to be up for briefing at 0530. Ours was a quiet Mess that night, only admin officers were drinking more than lemonade and all air crews were in bed by about 10 – most unusual for us!

'Rising before midday was a bit of a strain, but 0530 on Sunday found us all milling around the briefing room with an exceptional complement of 'braid and scrambled egg' among us. The tense gaiety and laconic humour of briefing are something one remembers but can't adequately describe. I can recall only two things. The CO's description of the purpose of the Arnhem landing (for that

66

was the cause of the trouble): 'If this one comes off the war will be over in 14 days'; and his description of the anticipated reception of the paratroops: 'They expect to slide down stocks of 40 millimetre'. A minor flap broke out while navigators struggled with maps, rulers, protractors and computers, working out tracks, courses, winds and other essentials to the successful combat of hostile gremlins, until at last there was a welcome break for a hasty bacon and egg breakfast. It was a hectic and hilarious meal, then we were back for a final route check and squadron briefing on formation and tactics.

Hester continues:

We were briefed for two tasks that day: First was to film the 613 Squadron raid, then after that, photograph the airborne drop at Arnhem. We took our usual 4 bombs in case we found an opportune target. Whilst in our aircraft sorting out our cameras etc just prior to 'engine start time', the Wing Intelligence Officer appeared and gave us an extra brief. 'Can you take off at once and attack an undefended telephone exchange in a disused barracks in the town of Arnhem?' He handed us a map of the town and the position of the barracks, adding that they had just found out that the German land-line communications would need to go via that exchange when the Para drop began. What could be simpler? We loved undefended targets and were used to hitting small buildings.

We took off about five minutes ahead of 613 Squadron. I think they probably thought my watch was wrong. Upon arrival over Arnhem we found the target. Good Boy. Good Boy. We made live one bomb only. The target was a haystack size building just inside the main gate of the barracks. Why not treat this attack as a practice bombing exercise and make four runs? We slowly descended for the first, and when we were established in a shallow dive, Ted Moore in the nose said 'Jesus Christ, look at that!' Now Ted was a very cool, quiet South African who seldom got excited about anything, so I realised that something was afoot. Taking my eye off the target, I saw that we were gently approaching some twenty Tiger tanks – all manned and firing at us!

We dropped our one bomb from an approach pattern we would not have used had we known the target was defended. As a result our aircraft was hit, and I got three bullets in my left leg, which stopped my left foot from working. Ted kindly fastened a field dressing around the outside of my trousers and we continued the exercise. Fusing the other three bombs, we made a further attack on the telephone exchange, but did not wait to see if we had hit the target. We were now too late to film the attack by 613 Squadron, so with regret, we continued to the Para dropping zone, found, and filmed considerable German armour etc surrounding the dropping area, and decided to head for home. There was no way I could break radio silence and even if I had, no single aircraft transmission could have put a stop to such a large operation as Market Garden. On arrival back at Lasham, our AOC, AVM Basil Embry, was on base. With no food for several hours, I hobbled into de-briefing. Noting my state, Basil Embry handed me a half-pint glass full of issue rum, and proceeded to take our report. Ted Moore went off to process the films, which were flown to Monty within hours.

Meanwhile, at Lasham the Mosquitoes of 138 Wing had taken off, but only after a few last minute hiccups, as Nigel Gilson recalls:

Time for take-off was altered twice, but at last we went to our aircraft where tired ground crews, who'd been working half the night, were just finishing bombing and arming up. Flying Officer Phil Slayden, my pilot, and I sat on the grass waiting for the signal to get into our aircraft. In the peace of a brilliant Sunday morning war seemed very far away. Only Dougie, who'd come to the squadron the day before, remarked on the incongruity of it all; the strains of 'Abide With Me' from a nearby hangar service sounded too ominous to his unaccustomed ear to pass unnoticed! The ground crew gave us the usual strict orders to do a good job with their aeroplane and wished us a brief but sincere 'Good luck', and we taxied out. We took off into a clear sky already filling with squadrons of ungainly gliders and tugs, took up formation and set course. Soon the English draught-board gave place to a sea of rippled blue, and finally that to the deeply cut green flats of Holland.

Arnhem identified itself for us – the natives, or their uninvited guests were distinctly hostile – but we rejoiced in our speed and ploughed in. At first one could watch things quite objectively; one gun team was firing explosive shells, with tantalizing persistency, right on our track, and I wondered absent-mindedly by how much they would miss us. Then we dived to attack. I bent to switch on the camera, began to rise, then instinctively ducked again, only to be conscious of an explosion and a shower of perspex splinters. I jerked up, looking anxiously at Phil, and heaved a sigh of relief when I saw that he was OK and that we were climbing again. At least, I think we were climbing – neither of us was quite sure what happened in those 30 seconds. A glance showed that the gun team had been robbed of their prey by the dive, and the shell had burst above us, merely shattering our cockpit cover.

Suddenly Phil called, 'Hey, the bomb doors are shut, we couldn't have dropped the bombs!'

I jammed them open and he pressed the tit to drop the bombs; we looked behind for the flash, but there was none, and then we remembered that we'd opened the doors before the dive and must have closed them instinctively during the attack. But the look behind had shown us one thing – an aircraft with our markings suddenly catching fire in the starboard petrol tank. The flames spread rapidly to the port, covering the cockpit; the aircraft lost height and finally hit a house and overturned into the river. We shall not forget that quickly. Woody and Mac were in that mass of flame.

It was only a matter of minutes before we were over the Zuider Zee again, flying below formations of gliders and tugs. We felt sorry for them – they hadn't our speed, they had to fly straight though the flak, and their occupants had to go down on 'chutes or without engines or guns – no future in that.

The CO called up to check formation. As we called 'Here' to our own call sign we waited anxiously to hear who was missing. Two failed to reply – two out of 14. Woody and Mac, Ted and Griff had bought it – tough luck; we should miss them.

Late in October another daring low level raid, this time on Aarhus University, the HQ for the *Gestapo* in the whole of Jutland, Denmark, was ordered. The University consisted of four or five buildings just next to an autobahn which ran ten miles in a straight line up to the buildings. In College No.4 was also the HQ of the SD, the police service of the *Nazi* party. The precision attack was scheduled to be carried out on 31 October by twenty-five FBVIs of 21, 464 and 487 Squadrons, each carrying 11-second delayed action bombs. Included in the Mosquito formation, which was led by Group Captain Peter

Wykeham-Barnes, was AVM Basil Embry and his navigator, Peter Clapham. Escort was provided by eight Mustang IIIs of 315 (Polish) Squadron, 12 Group, which flew to Swanton Morley from their base at Andrews Field in Essex, led by the CO, Squadron Leader Tadeusz Andersz.

Australian Ern Dunkley, a 464 Squadron pilot on the raid, recalled:

We made landfall at a lake where we made a rate one turn. The first six aircraft took off for the target followed at short intervals by the other three boxes of six. It was a very well planned run really, except that the wind was blowing right down the autobahn. The blokes who went in first had a good picture of the target, whereas those following had dust and smoke obscuring the target. By the time we got there the place was a mess. There was a hospital not very far along the road on the other side and a lot of people must have got a hell of a shock from the noise but not a single bomb landed in the hospital area. On the way home I lost track of our CO [Wing Commander A. W. Langton DFC] and had called over the radio, 'Has anyone seen the old man?' He came back saying, 'We are not home yet, shut up!' The whole flight took four hours 45 minutes.

Inside one of the college buildings, forty-year old Pastor Sandbäk, arrested in September on suspicion of complicity in acts of sabotage, was about to have his final interrogation, the longest interrogation being thirty-nine hours without any rest, after days of whipping and tightening of string around his handcuffs. 'Suddenly, we heard the whine of the first exploding bomb while the planes thundered across the University. Werner, my interrogator's face, was as pale as death from fright. He and his assistants ran without thinking of me. I saw them run down a passage to the right, and instinctively I went down to the left. This saved my life. Shortly afterwards the whole building collapsed. Werner and his two assistants were killed. I heard two bangs and everything went blank. When I awoke again I was buried under bricks.' Pastor Sandbäk was later spirited across to Sweden.

The operation was carried out at such a low altitude that Squadron Leader F. H. Denton of 487 Squadron hit the roof of the building, losing his tail wheel and the port half of the tail plane. Denton nursed the Mosquito across the North Sea and managed to land safely. Flight Lieutenant Stembrowicz concludes: 'We saw explosions and very light

70

ack-ack coming up in the Mosquitoes wake. All of us went to the right and put ourselves between the Mosquitoes and the German airfields. This time we were higher. We saw no fighters and the flight home was uneventful.' The university and its incriminating records were destroyed. Among the 110–175 Germans killed in the raid was *Kriminalrat* Schwitzgiebel, head of the *Gestapo* in Jutland and SS *Obersturmbannfuehrer* Lonechun, Head of the Security Services.

Chapter Five

New Found Offensive

The FBVIs of 21, 464 and 487 Squadrons in 140 Wing, 2nd TAF were to remain at Thorney Island until December 1944 when the Australian and New Zealand squadrons both sent advance detachments to Rosières-en-Santerre, France. At Lasham meanwhile, 2nd TAF's other Mosquito fighter-bomber wing – 138 – comprised Nos. 107, 305 (Polish) and 613 Squadrons, which late the previous year had re-equipped with FBVIs after flying Bostons, Mitchell IIs and Mustangs respectively. It was planned to transfer 138 Wing to airfields in France when the breakout from the Normandy beachhead came. 2nd TAF was further strengthened early in 1944. 85 (Base) Group was formed for the purpose of providing fighter cover over the continent leading up to and after, D-Day. 85 Group was created by the transfer from Fighter Command of Nos. 29, 264, 409 'Nighthawk' Squadron RCAF, 410 'Cougar' Squadron RCAF, 488 Squadron RNZAF and 604 Squadrons. The first Mosquito fighter squadron to transfer to 85 Group was 264 Squadron, in January 1944, which went to 141 Wing. (The last, 219 Squadron, would transfer from Fighter Command to 147 Wing on 28 August.) As part of the newfound offensive, the main work for the NFXIIs and NFXIIIs of 85 Group and the FBVIs of 138 and 140 Wings was Day and Night Ranger operations and Intruder sorties from England.

One of the main proponents of Day Ranger operations over France and the Low Countries was 418 (City of Edmonton) Squadron RCAF, which had re-equipped with Mosquitoes in March 1943 and had flown Flower Intruder operations out of RAF Ford, Sussex, using AI Mk IV and Mk VIII. 418 flew their first FBVI operation on 7 May 1943. Since January 1944 the Canadians had reaped a rich harvest of

72

victories on Day and Night Rangers, and the high point came in April-May when they shot down thirty aircraft in the air and destroyed a further thirty-eight on the ground. By May the Canadians, based at Holmsley South, had claimed 100 victories and would have the distinction of destroying more enemy aircraft both in the air and on the ground than any other Canadian squadron, in both night and daylight operations.

Flying Officer Bernard Job, Flying Officer Jack Phillips' navigator in the squadron, recalls:

Being one of the pioneers in Intruder operations, the squadron worked at perfecting techniques aimed at surprising and intercepting enemy aircraft over their own airfields at night and generally disrupting airfield activity. Given opportunity, ground targets were strafed. The absence of AI equipment in the aircraft plainly made the task of interception much more challenging, but, as results showed, hardly impossible, given the acute observation and perseverance demonstrated by crews.

What made this type of offensive operation so different from many others was that, having been assigned designated patrol areas, often a group of airfields in France or Germany, crews were then free to plan their own routes to and from these areas. Intruder aircraft almost always flew at low altitude, firstly in order to avoid unwanted enemy radar detection but also to arrive on target at something like aerodrome circuit height. There were of course, variations on the theme of night intruder patrols. One of these was that of a Ranger where by a single Mosquito penetrated free lance deep into enemy territory, even as far as Poland and southern Bavaria. Later, Day Rangers took place, usually by pairs of aircraft surprising and destroying enemy aircraft both in the air and on the ground, far afield. The Baltic States became a favourite run, thereby exploiting the Mosquito's long endurance at low speed.

On 27 January 1944 Flight Lieutenant James Johnson RCAF and Pilot Officer John Caine, and Pilot Officer Earl Boal, in FBVIs, attacked Clermont-Ferrand airfield. Johnson shot down a Ju88 and damaged a Ju86 and shared in the downing of two JuW34s with Caine, who also destroyed a Ju88. By 8 May, Caine had destroyed twelve aircraft on the ground or water, with five more damaged on the ground or water. (In April-May 1945, Caine, now with 406

Squadron, and flying NFXXXs, destroyed a Ju88 on the ground and damaged four other aircraft on the ground). In the meantime 418 Squadron had also been busy. On 21 March American Lieutenant James F. Luma and Flying Officer John Finlayson, and Flight Lieutenant Donald MacFadyen and 'Pinky' Wright flew a long-range Ranger over France. Luma and Finlayson attacked Luxeuil airfield, where they shot down a JuW34 liaison aircraft and a Ju52/3m transport and damaged two Gotha Go242 glider transports and two Bf109s on the ground, while MacFadyen and Wright shot down a Bv141 which was coming into land. Moving on to Hagenau airfield, MacFadyen proceeded to destroy nine Go242s and a Do217 on the ground. MacFadyen later operated in 406 Squadron where he flew the NFXXX on Night Intruders, finishing the war with seven aircraft and five VIs destroyed, and five aircraft destroyed and seventeen damaged on the ground. Luma finished his tour in April and was awarded both a British and US DFC.

On 14 April Squadron Leader Robert Kipp and Flight Lieutenant Pete Huletsky, also of 418 Squadron, shot down two Ju52/3m minesweepers fitted with de-gaussing rings, and two Do217s on the ground, plus they damaged one more. Kipp finished the war with a large bag of victories, which included ten aircraft shot down, and seven and eight destroyed and damaged on the ground. Meanwhile, Stan Cotterill and 'Pop' McKenna destroyed four in a night sortie, and Charlie Scherf in three months, January-16 May 1944, racked up twenty-three destroyed, thirteen of them in the air. In fact, during April-May 1944, 418 Squadron shot down thirty enemy aircraft in the air and destroyed a further thirty-eight aircraft on the ground. 418 scored their 100th victory in May and in June flew anti-Diver patrols at night.

On 5–6 June, the eve of D-Day, 2nd TAF's Mosquito fighter and fighter-bomber squadrons performed defensive operations (264 Squadron flew jamming patrols before they went looking for enemy fighters) over the invasion coast. *Luftwaffe* activity on 5–6 June was almost non-existent. Flying Officer Pearce and Flying Officer Moore of 409 Squadron in a NFXIII claimed a probable. There was also another role for the Mosquitoes, as Bernard Job of 418 Squadron recalls:

The squadron was stationed at Holmsley South near Bournemouth and six aircrews were detailed to act as 'Flak bait' to cover the para-troop and glider drops in the Cherbourg Peninsular, by drawing searchlights and Flak away from these more vulnerable aircraft. So successful was this that two of the six were hit, one so badly that it crash landed near base and burnt up. The crew ran!

Fewer than fifty plots were made on 5–6 June and only Flying Officer R.E. Lelong RNZAF and Pilot Officer J. A. McLaren, of 605 Squadron in a FBVI scored a kill, when they destroyed a Me410 seven miles south-east of Evreux airfield. On 6–7 June Flight Lieutenant E. L. Williams DFC of 605 Squadron in a FBVI shot down a Ju88 at Orleans-Bricy airfield. Flight Lieutenant Don MacFadyen DFC RCAF and Flight Lieutenant 'Pinky' Wright, of 418 Squadron, flying HR155, destroyed a Ju52/3m north of Coulommiers airfield. Wing Commander Keith M. Hampshire DSO, CO, 456 RAAF Squadron, and Flight Lieutenant T. Condon, in NFXVII HK286, destroyed a He177 three miles east of Barfleur. On 7–8 June when Mosquito night fighters shot down eight enemy aircraft over France 456 Squadron destroyed four He177s and three more on 8th. On 9–10 June 456 Squadron shot down a He177 and a Do217. (On 5 July the Australians claimed three enemy aircraft to bring its score to thirty victories since 1 March).

On 6–7 June Flight Lieutenant Allison and Flying Officer Stanton of 29 Squadron destroyed a Ju52/3m and an unidentified over Coulommiers. 604 Squadron alone destroyed ten aircraft on 7 and 8 June (on 6 August 604 became the first fighter squadron to move to France.) On 8–9 June Flight Lieutenant J. C. I. Hooper DFC and Flying Officer Hubbard DFM of 604 Squadron, in NFXIII MM500, destroyed a Bf110 north-east of Laval and Flying Officer Wigglesworth and Sergeant Blomfield of 29 Squadron downed a Ju88. On the night of the 9–10th, 29 Squadron destroyed two more enemy aircraft and 409 and 410 Squadrons destroyed two Ju188s. By the end of June the night fighters and fighter-bombers of 85 Base Group had destroyed seventy-six enemy aircraft and claimed five probables. In June 264 Squadron claimed sixteen aircraft destroyed, one probable and three damaged all in the vicinity of the beaches. On 19–20 June Squadron Leader F. J. A. Chase and Flying Officer A. F. Watson destroyed a Ju88 over the Channel. July opened well and 264 Squadron claimed six more destroyed by the 14th with a probable and a couple damaged. On the night of the 14th 264 changed over from the beachhead patrols to defensive patrols against flying bombs. A very busy fortnight followed, during which they destroyed nineteen – no mean feat with the lack of speed superiority by the Mosquito. Flying Officer Brooke distinguished himself by getting six. On 26 July 264 Squadron moved to Hunsdon, while 142 Wing, who had recently taken over from 141, went on ahead to France.

On 14–15 June Squadron Leader Russ Bannock and Flying Officer Bob Bruce of 418 Squadron achieved their first victory since joining the Squadron. Bannock recalls:

I joined 418 Squadron at Holmsley South airfield in May 1944 after completing a Mosquito OTU course at both High Ercall, Salop and Greenwood, Nova Scotia. 418 Squadron had been engaged in Night Intruding against enemy airfields as well as conducting low level Day Rangers against airfields when operating in pairs. Prior to training on the Mosquito I spent four years in the Joint Air Training Plan in Canada training Flying Instructors at Central Flying School, Trenton, Ontario and No 3 Flying Instructors School at Arnprior, Ontario. While at Greenwood I teamed up with my navigator, Robert Bruce, who came to Canada for navigator training.

Bruce adds:

The war had been going on a long time when we reached operational flying and we were both 'fully primed'. In 1939 I was a graduate of Edinburgh University with a first in Music, a brilliant outlook and no money. Deeply influenced by the poetry of Wilfred Owen, who was killed in action in November 1918, I joined the Friends Ambulance Unit (as gallant a bunch as any military). But after two and a half years I knew the war was ruinous, and I must be part of the ruin. I was accepted for aircrew training. I was almost 28. Russ on the other hand was young in years – 23 – and old in flying experience and leadership. I arrived at Holmsley South about the 10th of June, Russ a few days earlier.

We wasted no time and after practice trips on the first three days, set off on the night of 14–15th June on our first Intruder, a two-hour patrol off Bourges-Avord airfield. Luck was with us, and after some time we spotted the exhaust of a night-fighter as it passed overhead. We picked it up as it turned on final approach but had to break off to the south due to heavy anti-aircraft fire. Fortunately

76

for us the pilot switched on his landing lights. We attacked in a shallow dive and fired a burst of cannon and machine guns. As it exploded and caught fire we recognized it as a Me 110. We were subjected to a barrage of AA fire from the north side of the airfield and we turned sharply to the left to avoid this wall of fire, but Russ was reefing so hard on the elevator we did a high-speed stall just as we almost turned 180 degrees. The aircraft flicked (rolled) to the right and I caught it after we rolled almost 180 degrees. We then exited to the west of the field.. At that time I had never heard of a high-speed stall and was blissfully unaware of it, nor did I hear of it for 40 years, till Russ casually dropped the term in conversation. I believe the key word is 'I caught it'. We both remembered seeing pine trees illuminated by a searchlight, standing, just off our right wing tip. Surprisingly I emerged from these manoeuvres with no debilitating sickness, and I recall a moment of smug gratification when I had to exert my authority by calling a course for the pinpoint on the river Loire! We were, by the way, still carrying two bombs under the wings, and by the time we reached Holmsley South our fuel reserves were getting low. It was a memorable first trip.

On 24–25 June 1944 488 RNZAF Squadron crew Flight Lieutenant George Esmond 'Jamie' Jameson DFC RNZAF and Flying Officer A. Norman Crookes, his navigator from Derbyshire, were on patrol from Zeals in NFXIII MM466 R for Robert over France covering the advance of the Army near Lisieux. Jamie had flown Beaufighter IIs and VIs in 125 Squadron and had his first combat during night raids on Cardiff and Swansea in the summer of 1942. After a He111 had bombed his own airfield, Jamie pursued the enemy aircraft and shot it down into the Bristol Channel. He landed to find that the bombs had killed the WAAF fiancée of his squadron friend. In August Jamie destroyed another He111 and while on detachment in the Shetlands he claimed a Ju88 as 'damaged' although later information indicated that the bomber had crashed on landing at Stavanger. He was credited with the destruction of a Do217 on 11–12 February 1943 and he then went on 'rest', becoming a gunnery instructor. In January 1944 he joined No. 488 Squadron, which lost nine crews in flying accidents for just two enemy aircraft destroyed. Morale was very low and, although Jameson and Crookes patrolled night after night along the east coast, very little activity came their way. All this was to change on 24–25 June. Crookes picked up a stray contact twenty miles south-west of Bayeaux and closing in quickly, Jameson shot down a Me410.

Four nights later, on 28–29 June, Jameson and Crookes destroyed a Ju88 ten miles north-east of Caen as it was about to bomb British Forces landing at Arromanches. Crookes' DFC was announced for his share in three of Jameson's victories. In June 488 Squadron was credited with nine victories over the beachhead area. At the end of July the New Zealand squadron moved to Colerne near Bath, where Jameson was devastated to learn that his both his brothers had been killed. His elder brother was serving with the New Zealand Army in Tunisia and his younger brother died in a Beaufighter during training at East Fortune. Tragically a cable from New Zealand informed Jamie that his father had died on hearing the news of the death of two of his sons. Jameson's mother immediately appealed to the New Zealand Government to allow Jamie to return home and take over the family farm of nearly 2,000 acres in Rotherham near Canterbury. The High Commissioner, Mr (later Sir William) Jordan, visited 488 Squadron and told Jamie that he had done more than his duty and that he should return to his mother. Jamie was persuaded to apply for a passage on the next ship repatriating time-expired New Zealanders and Australians via the USA and Panama. However, before Jameson departed he was determined to avenge the untimely deaths of his brothers.

On the night of 29–30 July the Kiwi and his faithful navigator Crookes took off in *R for Robert* to patrol the Coutance-St Lô area when they saw an unidentified aircraft approaching head-on at 5,000 ft. Jameson wrote:

> Against the dawn I saw that it was a Junkers 88 and as I turned hard to port I followed him and he skimmed through the cloud tops. I closed to 300 yards and there was a series of explosions from the ground caused by the Junkers dropping his bombs (earmarked for our troops) as he tried to get away. I gave two short bursts as we came to the next clear patch and after a fire in the port engine and fuselage, the Ju 88 went down through the clouds vertically, hitting the ground near Caen.

Jameson circled the crash scene when Crookes picked up another contact on his radarscope. A visual sighting was soon obtained of an aircraft flying just over the clouds at about 280 mph. Whilst closing on it, another Ju88 suddenly appeared through the cloud about one mile ahead, flying in the same direction as the first aircraft. As Jameson drew closer the second Ju88 seemed to see him and did a hard port turn, diving towards cloud cover. Jameson and Crookes followed on the turn and opened fire from dead astern at 350–400 yards range. A large fire started in the Ju88's starboard engine and it disappeared vertically through clouds, well ablaze. Later it was confirmed destroyed by a navigator of No. 410 (RCAF) Squadron who saw the Ju88 hit the ground five to six miles south of Caen, explode and burst into flames.

Jameson and Crookes continued on patrol. Jamie reported:

> Almost immediately I obtained a brief visual on an aircraft crossing from port to starboard some 5,000 ft away and identified it as a Ju 88. My navigator confirmed this and took over on his 'box-of-tricks' keeping me behind the enemy aircraft, which was now taking most violent evasive action and at the same time, was jamming our equipment. When we were down almost to tree-top height I regained the visual at only 250 yards, opening fire immediately and causing the Junkers to pull up almost vertically, turning to port with sparks and debris falling away. The Ju 88 eventually stalled and nose-dived into a four-acre field where it exploded. This was near Lisieux and as the time was now 0515 hours I climbed to 5,000 ft and requested Control to vector me back to any activity, as I had already observed further anti-aircraft fire through the clouds ahead.

Norman Crookes soon obtained two more contacts and Jamie decided to take the nearest, chasing this until a sighting was obtained at 4,000 feet range where it was identified as a Do217. The Dornier pilot evidently spotted the Mosquito at the same time because he immediately began intensive evasive weaving and climbing before entering cloud where he straightened out just as Jameson opened fire at 300 yards. Strikes were seen on the Dornier's fuselage, which began to burn furiously as the enemy aircraft turned its nose up and to starboard with the rear-gunner opening fire, but the gunner's dying burst missed and the aircraft dived into the ground with a terrific explosion. Jameson had fired 320 20-mm shells to destroy all four aircraft in the space of just twenty minutes,

79

a feat which took the New Zealander's score to nine enemy aircraft destroyed.

In July the six squadrons downed fifty-five enemy aircraft and claimed two probables. In July 1944 NFXVIIs of 219 Squadron in Fighter Command based at Bradwell Bay shot down six Ju88/188s in and around the beachhead. Flying Officer D. T. Tull got two of them. In August seventy-seven enemy aircraft were destroyed in the air by the seven night fighter and fighter-bomber squadrons. On 1–2 August Canadians Squadron Leader James D. Somerville and Flying Officer Robinson of 410 (RCAF) Squadron in NFXIII MM477/'U' equipped with AI VIII shot down of a Ju88 north-east of Tessy at 01.00 hours. Somerville reported,

We took off from Colerne at 2310 hours and went to Pool 2. Handed over to Robust and given vector of 100 degrees then over to Circular and later to Radox GCI. We intercepted a Stirling on southerly vector and then told to vector 190 degrees, 140 degrees and finally 230 degrees from the Seine estuary. Control told us they had a Stirling. In the meantime having crossed inland we pulled over to starboard of the Stirling and was immediately given patrol vector of 280 degrees. After flying on this course for 2/3 minutes chandelier flares were seen N/W of us. Immediately Radox told us to vector 320 degrees as my 'turkey was gobbling' and they could not help us much. Whilst still on 320 degrees contact was obtained 3 miles range 5 o'clock 40 degrees. Closed in to 2,000 ft, when visual was obtained on an a/c weaving 30 degrees on either side of 320 degrees. A straight course was flown on visual when a/c cut across in front of Mosquito on one of the jinks, range dropped to 600 ft. A/C now identified as Ju.188. The enemy crew evidently saw us at approximately the same time and did a violent peel off to starboard, but luckily peeled off directly into the chandelier flares and visual was maintained during the dive. E/A pulled up into steep climbing port turn. We turned a little harder than E/A and the range dropped to approx. 900 ft where I opened fire allowing 1 ring deflection. After what appeared a short burst the port wing of the E/A disintegrated outward of engine nacelle. The E/A flicked over into a steep half spiral to starboard and dived vertically into the ground approx. 10 miles N/E Tessy. There a violent explosion followed. No return fire experienced. Landed back at Colerne 0500 hours.

The night following, 2–3 August 1944, Squadron Leader F. J. A. Chase and Flying Officer A. F. Watson of 264 Squadron got their fifth enemy aircraft since D-Day when they destroyed a Ju188 (or 88) ten miles west of Argentan. Somerville and Flying Officer Robinson 410 (RCAF) Squadron in MM477/U scored their third victory when they shot down a Do217 six miles north-west of Pontorson at 22.55 hours. Somerville wrote:

I was first given vector of 190 degrees after a group of bogies then vectored 170 degrees and finally on 150 degrees from 20 miles NE of Avranches. Contact obtained 3 miles range 50 degrees off and to starboard height 7,000 ft ASI 220 mph. Target was doing a gentle weave. I closed to 1,000 ft and identified as a Do 217 by pulling off to starboard and getting a silhouette against a bright northern sky. I pulled back into line astern and opened fire at approximately 800 ft. it appeared that E/A must have seen me at the exact split second as I opened fire as it started a fairly hard starboard turn. On the first burst half of the E/A port tail plane and the port rudder flew off and evidently I must have holed his oil tank, because my windscreen and A/C became smothered in oil. I experienced great difficulty in maintaining a visual through the film of oil. E/A then started doing a steady starboard orbit and losing height rapidly as if the pilot had been killed or was having difficulty in controlling his A/C. After the first burst the combat developed into a dog fight as return fire was experienced from the dorsal and ventral guns of the E/A. No hits appeared to register although the fire appeared to be uncomfortably close. I reopened fire every time I got close enough to see the E/A through oil, which was gradually clearing due to the slipstream, at the same time E/A kept firing back at me. It appeared that the E/A dived vertically into the ground from 3,000 ft at the precise moment when I had used all my ammunition. I orbited port and saw the E/A strike the ground and burn furiously. (Position approx. 6 miles NW Pontorson). No parachutes were seen to leave the E/A but my navigator on the last burst told me he saw the other half of the tail plane leave the E/A. Intermittent flak was experienced throughout and on returning to base found that my main plane had been hit by a 13 mm shell inboard of the port engine nacelle.

Flight Lieutenant 'Jamie' Jameson DFC's tenth victory on 488 RNZAF Squadron came on the night of 3–4 August when he shot down a Ju88 which was about to dive-bomb British Army troops near St Lô. He fired just sixty 20-mm cannon shells to down the Junkers. Next day came news of his sailing date for New Zealand. On 6 August Jameson and Norman Crookes took off on their last sortie together in *R-Robert*. The Controller informed them that 'Bandits' were making for the front line. Jameson gave a 'Tallyho' (enemy sighted) over his R/T and he claimed a Ju88 damaged five miles west of the Vire before notching his eleventh victory, a Ju88 fifteen miles east of Avranche. *R for Robert* landed back at Colerne to a rapturous welcome. Jameson returned to New Zealand and the award of a DSO followed. Crookes, who after the war became a teacher in Kent, received a bar to his DFC. Jamie's score made him the highest scoring New Zealand fighter pilot of the war.

On the night of 6–7 August Wing Commander J. D. Somerville (RCAF) DFC and Flying Officer G. D. Robinson (RCAF) DFC of 410 (RCAF) Squadron in NFXIII MM566/'R' equipped with AI VIII shot down a Ju88 at St Hilaire to take their personal victory score to four. Somerville wrote:

Took off from Colerne at 0050 hr landed back at 0325 hrs. I was put on patrol east-west (south of St. Malo). I was given a vector of 060 degrees and after being on this vector for a short time Tailcoat told us to vector 280 degrees, as he had something for us. I did several one-off vectors until finally on 240 degrees contact was obtained at 2 miles range, 30–35 degrees above, 12 o'clock. My observer told me to climb hard as E/A was considerably above us. Our height was 4,000 ft. My starboard engine was missing badly but we managed to climb to about 5,500 ft where a visual was obtained about 1,000 ft above, dead ahead. Flak was starting to emanate ahead of E/A which seemed to frighten him somewhat and he did a turn to port and started to let down slowly, which suited us as the starboard engine was giving considerable difficulty. When I saw him start to turn I cut across the inside of his turn and pulled in to about 900 ft, slightly below, where I recognized him as a Ju 88. Pulled in a little close and saw two large bombs carried externally inboard motors. Pulled up and opened fire at approximately 700 ft. A few strikes were seen on the starboard engine, which caught fire. E/A did a wide sweeping spiral to port from 3,000 ft and struck the ground with an extremely violent explosion, scattering debris over a large area. Tailcoat fixed us at

1. Wing Commander Bertie Rex O'Bryen 'Sammy' Hoare DSO DFC★ one of the leading Intruder pilots of his generation.

2. Mosquito NFII DZ238 of 23 Squadron in July 1942.   (via Kelvin Sloper)

3. 85 Squadron's Squadron Leader Wilfrith Peter Green DSO DFC, OC A Flight, Wing Commander John Cunningham DSO★ DFC, CO, and Squadron Leader Edward Dixon Crew DFC★, OC B Flight, at Hunsdon on 5 May 1943.   (via Mick Jennings)

4. Mosquito FBVI crews study a map of the continent before setting off on another daylight operation. *(via Mick Jennings)*

5. A photographic still of the Amiens prison raid 18 February 1944 taken from Wing Commander Bob Iredale's Mosquito MM412/SB-F. The aircraft following is MM402/SB-A flown by Squadron Leader W. R. C. Sugden and Flying Officer A. H. Bridges. *(via John Rayner)*

6. On 24-25 March 1944 Flying Officers Edward R. Hedgecoe and N. L. Bamford of 85 Squadron were forced to fly through the fireball created by the sudden explosion of a *II./KG54* Ju88 that they had been attacking just seconds before. Upon returning to West Malling the true extent of the damage to their NFXII was revealed. *(via Philip Birtles)*

7. Mosquito VI MM417/EG-T of 487 Squadron RNZAF. On 26 March 1944 this aircraft, which was being flown by the CO, Wing Commander Irving S. 'Black' Smith RNZAF, was shot up (accidentally) by a following Mosquito flown by Claude Pocock, who was on his first Noball operation. MM417 landed at Hunsdon whereupon it broke up into three pieces. That evening, still thinking he had been hit by enemy fire, Smith and his navigator, Ronnie Marsh, went to examine the wreck. Marsh dug some 20-mm ammunition out of the wing and examination of NS828's camera gun film proved that Pocock had shot down his CO! *(IWM)*

8. Flying Officers John Barry and Guy Hopkins of 29 Squadron leaving their crewroom to take their Mosquito on the obligatory NFT (Night Flying Test). *(Ken Lowes)*

9. Mosquito FBVI LR366 of 613 'City of Manchester' Squadron, 2nd TAF, refuelling at RAF Swanton Morley, Norfolk early in 1944. This aircraft was lost flying with 107 Squadron on 17 September 1944. *(via Jerry Scutts)*

10. Flying Officers John Barry and Guy Hopkins of 29 Squadron ready for the off. *(Ken Lowes)*

The text visible on the blackboard:

PILOT	NAVIGATOR	A/C			REMARKS
...SHAM	F/O ELLIS				
...RY	F/O HOPKINS	413	18.10	2030 2.20	
...TERS	F/Lt GUNN	168	18.45	2050 2.05	
...KLAND	F/O RASPIN	515	2200	2310 1.10	
...GETER	F/Lt FELL	167			
...NGLE	S/Lt PORTER	403	2245		
...TEWARD	F/O MAIN	165	2340		
...OVAN	W/O NICOL	174			
...LLIPS	F.I.U.	515			
...SSWELL	F/S McDOWALL	Mos			
...UNE	F/O FHL	189			
...NGLE	Sgt NUTSHY				

11. Squadron Leader Clive Kirkland A Flight commander, 29 Squadron, is receiving the first warning of a possible approaching raider force. The two bottom lines were frivolous additions and have oblique references. Pilot Officer Prune seemed to serve on every RAF squadron. He dropped all the clangers and was responsible for all the mishaps. He never grew up and never got promoted.   *(Ken Lowes)*

12. 29 Squadron crews on readiness before twilight until dawn. The only card game that was universally played was poker and there were few abstainers. *Left to Right:* Flying Officer Guy Hopkins, Flight Sergeant Athol Cresswell, Sergeant Eric Haines, Flight Lieutenant Reggie Pargeter, Flying Officer Bill Ellis, Flight Sergeant McDowall, Flying Officers Ron Bensham (KIA June 1944) and John Barry, who is wearing special goggles with dark red lenses for darkness adaptation. When an aircrew was called out on a scramble, dashing out from artificial indoor lightning into the darkness outside was hazardous. The pictures on the walls are mostly pages from the American magazine Esquire. *(Ken Lowes)*

13. Servicing of a Mosquito the morning after operational flying. *(Ken Lowes)*

14. Having flown his stint for the night, a pilot was nevertheless still on standby so he went into the bunker to have a nap. After dawn he could go to his own bed in the Officers' mess, a former girls' boarding school about a mile away where the aircraft noise was much less than in the bunker on the airfield. *(Ken Lowes)*

15. Captain Ken Lowes, the Army Liaison Officer, with crews of 29 Squadron. *(Ken Lowes)*

16. 29 Squadron crews at RAF Ford on 24-25 February 1944 - 'The Big Night' - the squadron's most successful searchlight operation night with claims for nine shot down plus one shared, two destroyed and two probables. *Back Row:* Flight Lieutenant R. L. Fell; Flying Officers John E. Barry; Guy Hopkins; Dicky Raspin; Warrant Officer Nicol. *Front Row:* Warrant Officer Kershaw; Flight Lieutenant Ted Cox; Squadron Leader Clive Kirkland; Flying Officer W. W. Provan; Flight Lieutenant Reginald Clive Pargeter. *(Frank Pringle via Theo Boiten)*

17. Flying Officer John Barry (left) explains to the other crews in 29 Squadron how he shot down two enemy aircraft that night. *Left to Right:* beside Barry are navigator Bob Stainton, his pilot Ernest Mutters, Flying Officer Guy Hopkins and navigator Flight Sergeant McDowall. *(Ken Lowes)*

18. On the night of 24-25 February 1944 Squadron Leader Clive Kirkland and Flying
    Officer Dicky Raspin of 29 Squadron in Mosquito XIII HK413 shot down a Do 217M
    over the Dorking Hills, Surrey. Raspin got the chance to go souvenir hunting as the
    crash site was only thirty miles north of their airfield at Ford. Having taken this pic-
    ture, Captain Ken Lowes, an Army liaison officer attached to the squadron, went
    towards the wreckage with a view to taking one or two close-ups. As he got nearer he
    realized that the aircraft was 'ticking' like an alarm clock.   *(Ken Lowes)*

19. Mosquito XVII
    flown by the CO of
    456 Squadron
    RAAF, Wing
    Commander Keith
    M. Hampshire DSO★
    DFC, who finished
    the war with seven
    confirmed victories
    and one probable, all
    scored flying
    Mosquito XVII air-
    craft. When the four
    cannons were fired
    the first shells burst
    through the stream-
    lining material which
    is being applied and
    easily replaced the
    following morning.
    (Ken Lowes)

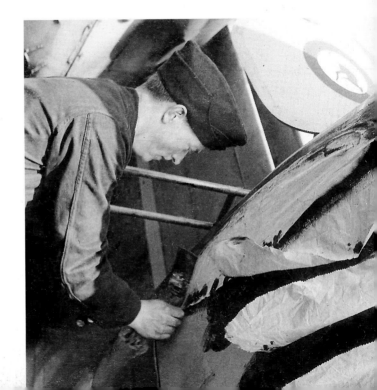

20. 464 Squadron RAAF CO Squadron Leader Gordon 'Peter' Panitz of Queensland, Australia, and Flying Officer Richard Williams of NSW. Panitz and Williams were one of eighteen crews from 21, 464 and 487 Squadrons who successfully attacked Bonneuil Matours, a collection of six buildings inside a rectangle just 170 x 100 feet, close to the village which had to be avoided, on Bastille Day, 14 July 1944.

(via Paul McCue)

21. The railway marshalling yards at Lyon, France under attack by two Mosquitoes of 107 Squadron in July 1944.

(Vic Hester)

26. Battle of Britain veteran Michael Hugh Constable-Maxwell (pilot) and his navigator Sergeant (later Flight Lieutenant DFC) John Quinton. Constable-Maxwell (later Wing Commander DSO DFC) scored six victories, one shared destroyed, and four probables in the Second World War, four of the kills being obtained flying Mosquitoes. Quinton was killed in a Wellington crash on 13 August 1951 after he had selflessly given his parachute to an ATC cadet.
(via Ron MacKay)

27. On 31 October 1944 a precision attack was carried out on Aarhus University, the HQ for the Gestapo in the whole of Jutland, Denmark, by twenty-five FBVIs of 21, 464 and 487 Squadrons, each carrying eleven-second delayed action bombs, and led by Group Captain Peter Wykeham-Barnes. The operation was carried out at such a low altitude that Squadron Leader F. H. Denton of 487 Squadron hit the roof of the building, losing his tail wheel and the port half of the tail plane. Denton nursed the Mosquito across the North Sea and managed to land safely. The university and its incriminating records were destroyed. *(via Derek Carter)*

28. The *Shellhaus* in Copenhagen. Above, during the raid.　　　*(via Derek Carter)*

29. Below, after the raid.　　　*(via Derek Carter)*

180 degrees beacon FM 55 miles (St. Hilaire du H. area). No return fire or evasive action experienced. I claim 1 Ju 88 destroyed.

On 6 August 604 (County of Middlesex) Squadron at Zeals, which had joined 141 Wing, 2nd TAF, in April, transferring to 147 Wing 85 (Base) Group, on 3 May, became the first Mosquito fighter squadron to move to France, when it transferred to A.8 at Picauville. On the 11th 264 Squadron moved to Picauville on the Cherbourg Peninsula having been beaten to it by 604 Squadron by a few days. Flight Lieutenant J. A. M. Haddon of 604 Squadron recollects:

By the time 2nd TAF came into existence the Allies had had four years of night warfare experience to devise airfield systems that could function well at night as well as protect aircraft on the ground from attack, largely using wide dispersal, aircraft blast sheltering, and minimal visibility from the air as defensive systems. As aircraft became heavier, grass surfaced fields fell out of use. By D-Day engineers had perfected systems of construction that could carry entire airfields overseas, not too different in facilities from any modern field of that time. One invasion airfield, A8 at Picauville, west of St Mere Eglise in the American sector was built in about 48 hours, including runway, dispersals, taxi paths, control and refueling, using a base of sand covered with tar paper. Designed to last 30 days, it lasted 55 or so and was home to three American day fighter-bomber squadrons and two RAF night squadrons. The RAF was doing night cover from A8 because someone, quite wrongly, had convinced the planners that the US night fighters were inadequate. I heard that the A8 designer was a Canadian. Again by 2nd TAF time, aircraft carrying heavy radar and equipped with cannons firing 2,400 rounds of 20mm ammunition a minute could be operated out of such fields in all-but-total darkness. As far as I know there was only one fatal crash in the 55 days of A8's existence.

Like most wartime flying operations, the longer a night-fighter crew had survived, the longer it would continue to survive. Crews of 604 and 264, the first night squadrons on the beachhead, had no less than one full tour of duty each behind them. As I recollect it, 604 shot down some 50–60 hostiles for the loss of two or three crews from D-Day to VE Day. Life for aircrew wasn't all that bad in Normandy. There were so many experienced crews available, and food was so much easier to furnish in the UK than on the beachhead, that for one period we got ten days home leave every three weeks. As usual, staff seemed to get better quarters than fighting forces. At A8 the staff lived in the former German Army Commander's HQ, known as the Chateau, while aircrew were put into a centuries old, partly burned-out insect-ridden farmhouse known to us as the 'Shiteau'. We eventually rebelled and moved into tents.

Although fast scrambles had been additional ways of getting nightfighters airborne, the usual procedure was to have aircraft constantly on patrol at about Angels 10, positioned to intrude into hostile air space when required, with minimum loss of time. The speed difference between a Ju 88 and a Mosquito was sufficiently slight that the long stern chases of earlier years were out of the question. Security considerations had prevented the very latest airborne radar from being operated from bases so close to enemy lines, so the squadrons operating from Normandy had to use a radar that could only see in a cone (like an ice cream cone) looking forward, which limited their interception capabilities. I now forget the maximum range of that radar but probably it was two or three miles.

A time-saving manoeuvre, if a ground controller had been good enough to put you onto a bandit on a closing angle, was to wait for your RO to get radar contact and assess the targets course and speed as it came towards you, then at the critical moment determined by the RO, turn hard across the face of the bandit and continue turning until hopefully it re-appeared in the radar cone in front of you. If you turned too soon, you got in front of him, not a good thing if he was also a night fighter; if you turned too late it meant a long stern chase. It was the RO's skill and the crew's total integration that determined success or failure. Most crews had spent years perfecting their techniques.

On a good moonlight night a normal night fighter pilot could (visually) see an aircraft as a dot at about 4000 ft; on a black night 1,500–2,000 ft was pretty good. The RO's job was to get his pilot to that range, nicely positioned for the kill. Under the operating conditions of normal static warfare, ground control could reasonably assure a crew whether or not a target was hostile. Under invasion conditions such as Sicily or Normandy, the chances of a target being hostile were perhaps ten or twenty-to-one against. I was told that when we were airborne at H-hour-6 of D Day, and over a beachhead- and sea area some thirty miles long by twenty miles deep, there were up to 20 other TAF night fighters-as well as Dakotas towing gliders, the odd bomber and quite a few Fighter Command aircraft trying to get into the act. My logbook shows much the same to be true for the next two weeks as we covered the fleet and invasion area. Sorting things out wasn't easy.

Experienced night crews knew that it was vital to treat any interception as a technical exercise and make full identification, rather than go blustering in and shooting down some unfortunate Allied crew while the adrenaline was flowing. The only exception to this identification-first principle came from US anti-aircraft gun crews on the beachhead who generally fired at anything within range, especially before they got used to having night fighters based in their midst.

On the night of 5–6 August Flight Lieutenant J. A. M. Haddon and his navigator, Flying Officer R. J. Mcllvenny, flying XIII MM514 took off on a night patrol. Haddon wrote:

Mcllvenny and I had taken off from A8 at 2200 hrs on our first night sortie from the American beachhead, and ground control was using us to calibrate some new radar on the British beachhead. Our patrol line lay about 50 kilometers south of Caen at about 5,000 ft. Unknown to us a Junkers 188 was on a westerly course, fairly well east of the British Sector. An 88/188 would follow him some twenty minutes later. Both could have been aiming at targets anywhere in the American Sector. Patton had just made his breakout of the beachhead towards Rennes in the extreme west but the Canadian and British forces were still being held fast somewhere south of Bayeaux and Caen. Falaise was still in enemy hands. We could see ground artillery fire from that Sector. It was a brilliant moonlit night, a little before midnight.

Control told us there was trade coming up flying much higher than we were and gave us several southerly courses to steer. Because we had been unusually low and had to climb as we tried to reach our target we found ourselves having difficulty catching up with it, but it made things easier by gradually turning from west to NNW towards the general direction of our own airfield. We were pretty sure we were after a fellow Mosquito and that our interception would be no classic encounter – just another tail chase. Controllers who put you in such a position weren't high on aircrew popularity lists.

Mac had the bogey on radar for some minutes before I saw a tiny speck ahead in the sky at a distance of 3,500 ft. At 2,000 ft Mac voiced the opinion that it could be a Ju 88. He was using night glasses. Pilots seldom believed that navigators could tell a Lancaster from a Lysander but, as Mac was much above average, discretion became the better part of valour. We slid well to one side and below so that we weren't silhouetted against the moon as we had been, which also gave us a chance to see the aircraft from the best angle. As we closed it was clear that our target was a 188 and that he didn't know we were there, a very desirable situation. Keeping it that way, I got in to 800 ft and checked for the tenth time that the guns were set to fire, the props were in near fine pitch and the gunsight dim enough to see through. I then pulled up behind him and opened up. I first hit his port engine, then the fuselage, and we ducked when something left the aircraft. It was on fire on the way down, then its pyrotechnics blew up and finally it went in near somewhere called Domfront.

Before we had time for the usual mutual admiration to begin we got a call from Ops to turn south east again because there was more trade at 25 miles and below us. I put the nose hard down and eventually Mac got a number of contacts. I ended up overshooting and needing more help from Ops and Mac. It was clear that this was no sitting duck. He knew we were there and what he had to do about it. After several visuals on an 88 that was all over the sky, doing steep turns, climbing and diving, I finally managed to hold him visually, and fly as in a day combat. Now night aerobatics are not to be recommended because you topple your major instruments and lose them when you need them most. It is also very easy to lose speed and spin-in. However, Mac and I had developed a drill for such circumstances and he called height and airspeed to me every few seconds so that we would not fly into the ground. As I tried to turn inside the 88 to get my gun-sight on him I found him flying in a very tight turn, much too low for comfort. Suddenly he went on his back and dived, perhaps having stalled. Shortly afterwards there was a great flash from the ground and both Ops and Mac lost contact. Later the French Underground confirmed time and place near Antrain where it had gone in.

On 7–8 August Flight Lieutenant Davidson and Flying Officer Willmott of 264 Squadron had to fly through the explosion of their Ju88 which blacked the entire aircraft and burnt off the rudder fabric. Nothing daunted they landed their Mosquito safely on a strip just behind the beachhead. On the night of 14–15 August Squadron Leader Somerville DFC and Flying Officer G. D. Robinson DFC of 410 (RCAF) Squadron in NFXIII MM477/'U' equipped with AI VIII went in search of their fifth victory. Fifteen miles due west of Le Havre they picked up a contact as Somerville relates:

> I pulled in behind the E/A, range about 1½ miles and started to close. E/A at this time began to climb and do about a rate half turn to starboard. We maintained contact on the AI, closing the range till finally the E/A leveled off at approximately 10,500 ft after turning a complete 360 degrees. At this time I was very well shrouded. The range at this time was about 1800 ft, almost directly above. I started to pull up and on decreasing the angle off the exhausts disappeared, visual being lost. However the visual was regained at approximately 800 ft range 20 degrees, off. I pulled into 600 ft and recognized E/A as a Ju 88. During this period my navigator was getting his Ross Night Glasses and from directly underneath the E/A he confirmed my recognition. At this range I noticed two heavy calibre bombs slung externally inboard of the engines. I dropped back to 450 ft, pulled up to dead astern and opened fire at this range. The fuselage of the E/A burst with a violent explosion and disintegrated into the air. No return fire was experienced. The majority of the debris fell off to port. I pulled up in a very steep climb and broke to starboard. I asked control for a fix and was given 15 miles due west of Le Havre. Time 2325 hrs. I claim this E/A destroyed.

Somerville was promoted to wing commander and given command of 409 (RCAF) Squadron.

On 26 August 219 Squadron joined 147 Wing, 85 (Base) Group, 2nd TAF and on 3 September 264 Squadron made a move to Caen/Carpiquet with the first patrols flown over the Paris area and later over Brussels. The only real excitement was when Flight Lieutenant Moncur and Flying Officer Woodruffe did not return from a low flying exercise on the afternoon of the 19th. They did come back a week later having been shot down in the St Nazaire area. On the

14th 264 Squadron flew back to Predannack, ostensibly to re-equip, but anyway by then the war had got too far out of sight. Victories in September and October did not match those scored in June and July but the night fighters nevertheless maintained a credible response. During September they destroyed twenty-eight enemy aircraft of many types, and in October, a further fifteen were destroyed.

Though V1 patrols had occupied most of 418 Squadron's time in July and August they were interspersed with other types of activity, 418 reverting, in September, to Rangers, and abortive Big Ben patrols (trying to 'jam' V2 rockets). 418 finished the war with the distinction of destroying more enemy aircraft both in the air and on the ground, than any other Canadian squadron, in both night and daylight operations as, Bob Bruce, Russ Bannock's navigator, recalls:

We did Flowers harassing enemy bases in support of the invasion or of bombers, and Day Rangers hunting in pairs. These were carried out at low level, and ideally with cloud cover at 1,000ft or more, to facilitate evasion if attacked. Our first of these was on 28 June1944 led by Flight Lieutenant C. M. Jasper (Long Beach, Ca.) and his navigator Archie Martin. Jas was one of several American pilots who joined the RCAF. Crossing Denmark at treetop height, we found a Ju 88 crossing the Baltic, close to a fair sized vessel. Jasper destroyed the Junkers in the air, but was caught by the ship's fire. I vividly recall his blazing tailfin above the seemingly static ship. The damage was limited and he flew home successfully.

Night Rangers and Flowers gave similar opportunity, if we were lucky enough to detect enemy aircraft. For a higher success rate AI was needed, with which 406 Squadron were equipped. But we were lucky sometimes, and Russ's shooting was deadly. Sometimes bad weather intervened. On 15 August en route for Avignon we met such thunder and up draught over the Massif Central that we had to pull out and return. We had gained 4,000ft over the mountains in a few seconds; we might equally have lost them. Russ compared the stresses he encountered there with the worst ever in his subsequent career as a test pilot. (On another trip to Breslau in October we flew 5.25hrs without a pinpoint and of course no result. Good D.R. depends upon accurate flying).

We did two other Day Rangers, one to Copenhagen with Sid Seid (another Californian) and Dave McIntosh with gratifying result, the other alone arriving at Parow, 'on the Baltic coast at sunrise.

We found an OTU in full operation. After destroying two Me 108's in the circuit we were attacked by another older type Me 109. We broke off at treetop height but our port engine caught fire (due to debris holing the radiator). We feathered and returned on one engine landing back at Hunsdon after 7hrs 15 mins. 418 had established a high success rate in Day Rangers during the first six months of 1944. On the night of 29–30 August, Russ Bannock and Bob Bruce, paired with Flying Officer Sid Seid and Dave McIntosh, blew up a Ju88 on the ground at Copenhagen-Kastrup, and a Bf110 at Vaerose airfield.

Seid, who scored hits on a line of three aircraft, observed a mechanic working around the tail section of the Bf110 as they approached. 'After one look at us,' Seid recalled, 'the "Erk" broke all speed records during a sprint in an easterly direction. During my attack, another "Erk" was observed descending a high ladder near the roof of a hangar. Upon seeing us the speed of his descent was suddenly and forcibly increased by a backward fall from near the top of the ladder. I claim this "Erk" as "probably destroyed".'

Life for Dave McIntosh was never dull flying with Sid Seid. McIntosh recalls that:

Shortly after dawn on 15 October 1944, Sid and I were flying in a Mosquito fighter over our target, Stargard, a German airfield north-east of Berlin. We were a long way from home (Hunsdon, an airfield thirty miles north of London) and still had farther east and north to go to a second target, Kolberg, another German aerodrome, before we could head back to England. 'Heading back' were the sweetest two words, I knew during the war, apart from 'arrival Hunsdon' (or any other friendly base). We were in the process of attacking Luftwaffe planes on the ground – we had seen none in the air, thank heaven – and there was a whole array of them for our picking: Messerschmitt fighters, Junkers night-fighters, Stuka dive-bombers and Focke Wulf fighters. We had flown low (treetop) level, pulling up over power lines, and had so completely caught the Jerries by surprise that a hundred of them were drawn up for what we surmised was a Sunday morning (which was what it was) church parade. I say surmise because neither Sid nor I ever went to church (in his case, synagogue) except, perhaps, to give the squadron padre a lift occasionally when he was particularly down in the mouth because of heavy non-attendance at his services in gymnasium, hangar or open air. Fear of death in war might have driven some fliers to God, but it didn't drive them to church.

Sid dived at one group of planes, aiming at the wing roots where the fuel was located, and blazed away with our 20-mm cannon. He blew up a Messerschmitt with a one-second burst on our first run. We got turned around for another run at the field and Sid fired a two-second burst at three planes, one exploding. As he finished the salvo, he spotted two more planes, one a Stuka, on the south side of the field. He got in a quick burst and the Stuka exploded just as we started going over on our port side. We were only 20 ft off the deck and when Sid tried to correct our roll we stalled and the stick flew out of his hands.

We should have been dead right there and then, spread in little pink and red pieces all over Stargard airfield. If the Germans could find anything at all to pick up, the two of us would have fitted easily into one shoe or cigar box. But the Mosquito in an unexplained flick righted itself and we were flying straight and level at a height of ten feet. The explanation for this baffling Mosquito self-manoeuvre didn't interest me; only the result did. Later, I wondered vaguely whether our plane's call sign, Credo 29, had anything to do with our survival: Belief, resulting in a perfect cribbage hand. When my nerves steadied (as much as they ever did – a controlled jangle) a few minutes later as we raced over the sunlit autumn leaves toward Kolberg, I said to myself: 'Boy, the rest of your life is pure gravy. Every minute after flicking out of the lethal stall is an unearned bonus.'

On 2 October 1944 Flying Officer R. Lelong of 605 Squadron took off from his forward base at St Dizier and over the Baltic claimed six enemy aircraft destroyed, plus one 'probable' and five 'damaged'. Lelong returned to base on one engine. (Five days later, on 7 October, two Mosquitoes of 605 Squadron destroyed ten enemy aircraft near Vienna and damaged six more.) At this stage of the war the *Luftwaffe* had become increasingly wary in its use of its dwindling aircraft resources. Consequently, the Allied air forces had to employ imaginative tactics to find and destroy them. Since the *Luftwaffe* was doing less and less flying, Flight Lieutenant F. A. 'Ted' Johnson DFC RCAF and his navigator, Flight Lieutenant N. J. 'Jimmy' Gibbons, of 418 Squadron had speculated that it should be possible to catch them on the ground at night. After some experimentation they had established that on nights when there was a full moon there was sufficient light to carry out an air-to-ground strafing attack in a shallow dive from about 1,500 feet above ground level. Any higher and it was difficult to see objects on the ground, while any lower would give insufficient time to aim the Mosquito's guns, fire a burst and pull out from the dive before striking the ground. Best visibility was obtained by positioning for the attack with the moon on the opposite side of the target. The Mosquito crew had studied intelligence reports of *Luftwaffe* flying activity and had noticed that in recent weeks there had been several indications of aircraft flying in the vicinity of Erding airfield. Although it was deep within Germany on the far side of Munich at the limit of the Mosquito's range, they had calculated that if they pre-positioned their aircraft from their operational base at Hunsdon to Ford airfield in Sussex, and re-fuelled and launched from there with full tanks, they could make the round trip. So at the next full moon phase they re-checked all factors, obtained authorization for the operation, on the night of 2 October 1944, moved their Mosquito to Ford in the late afternoon, re-fuelled, then took off at 20.15 into a hazy autumn night. The moon had not yet risen but it would be up in an hour and the Met forecast had said that although there was a weather front over Germany it should be well east of their target by the time they arrived and the skies should be clear.

The Met man was wrong. After flying for three hours at 500 feet in the hope of avoiding being picked up by German radar, Johnson and Gibbons arrived in the area to find the sky completely obscured by thick, low-hanging clouds. There would be no help from the moon. Determined not to return without trying to attack their target, they flew north of the enemy airfield to a predetermined sharp bend in the Isar River, which could be seen even on this moonless night, and using an accurate course heading, airspeed and time made their first abortive pass. The Germans did not react as they overflew the airfield, so Johnson and Gibbons speculated that no radar alert had been given to the defences and, indeed, they might still be uncertain if this was a hostile aircraft or one of their own with radio communications problems. As their Mosquito streaked close to 300 mph through the night sky a few miles east of Munich, searchlights flicked on to the southeast at Erding airfield and nervously probed the dark clouds above. Johnson said, 'Jim, turn our navigation lights on and off a few times. The natives are getting restless.' A few flashes of the nav lights and the German crews doused their searchlights and waited and wondered.

Again they reached their pinpoint over the river bend and carefully turned so that when they re-crossed in a southerly direction they would be on the desired course at exactly the selected height and airspeed. The Mosquito passed over the river – precision was essential to success under these adverse visibility conditions. Gibbons clicked his stopwatch and breathed into the microphone mounted in his oxygen mask, 'Two minutes 28 seconds to go.'

Ted Johnson grunted acknowledgement and re-checked that the safety guards were off on both the cannons and the machine guns. He tweaked the dimmer control lower on the reflector gunsight to reduce the dim glow of the circle of light with its central dot on the wind-screen that was his aiming guide. He needed the gun sight as dim as possible to maximize his chances of seeing something on the ground in the target area. Dim outlines sped under the Mosquito as the two Merlin 25s growled their power across the night sky. Wispy cloud flicked by. Tension in the dimly lit cockpit mounted as the crew strained forward in their safety harnesses, striving to see objects on the ground. The airfield ahead remained totally blacked out. There was no sign of hostility. Johnson re-checked speed, course and alti-tude. Gibbons glanced at his stopwatch and said, '30 seconds', then began a countdown at ten-second intervals. As he called out, '10 seconds', Johnson replied, 'Airfield in sight!' and eased forward slightly on the control column, anticipating the need to initiate a quick dive as soon as a target was seen. His right thumb and forefinger tensed over the button and the trigger on the control column that would fire the cannons and machine guns. Suddenly the vague outline of a single-engine aircraft sitting on the airfield swept under the Mosquito's nose and the pilot made a spasmodic movement to start a dive but in the same second knew it was too late. 'Damn!' was all he said as the airfield continued to race away beneath and the indistinct outlines of hangars on the southern boundary were left behind. Still no reaction from the airfield defences.

The Mosquito made a wide sweeping turn westwards and continued around on to a northerly heading. Gibbons spoke. 'What kind of aircraft was that?'

Johnson replied, 'I'm not sure. Could have been a Me 108, an advanced trainer. I couldn't see in time. Let's have one more go.' A green Aldis-type hand-held signal light directed a series of dots and dashes toward them from the airfield control tower. The Mossie crew was unable to decipher the message since, whatever it was, it was in German. 'Jimmy', said Johnson, 'I think they believe we want to land. Give them a few more flashes on the nav lights, then leave them on steady.' Then, as an afterthought, he added, 'Make damn sure you switch them off the instant I fire the guns!'

Over the kink in the river they commenced their third run. Johnson eased the Mossie down 100 feet hoping to improve the ability to see objects on the ground, and concentrated on holding the air speed and heading. He turned the ultraviolet cockpit instrument lighting a notch dimmer and eased forward on the hard dinghy pack that was numbing his buttocks after three hours. The airfield ahead remained in total darkness. A trickle of sweat itched its way down the pilot's back. His open mike picked up the navigator's rapid breathing. '20 seconds to go,' said Gibbons tensely. A moment later Johnson saw the blurred outline of a tree on the airfield perimeter and realised that he had seen it on their second pass. The parked aircraft had to be just ahead! Without waiting to actually see his target he pushed the Mossie's nose down into a shallow dive and at the same moment saw the shadowy outline of the German aircraft. Rapidly he brought the central 'bead' of his reflector gunsight on to it and squeezed both triggers.

The cockpit floor vibrated under their feet from the thunderous bellow of the four 20-mm cannon, each spewing rounds at the rate of 600 a minute. Simultaneously the four .303 machine guns chattered their deadly hail. Streams of glowing tracers lashed forward from the Mosquito's nose and immediately a pattern of strikes from the mixture of ball, incendiary and explosive shells were seen to envelope the German aircraft. The stench of cordite fumes filled the Mossie's cockpit.

On the ground the suspicious anti-aircraft crews were tracking the mysterious intruder in their sights, and instantly the Mosquito fired they loosed a barrage at it. Yellow, white and red fiery streams venomously arced through the darkness, clawing to destroy the attacker. As they pulled from the dive, the Mosquito crew heard a loud bang. Their aircraft shuddered. They had been hit! Johnson concentrated on controlling his aircraft and keeping as low as he dared without running into the hangars on the edge of the field. The German flak continued to hose up at them from all sides, but he knew that they could not fire too low lest they strike their own buildings. The volume of incendiary bullets slashing the sky actually provided enough light to see the oncoming hangars well enough to pass over them with minimum clearance. Rapidly they swept away from the hostile area and the ground fire ceased. It as only then that Johnson glanced out toward the left wing-tip and exclaimed, 'My God, Jimmy, you forgot to turn the nav lights out!' The Mosquito was vibrating badly. The rudder pedals were tramping back and forth so furiously that the pilot could not hold them, and he finally withdrew his feet from the battering. Slowing the aircraft reduced the severity of the vibrations somewhat, but did not stop them. Anxiously the navigator peered toward the tail of the Mosquito, but was unable to see the extent of the damage. Johnson set course to pass south of the heavy defences around Munich, then turned for England while watching the engine temperature gauges for any sign of overheating, and the fuel gauges for loss of fuel. At the reduced speed it would take over three hours to reach home base. Would the Mosquito hold together that long?

Knowing that they had thoroughly stirred up the enemy defences, they kept as low as they dared and maintained a watchful eye over their tail for German night fighters. It was a long flight home. The official maximum endurance of this version of the Mosquito was six and a quarter hours. They landed back at Hunsdon after six hours fifteen minutes! The fuel gauges all read nearly zero. Upon wearily clambering down from the cockpit, Johnson and Gibbons were able to see by the aid of their ground crew's flashlights the damage to their beloved Mosquito. The tailplane and elevators were sieved with shrapnel holes, there was a ragged one foot hole in the starboard tailplane, and the rudder was but a skeleton of ribs, but it had brought them home. As they trudged towards the operations room for de-briefing by the Intelligence officer, they heard one of the ground crew remark, 'They sure build these Mosquitoes tough!' In all Johnson flew forty-three operations as a pilot with 418 Squadron but none were as eventful as this.

Bob Bruce meanwhile, 'When near the end of November 1944, 418 were posted to 2nd TAF, Russ went to take command of 406 Squadron, equipped with Mk XXX AI Mosquitoes, at Manston. They had been on home Night Fighter duties for some time. I went along as Navigation Officer, non-operational, and Squadron Leader Don MacFadyen as Operations Officer. We set up lively ops' room, with all the Intelligence available. The Squadron had considerable success with the use of AI but with 418 tactics and morale rose beyond all possible expectation. But that would be another story, and would begin to overlap the experience of 100 Group.'

By November 1944 Nos. 107, 305 (Polish) and 613 Squadrons of 138 Wing finally arrived in France, to be based at Epinoy near Cambrai. By this stage of the war the *Panzers* and other German troops were being given no respite in the daylight raids by Mitchells and Bostons and the nightly visits by Mosquitoes. Flight Lieutenant Eric Atkins DFC* KW* (*Krzyz Walecznych*, the Polish Cross of Valour), a Mosquito pilot in 305 (Polish) Squadron at this time, recalls: 'Prisoners captured complained, "We are attacked all day and then the Mosquitoes harass and bomb us at night. We cannot 'em Schläfchen machen' (take a nap) or 'eine Scheiesse machen' (have a crap) – we are caught with our pants down!"' The Mosquito, and its crews, coped well with the upturn in operations, as Flight Lieutenant Eric Atkins, remembers:

Being small and light, the Mosquito could fall foul of bad weather conditions. On the other hand, in emergency conditions when caught in flak, searchlights or being attacked by enemy aircraft, it could be flung around the sky in almost impossible manoeuvres that a pilot might think twice about in daylight. The Mosquito responded to the controls like a thoroughbred racehorse, with speed, precision and a sixth sense of judgement linked to that of the pilot. I have also known the Mosquito to turn in such a tight circle at night to get away from searchlights and Flak beamed onto it, that it virtually 'disappears up its own orifice'.

A Mosquito could fly well on one engine, providing you had the speed and height to gain a level flight over a long distance. Many a Mosquito pilot flew from Germany on one engine but the landing could be tricky and you never knew whether the other engine would overheat and pack up! A Mosquito would also do a safe belly landing, providing you remembered to come in without any undercarriage and flaps – then it would probably turn over. I landed at night on a grass 'drome at Epinoy, France, with no under-carriage, no flaps and a bomb aboard! The only annoying thing was that the ambulance and M.O. took over half an hour to reach us. They were waiting to see whether the bomb went off! The aircraft had only minor damage and was soon returned to service again. Other Mosquitoes landed with half a wing missing. Despite its wooden construction the Mosquito had strength and endurance and was easier to repair. You simply spliced another wing on! The speed of the Mosquito also meant that the operational time was less (unless you were Ranging) and the turn-around time was such that when German light vehicles were piled up around Rouen and an all-night attack was called, we did three operations in one night, landing, refuelling, arming and away again – a dusk to dawn hat-trick!

On 21 November, 136 Wing was created within 2nd TAF by the arrival, from Fighter Command, of Nos. 418 and 605 Squadrons, which transferred to Hartford Bridge. That month fourteen enemy aircraft fell to the guns of the 2nd TAF Mosquito night predators.

The signs in December 1944 were that the weather and other factors would limit Mosquito night fighter activity over the *Reich*. Only three Ju88s and two Bf110s were destroyed between 4 and 18–19 December. On the last, Flight Lieutenant C. E. Edinger RCAF and Flying Officer C. C. Vaessen of 410 Squadron in NFXXX MV527, shot down a Ju88 south of Bonninghardt. Wing Commander James D. Somerville DFC, now in command of 409 Squadron, scored his sixth confirmed victory, flying NFXIII MM456 with Flying Officer G. D. Robinson DFC, when they dispatched a Ju88 in the Kaiserworth area. Somerville wrote:

While patrolling at Angels 10 under 15119 Control (Squadron Leader Allen) we were vectored south as the Hun was reported to be active in the American Sector. We were then advised of trade and after receiving initial vectors of 130 and 280, we were vectored 190. Controller advised us that he was keeping us on a slightly converging course to bring us in behind the target beyond the 'Hot Spot' at the same time, instructing to reduce to Angels 7. We started down but as the Control then advised that the target had started to climb, we levelled out at Angels 9. AI contact was obtained at a range of 5 miles and closing rapidly, I obtained a visual at 1600 ft. Closing to 800 ft below and directly beneath, both my navigator and I recognized the target as a Ju 88, flying at approximately 160 mph indicated, which necessitated my lowering my under-carriage to prevent overshooting. At this juncture, the E/A turned west and started to dive.

I followed, and overtook the E/A with an indicated speed of 270 mph. I closed to 600 ft and pulled up, but did not fire as I momentarily lost visual owing to a dark cloud in the background. I closed to within 300 ft and opened fire. I observed strikes on the fuselage but no flames. I attempted to re-open fire but my guns had jammed so I continued to follow the aircraft down, which by this time was doing hard evasive – making hard peel offs to starboard and port, until it finally dove in from 1500 ft. my navigator and I both saw it hit the ground and explode with a brilliant flash but it did not appear to burn on the ground.

Christmas drew near and 2nd TAF had a very eventful Yuletide. On the night of 22–23 December Wing Commander Peter Green DSO DFC and Flight Lieutenant Oxby DFM** of 219 Squadron, in NFXXX MM792, shot down a Ju88, and bagged another, south of Huy, on the night of 23–24 December. Two other crews in 219 Squadron destroyed two more Ju88s. Altogether, 2nd TAF NFXXX and NFXIII crews knocked down ten enemy aircraft on 23–24 December. Flight Lieutenant McPhail and Flying Officer Donaghue of 409 Squadron destroyed a Ju188, Flying Officer Mackenzie and Flying Officer Bodard of 410 Squadron brought down two Ju88s. Four others and one damaged fell victim to 488 Squadron RNZAF at B48/Amiens-Glisy. Wing Commander R. G. Watts, the CO and Flying Officer I. C. Skudder got a Ju188, Flight Lieutenant Johnny Hall DFC and Flying Officer J. P. W. Cairns DFC shot down a Me410 in the US Sector, and the two other victories this night went to Flight Lieutenant Kenneth William 'Chunky' Stewart, a solicitor from Dunedin, and his navigator Flying Officer H.E. 'Bill' Brumby in NFXXX MM822.

Flight Lieutenant Al Gabitas, who had trained at Levin in New Zealand with Stewart in 1941 recalls:

His legal studies behind him, he seemed to radiate savoir faire together with a degree of assurance that was to be envied by other recruits. He had a great sense of humour, was never at a loss for words and with a fund of funny stories was something of an enter- tainer in the canteen at the end of the day. He was solidly built and played a good game of squash, but at 5ft 2½ ins in height he was the shortest man on the base at Amiens, but unlike many short people he was not over-assertive or unduly aggressive in nature. I am not sure who it was who came up with 'Chunky' as a nickname but it seemed to be so apt that it stuck. After the arrival of 488 Squadron at Amiens in November 1944 things were relatively quiet for a while. Later, on 23rd December, Chunky was to demonstrate the remarkable initiative and unusual persistence, which lay behind his generally relaxed and amiable disposition. There may have been a strong element of chance in this first night encounter with no less than two enemy aircraft in succession, but there was no doubt about the matter-of-fact manner in which he dealt with them. In this last six months of the war he was to pursue this winning streak with great determination, and, with the assistance of a particularly rapid reacting radar operator in Bill Brumby, brought his final score to five destroyed and one damaged. This earned him the title in the squadron records of 'the Last of the Aces'.

Chunky Stewart described the events of 23–24 December in his report:

While on patrol near Roermond I noticed clusters of white flares and obtained permission to investigate. The controller said that there was no activity in that direction but my navigator succeeded in putting me on to an aircraft and after a short chase, with the target taking mild evasive action, we both identified the objective as a Junker 88, but for positive identification I closed to 100 ft whereupon the enemy aircraft fired off a red flare which illuminated the black crosses on the fin, fuselage and mainplane. I dropped back to 150 yards and fired a short burst observing strikes between the port engine and fuselage. With a second burst the port engine caught fire and the Hun spun down in flames, exploding before hitting the ground near Maeseyck. The controller told me to climb to 7,000 ft and whilst doing so I saw further flares and again requested permission to chase. After changing Controls my navigator seized an opportunity and, after the enemy aircraft had throttled back, turned, climbed and straightened out, I obtained a visual at 2,000ft which my navigator confirmed with his glasses as another Junkers 88. At 300 yards this aircraft also dropped reddish flares and we plainly saw black crosses and also the bomb racks. I close in to 200/150 yards and gave two short bursts, which started a fire in the fuselage. The enemy did a diving turn to starboard and when I was down to 1,000ft he hit the ground and exploded.

On Christmas Eve 1944 eighteen German aircraft were shot down, five of them by four Mosquito crews of 100 Group. The rest were shot down by Mosquitoes of 2nd TAF, which dispatched 139 Mosquitoes on that night to targets in south-west Germany. 613 Squadron dispatched some thirty Mosquitoes; LR374, crewed by Warrant Officer Baird, pilot, and Sergeant Whateley-Knight, navigator, failed to return from a sortie to harass German movement behind the enemy thrust in the Ardennes. Also, thirty-seven Mosquitoes of 2nd TAF patrolled the areas of Aachen, Arnhem and the Dutch Friesian Islands, and flew close support sorties over the front lines. None of these Mosquitoes was lost, and they destroyed fifty vehicles and six trains. 410 RCAF Squadron at Lille/Vendeville (B.51) dispatched nine Mosquitoes on front-line patrols between 17.50 hours on Christmas Eve and 05.30 hours on Christmas Day. Three of the Canadian crews claimed two Ju87s of *Nachtschlachtgruppe* 1 (used for harassment of troops and transport) and a Ju88 destroyed. In the Wassemberg area Flight Lieutenant C. E. Edinger DFC and Flying Officer C. C. Vaessen DFC in NFXXX MV527 destroyed one of the Stukas and Squadron Leader I. E. MacTavish and Flying Officer A. M. Grant, flying NFXXX MT485, got the other. The Ju88 victory went to Flying Officer J. A. Watt and Flight Lieutenant E. H. Collis, who took off at 04.00 hours and patrolled the Roermond-Julich area for about an hour before they were informed of trade ten miles distant. Flying Officer Watt recalled:

A contact was obtained at 0605 hours, range 6 miles, 9,000 ft, slightly to port and well below. We lost height to 4000 ft and range to 1500 ft where a visual was obtained at 12 o'clock, 20 degrees. Range was closed to 300 ft dead astern, same level and the target was identified Ju 88. Identification was confirmed by the navigator with the aid of night glasses. I opened fire with two bursts but no strikes were seen. The E/A peeled off to port and the visual and contact was lost. I did a hard orbit to port and the target was regained almost immediately at 2 miles range. Height at this time was 4000 ft. The range was again closed to 1500 ft and a visual was obtained on target identified as a Ju 88 with the aid of night glasses. E/A was doing a diving turn to port. I closed in to 900 ft range, still closing and opened fire. Strikes were seen on the starboard engine, followed by an explosion. E/A went straight in from 3000 ft, exploding and burning on hitting the ground. Time 0618 hours. GCI fixed us at K.9363 (approximately Puffendt area). No action was employed by E/A during the first engagement, but

99

throughout the second engagement E/A employed quite violently evasive. No return fire was made. I claim 1 Ju 88 destroyed.

Watt fired a total of 410 rounds to down their victim, a Ju88 of 2./NJG2, which crashed near Roermond killing pilot Tetzlaff. Three of his crew survived and were made POW.

Two crews in 219 Squadron claimed three victories. Flight Lieutenant G. R. I. 'Sailor' Parker DFC DFM and Warrant Officer D. L. Godfrey DFC DFM took off from at Amiens/Glisy at 00.45 hours in NFXXX MM698 fitted with AI Mk.X. Parker continues:

Patrolled uneventfully for 1hr 20 minutes and at about 0250 hrs was informed that there was something to the south-east about 20 miles away. Voicebox obtained information from some other GCI and gave no vectors on to the target. Obtained contact range 4 miles target slightly below and on a northerly vector. My height at the time 3,000-ft. Closed under instruction of my operator to position slightly below and obtained a visual at 2,000 ft range, dead ahead. Closed to 200 ft, height 2,500 ft and identified as a Ju 188. Dropped back to 600 ft and gave a 2 second burst. Minor strikes observed on the port engine, which barely caught fire. Target continued mild evasive action and proceeded to climb to 150 mph. Gave 2 further bursts, no more strikes being observed. The fire, however, was gradually increasing. Then two parachutes – one black, one white, – were seen to drop from the e/a. Gave a further 2-second burst and many strikes were obtained on the port engine. The fire became intense. E/A continued to climb slightly and so I followed taking photographs only. I considered that as the crew had baled out, the e/a would crash without any further fire being necessary. It completed 3 orbits – height about 4,000 ft – when there was a small explosion in the port engine. The fire spread to the fuselage and the e/a crashed in a ball of fire about 34 miles east of Arnhem, fix supplied by Voicebox. Time of combat – 0300 hrs.

I continued patrol in vectors from Voicebox and at 0325 hrs I was given vector 100° and was ordered to descend to 6,000 ft as there was a bogey 10 miles ahead, travelling south-west. Voicebox gave me a crossing flight – port to starboard – interception. I was told angels 4, reduced to 3, and immediately obtained contact range 4 miles, crossing port to starboard, slightly below. Closed under instructions from my operator and obtained a visual at 2,000 ft, height of target then 3,000 ft. Closed to 200 ft and opened fire with a 2 second burst. The starboard engine caught well afire. Fired a further 2-second burst which set the port engine also well on fire. Flames immediately spread to the fuselage. E/a pulled up sharply, stalled and went over into a sharp dive, disintegrating in the air and crashing in about five pieces on the ground. Position approx. 12 miles SE of Eindhoven. Time 0335 hours. My operator immediately obtained head-on contact on starboard side and was informed that it was probably a bandit. Head-on contacts obtained 4 times but as I was getting short of fuel I decided to return. I claim 2 Ju 188s destroyed.

Parker and Godfrey landed at 04.00 hours, Parker having fired a total of 566 rounds to down his two victims. At the same moment Flight Lieutenant L. Stephenson DFC and Flight Lieutenant G. A. Hall DFC touched down at Amiens/Glisy ready to tell of another squadron kill. They had taken off at 00.50 hours and were taken under Rejoice control where they patrolled north and south thirty miles east of Hasselt. Flight Lieutenant Stephenson continues:

About 0230 hrs we were informed by control that there was an aircraft, probably friendly, 20 miles south east of us at 6,000 ft. We were given vector in that direction and lost height from 10,000 ft to 4,000 ft and increased speed. At about 6 miles range we were informed that the bogey had been proved friendly and so we prepared to turn back. A minute later the controller decided that we should investigate after all. We turned back on a vector of 100° and after a few minutes of well controlled interception we obtained a contact 4 miles range, slightly above, moving port to starboard. Our height was then 3,500 ft. Target did a few gentle turns but no real evasive action. Range was rapidly closed to 2000 ft when a visual was obtained on a twin-engined aircraft well above flying straight and level at about 235 mph. Our speed during the interception was 280 mph. Closed right in below and in the moonlight it was easily identified as an Me 110 with long range tanks. Dropped back to 750 ft and gave a two second burst from dead astern, height 4,000 ft. It immediately caught fire and dived steeply down hitting the ground with a large explosion. Just as it was in its steep dive the rear gun began firing vertically white tracer into the air. Time of combat 0245 hours; position as given by control F.0567. I claim this Me 110 as destroyed.

Stephenson had fired a total of fifty-two rounds to down his victim.

The other victories on Christmas Eve went to Wing Commander Russ Bannock DFC*, now CO, 406 Squadron, in NFXXX MM693, shot down ten kilometres west of Paderborn, Ju88G-l 714132 3C+CT of *9./NJG4*, crewed by *Oberfeldwebel* Manfred Ludwig and *Feldwebel* Hans Fischl (both KIA). Flight Lieutenant R. J. Foster DFC and Flight Lieutenant M. F. Newton DFC of 604 Squadron in NFXIII MM462 from Odiham claimed a He219 as probably destroyed, approximately five miles east of Nijmegen. Flight Lieutenant Stephenson and Flight Lieutenant Hall of 219 Squadron shot down a Bf110.

The *Luftwaffe* was powerless to stop the inexorable advance westwards but there was one last attempt to try to halt the Allies. Since 20 December 1944 many *Jagdgeschwader* had been transferred to airfields in the west for Operation *Bodenplatte,* when approximately 850 *Luftwaffe* fighters took off at 07.45 hours on Sunday morning 1 January 1945 to attack twenty-seven airfields in northern France, Belgium and southern Holland. The four-hour operation succeeded in destroying about 100 Allied aircraft, but it cost the *Luftwaffe* 300 aircraft, most of which were shot down by Allied anti-aircraft guns deployed primarily against the V-1s. One aircraft which escaped the bombing at Brussels was a NFXXX flown by Flight Lieutenant Chunky Stewart, who had landed the night before after getting badly shot up by the airfield defences at the German night fighter base at Rheine after following an enemy aircraft back to the base. With its hydraulics shot away Stewart's aircraft had headed for Brussels where it careered off the runway with a collapsed undercarriage, but the crew jumped out unhurt. Soon afterwards, as dawn approached, the Fw190s attacked. Tucked under the wing of a Flying Fortress the Mosquito escaped further damage, but was surrounded by burning aircraft.

During January 2nd TAF Mosquitoes exacted a measure of revenge, starting with the shooting down of three Ju88s on 1–2 January by Flight Lieutenant R. J. Foster DFC and Flight Lieutenant M. F. Newton DFC of 604 Squadron. By the end of the month 2nd TAF Mosquito night fighters had shot down seventeen enemy aircraft, including, on 23–24 January, two Junkers, which were dispatched by 409 (Nighthawk) Squadron NFXIIIs. At this time Ju88S-3s of

1./KG66 and *Lehrgeschwader 1* were carrying out bombing and mining operations against river traffic in the Scheldt estuary in an attempt to stem the flow of supplies to Antwerp. Pilot Officer M. G. Kent and Pilot Officer Simpson in NFXIII MM466 shot down a Ju88 of *LG 1* over the mouth of the Scheldt. *LG1* lost three Ju88s this night, including one flown by the *Gruppe Kommandeur, Hauptmann* Hecking (301348 L1+GK) and one flown by *Oberleutnant* Huber, *Stafelführer 6./LG1,* in 331294 L1+NP.

While there is some doubt about which was Kent and Simpson's victim, there is no question that the Ju188E-l, shot down three miles west of Dienst by the CO, Wing Commander James D. Somerville DFC and Pilot Officer A. C. Hardy in NFXIII MM456 was 260542 A3+QD, flown by *Obergefreiter* Heinz Hauck, who was on a clandestine mission for *KG200*'s *Kommando Olga*. Hauck took off from Rhein-Main and he successfully dropped two agents near Gilze-Rijn in the liberated part of Holland before heavy AA bursts and searchlights gave away their position to the Nighthawk crew, who were returning from patrol at 8,000 feet. Somerville and Hardy were directed by Rejoice, a GCI station, towards the bogey, now six miles distant at 4,000 feet. Somerville reduced height and Hardy was further assisted by Bricktile and then Laundry, GCI stations, until they came upon the Ju188E-1, which was now flying at 3,000 feet. Hardy had difficulty keeping their quarry out of the ground clutter on his AI Mk.VIII scope at their height of 2,500 feet until finally, he got a contact at two miles. Somerville closed to 1,500 feet for a positive identification. Satisfied, he closed still further and opened fire with his cannons at 200 feet. His first burst set fire to Hauck's port engine and the 20-mm shells caused a brilliant explosion which forced the Mosquito pilot, momentarily blinded, to break away. Somerville came in again for a second burst as Hauck desperately dived and stall-turned in a vain attempt to extinguish the flames. Somerville's second burst missed but his third ripped the Ju188's port wingtip off and the enemy aircraft dived steeply into the ground. It was Somerville's seventh and final victory of the war. Hauck, his observer, *Gefreiter* Kurt Wuttge, *Bordfunker, Unteroffizier* Max Grossman and *Feldwebel* Heinrich Hoppe, the dispatcher, baled out and were taken prisoner.

On 3–4 February Pilot Officer Kent and Pilot Officer Simpson added to their score by downing a Ju88, and Flight Lieutenant B. E. Plumer DFC and Flight Lieutenant Hargrove of 410 Squadron, in a NFXXX, dispatched a He219. On 6 February, 21, 464 and 487

Squadrons of 140 Wing left southern England and moved to Amiens and Rosières-en-Santerre. On 22 February all 2nd TAF crews and serviceable aircraft were pressed into action for Operation Clarion. This was intended to be the *coup de grâce* for the German transport system with 9,000 Allied aircraft taking part in attacks on enemy railway stations, trains and engines, crossroads, bridges, ships and barges on canals and rivers, stores and other targets. It was to be the last time that the Mosquitoes operated in daylight in such numbers. 2 Group put up every available aircraft, flying 215 sorties, 176 from the Continent and the remainder by 136 Wing in England. 138 and 140 Wings lost nine Mosquitoes and many more were damaged. 2 Group lost a total of twenty-one Mosquitoes on Clarion, with forty damaged.

The fighting continued into the night of 21–22 February and east of Stormede airfield Flight Lieutenant Don A. MacFadyen DFC RCAF of 406 Squadron, in NFXXX NT325, destroyed a Bf110. Flight Lieutenant K. W. Chunky Stewart and Flying Officer Bill Brumby of 488 RNZAF Squadron were patrolling over Holland when they were warned by ground control that they were being followed by a strange aircraft. Flight Lieutenant Al Gabitas, a fellow New Zealand pilot on the squadron, recalls: 'A sort of dog fight ensued in complete darkness between the two night fighters guided entirely by their own radar. With a great deal of weaving about Chunky managed to get behind the other aircraft. After brief visual contact it was identified as a Junkers 88G night fighter. Following a quick burst of cannon fire on a fairly wide deflection it blew up in mid-air. This was a duel to the death between evenly-matched opponents in which the outcome was determined by superior flying and gunnery skills and more than a slight edge on the technology.' (The enemy machine exploded near Groenlo.) Three nights later, on 24–25 February, Wing Commander Peter Green DSO DFC and Flight Lieutenant D. Oxby DFC DFM** of 219 Squadron, flying NFXXX MM792, shot down a *Stuka*, and on the 28th, Squadron Leader Don MacFadyen DFC in NFXXX NT325, claimed a unidentified enemy aircraft 'probably destroyed' at Halfingen.

Meanwhile, 264 Squadron had moved back to France, to 148 Wing at Lille/Vendeville. Its move had coincided with a snowstorm and the squadron had had to endure the weather with very little heating or comfort until the snow cleared early in February. Both January and February were complete operational blanks as the *Luftwaffe* was not keen to show itself at night at all, but near the end of February four pilots left for Gilze-Rijn to carry out Operation Blackmail. This was intensely secret at the time but it entailed carrying Dutchmen, Air Force and Army, and one woman over occupied Holland by day and night to maintain wireless communications with agents of their underground movement. This task was performed well and was particularly useful but had been refused by 2 Group who considered it to be too dangerous. March saw plenty of patrols being flown both from Lille and Gilze, but it was not until the 25th that any success was achieved; a Ju88 destroyed and another damaged, the first combat since 10 August. March in fact saw a heavy toll of German aircraft by 2nd TAF Mosquito night fighters. On 5–6 March Squadron Leader Don MacFadyen DFC RCAF of 406 Squadron, flying NFXXX NT325 destroyed a Ju88G at Gerolzhofen.

Chapter Six

Moskitopanik!

It is not perhaps very well known how successful the Mosquitoes who provided the Bomber Support as fighters in 100 Group were during the latter part of World War II. There were three stages in their harrying of the Luftwaffe night fighters. Some squadrons sent low level fighters to patrol the known German night fighter airfields. Others provided high level patrols near their assembly points, about 40 miles from our bomber stream, in order to shoot them down before they reached it, and a third wave of low level Mossies would arrive at their airfields as they were returning. At RAF Swanlington in Norfolk I was a member of 157 Squadron. We shared the station with 85 Squadron. In the comparatively short time we carried out high level patrols, our score was: 37 German night fighters destroyed, 6 probables and 13 damaged. We lost only 7, one of which was shot down by one of our own aircraft. The crew got back luckily and of course had several rounds of drinks from the offenders. 85 Squadron were even more successful and one of their Mossies bagged four German night fighters in one sortie. Very soon after the Bomber Support began operating, the Luftwaffe pilots started to use the phrase Mosquitopanik! and Ritterkreutz Height! The later referred to the fact that after carrying out their attacks against our bombers, they would immediately drop down almost to ground level, i.e. Ritterkreutz height in order to avoid the dreaded Mosquitoes. I believe they lost a few more planes with their low flying back to collect their Ritterkreutz.

Lewis Brandon

Intruder Mosquitoes, meanwhile, continued their Night Ranger operations over the continent and were rewarded with a mounting tally of victories. Some twenty-six aircraft were claimed destroyed by 100 Group Mosquitoes in July 1944. On the night of 4–5 July four enemy aircraft were shot down by 100 Group Mosquitoes. Over France on 5–6 July when FBVIs of 23 Squadron flew their first Intruder operation with sorties against enemy airfields, Ju88 751065 R4+2 of 5./NJG2 was shot down by Flying Officer P. G. Bailey and Flying Officer J. O. Murphy of 169 Squadron and it crashed near Chartres. *Oberfeldwebel* Fritz Earrherr, pilot and *Obergefreiter* Heinz Boehme, air gunner, were killed. *Gefreiter* Josef Schmid, radar operator, was WIA and bailed out. Bf110G-4 110028 C9+HK of 2./NJG5 crashed near Compiegne. It is believed that this was one of the two aircraft shot down this night by Squadron Leader J. S. Booth DFC* and Flying Officer K. Dear DFC of 239 Squadron. *Leutnant* Joachim Hanss, pilot, and *Feldwebel* Kurt Stein, air gunner, were killed. *Unteroffizier* Wolfgang Wehrhan, radar operator, was wounded.

Squadron Leader Graham J. Rice and Flying Officer Jimmy G. Rogerson of 141 Squadron meanwhile, had taken off from West Raynham at 23.17 hours on a Serrate patrol in support of Bomber Command attacks on St Lou D'Esserent and Vaires. Rice reported:

Enemy coast was crossed on track between Calais and Dunkirk at 0005 hours and patrol was uneventful until approximately 20 miles south of Abbeville at 0030 hours and 15,000 ft when an AI contact was soon dead ahead and slightly below. Aircraft turned hard port and contact passed overhead, when a visual was obtained on very bright exhausts. At 1,000-ft range contact was soon to be a twin engined aircraft travelling at high speed on a NNE vector and looked similar to a Mosquito. Aircraft switched on Canary but contact made no response. Contact was followed at full throttle but after 2 or 3 minutes it went right away and disappeared in interference and could not be recognised. As contact took no evasive action at any time and made no response to canary, it is thought contact was probably an Me 410.

Mosquito turned back on track and 5 minutes later when vectoring 147 degrees a head-on AI contact was obtained dead ahead and below. Contact was allowed to come in to 4,000-ft range and Mosquito went into a hard turn through 180 degrees and obtained contact dead ahead and still below at 8,000-ft range.

Contact was weaving gently and made 2 hard turns of 90 degrees to starboard with aircraft following hard and losing height to come in from below. No response was made by contact when Mosquito switched on Canary, after about 10 minutes chase a visual was obtained at 2,000-ft range at 10,000-ft height. Closing in quickly to 600 ft contact was seen to be an aircraft with twin fins and exhausts peculiar to an Me 110. At this moment enemy aircraft apparently became aware of the presence of Mosquito and took hard turn to starboard. Mosquito gave 1½ ring deflection and opened fire with a four second burst at 600ft range. Strikes were seen all along the top of the mainplane leading to a large explosion in the fuselage which was quickly well on fire. The E/A was now definitely established to be an Me 110. E/A turned over on its back and passed underneath Mosquito and was followed down to 3,000-ft range on AI then blip disappeared. Mosquito straightened up and orbitted to look for E/A and immediately a terrific explosion was seen directly below. Scattered pieces of E/A were seen floating down in flames and one large remnant hit the ground with a further explosion. Combat took place at approximately 8 miles N W of Amiens at 0050 hours at 10,000 ft. after combat AI was no longer wholly serviceable but improved after half an hour and aircraft made for the target area. Numerous green star cartridges were soon fired in the air on many occasions and aircraft attempted to investigate several times without success. Stoppages on port guns caused by foreign matter in breech. Claim 1 Me 110 destroyed Cat A (1)

Their victim was most likely Bf110G-4 730006 05+ of *2./NJG3*, which crashed five kilometres west of Chievres, Belgium. The German pilot and *Gefreiter* Richard Reiff, who was wounded, both baled out safely. *Obergefreiter* Edmund Hejduck was killed.

On 14–15 July, Warrant Officer Les Turner and Flight Sergeant Freddie Francis of 169 Squadron flew a Serrate patrol, their eighth trip since joining the squadron. Turner reported:

Took off from Great Massingham at 2310 hours in Mosquito M. Set course at 2315 hrs over base and crossed English and Enemy coasts on ETA. Arrived at Orbit point and patrolled for 80 minutes with no activity except for two fleeting AI contacts at maximum range which disappeared into ground returns before any pursuit action could be taken. At 0113 hours whilst on vector towards prang at Auderbelck obtained AI contact at maximum range ahead, well to port and slightly below, at patrol height. Turned port immediately and dived and after a few minutes chase closed range to 3,000 ft where target was held in dead ahead position. It was then ascertained that target was on port orbit and on closing to 2,000 ft visual was obtained on white light at first believed to be a tail light. Closed visually and when necessary on AI and on nearly overshooting saw that light was exhaust flames. Since target speed was approximately 160 mph throttled hard back and closed slowly in with my navigator calling out airspeeds. We closed to a position about 20 ft below enemy aircraft, which was recognized as a Me 109. I then dropped back to 150ft and opened fire, seeing strikes on starboard wing, and then fuselage caught fire. Enemy aircraft turned on its back and black crosses, blue camouflage and twin radiators could be seen as it passed underneath. A bright flash was seen as aircraft hit the ground. We took a Gee fix and plotted position. The combat took place at 0128 hours, at 13,000 ft, confirmed by Warrant Officer Schoolbread in Mosquito 169/G. Our patrol time being up we set course for Le Touquet at 0131 hours and returned to base uneventfully.

On 20–21 July Bf110G-4 730218 G9+EZ of *12./NJG1* was another victim of Wing Commander Neil Bromley and Philip Truscott of 169 Squadron. The aircraft crashed near Moll in Belgium. *Oberfeldwebel* Karl-Heinz Scherfling, the twenty-five-year-old pilot, who was a *Ritterkreuztraeger* since 8 April 1942 and who had thirty-three night victories, was killed. So too was *Feldwebel* Herbert Winkler, the thirty-one year-old air gunner. *Feldwebel* Herbert Scholz, the twenty-five-year-old radar operator, baled out seriously injured.

On the night of 23–24 July Bf110G-4 730036 G9+ER of *7./NJG1*, was shot down by Flight Lieutenant R. J. Dix and Flying Officer A. J. Salmon of 169 Squadron at very low level around midnight. The 110 crashed near Balk in Friesland Province in Holland. *Feldwebel* Heinrich Karl Lahmann, the twenty-five-year-old pilot, and *Unteroffizier* Günther Bouda, the twenty-one-year-old air gunner, both baled out. *Unteroffizier* Willi Huxsohl, the twenty-one-year-old radar operator, was killed. This same night two other *NJG1* night fighters were lost. At 01.25 hours Bf110G-4 730117 G9+GR of *7./NJG1* was shot down north of Deelen airfield. *Leutnant* Josef

Hettlich, pilot, *Feldwebel* Johann Treiber, radar operator and the air gunner all baled out safely. (Flying Officer N. Veale and Flying Officer R. O. Comyn of 239 Squadron claimed a Bf110 this night). The third Bf110 lost was 441083 G9+OR of *III./NJG1* or *7./NJG1*, which was shot down at 01.47 hours during landing at Leeuwarden airfield and which crashed at Rijperkerk, just to the north of the base. *Hauptmann* Siegfried Jandrey, thirty, pilot, and *Unteroffizier* Johann Stahl, twenty-five, radar operator, were killed. *Unteroffizier* Anton Herger, twenty-four, air gunner, was injured. A Mosquito of 2nd TAF possibly shot down this aircraft.

Pilot Officer Doug Gregory and Pilot Officer D. H. Stephens of 141 Squadron took off from West Raynham at 23.10 hours and set course for patrol area crossing enemy coast at 23.50 hours. Their destinations were the enemy beacons *Chameleon, Willi,* and *Biene*. At 15,000 feet an AI contact was obtained on an aircraft crossing starboard to port way below them at maximum range. Gregory reported:

> We turned in behind it and lost height. E/A was doing mild evasive action and half orbits. Chase continued for 10 minutes with A/C closing range giving fleeting visuals at 600 ft. closed further to 300 ft and E/A was identified as a Ju 88. We were now at 9–10,000. On identification panic set in and we desperately tried to get the sights on. Meanwhile, greater panic took hold of the 88 type who promptly peeled off and visual and contact was lost, although we also peeled off. Taking a psychological view of the situation we orbitted for ten minutes, hoping he would return. Sure enough he did and came in head-on well below. We opened up everything and got on to his tail. He was going very fast still weaving and it took us ten minutes to close range and get another visual when we again identified contact as a Ju 88. Due to slightly faulty elevation he appeared much more above than was expected.
>
> I said, 'He's miles above.'
>
> 'Stephens said, 'Gee, have a go'.
>
> Whereupon we stood on our tail and at a range of approximately 60 yards and I let fly with a one-second burst which exploded E/A's port engine. We continued upwards in a starboard climbing turn and watched the 88 spiral down in flames and, after going through cloud blew up on the ground with great gusto and much flame. He was still burning on the ground when we left ten minutes later.

Patrol completed we returned to base through the usual channels. Claim One Ju 88 destroyed.

Gregory fired just forty-eight rounds to down the Ju88.

Pilot Officer Doug Gregory and Pilot Officer D. H. Stephens were airborne from West Raynham again on the night of 28–29 July for another stint at 'bashing the beacons' when the bombers' target was Stuttgart. Gregory reported:

We took off at 2315 hrs, set course for enemy coast, crossing in at Overflakee at 16,000 ft at 2357 hrs. Route uneventful until leaving Ida on way to Christa. At 0031 hours at 16,000 ft we got an AI contact slightly port and below crossing port to starboard. We turned in behind him and went down. We closed and after an eight-minute chase obtained visual. Closing still further we got into various positions and finally when about 200 ft directly below, identified A/C as a Ju 88. He was flying quite straight at 14,000 ft without a clue. We pulled up to his level and at approximately 100 yards and let fly with a 1½-second burst. Our shells apparently found their mark for his port engine immediately gave up the ghost and burst into flames, and smoking pieces came back at us. We broke off to port and watched him burning satisfactorily and going down. He entered cloud at 8,000 ft and after a few seconds he lit up the cloud as he exploded on the ground. Time was now 0045 hrs and his grave may be found 16 miles NW of Metz. We then set course for base via Overflakee, crossing out at 0140 hrs. Here endeth the second lesson.

Ju88G-1 713649 R4+KT of 9./NJG2, flown by *Hauptmann* August Speckmann, pilot (KIA), with *Oberfeldwebel* Wilhelm Berg, flight engineer (KIA), and *Unteroffizier* Otto Brüggenkamp, air gunner (KIA) and *Oberfeldwebel* Arthur Boos, radar operator (WIA), was shot down over France. It was probably one of the two Ju88s destroyed by Gregory and Stephens and Harry White DFC* and Mike Allen DFC* of 141 Squadron.

Late in July 515 and 23 Squadrons at Little Snoring flew daylight escort duty for heavies attacking Bordeaux. In August they continued daylight operations with Day Rangers (operations to engage air and ground targets within a wide but specified area). The most successful 100 Group Day Ranger was on 29 October 1944. Flight Lieutenant

F. T. L'Amie and Flying Officer J. W. Smith, and Pilot Officer Terry A. Groves DFC and Flight Sergeant R. B. 'Doc' Dockeray DFM, of 515 Squadron, between them destroyed nine (three in the air and six on the ground) and damaged five enemy aircraft. In September the FBVIs of 23 Squadron briefly escorted Fortresses of 100 Group on Big Ben patrols.

Meanwhile, on 20 August, 85 and 157 Squadrons had resumed bomber support duties from Swannington. Even so, 100 Group Mosquito victories were on the wane, largely due to successful German countermeasures to the Serrate homing device used in the Bomber Support units. During August 100 Group Mosquitoes claimed only eight aircraft destroyed. It was the usual story for crews like Warrant Officer Les Turner and Flight Sergeant Freddie Francis of 169 Squadron. Though many trips were flown, kills were rare. There was no shortage of excitement though as Turner recalls:

Trip No.9 was to the Ruhr, No.10 to Kiel where we got severely frightened by flak. They had 'boxed' us and the normal evasive action seemed to have no effect. Eventually, I put the nose down with full throttle – we must have been pushing towards 500 mph (true) by the time I pulled out of the dive. It achieved the result, however. Trip No.11 was notable for the fact that we flew through the clouds loaded with static electricity. The first firework display from the radar aerials and across the windscreen from wipers to frame was impressive. Fortunately, I had been brought up on stories of St Elmo's Fire and knew what it was. The static display prevented me from getting a visual on the one radar contact we had.

Trips 12, 13 and 14, all record contacts but no visuals. On 15, we lost our radar and just stooged around Dijon. On No.16 we got coned by searchlights. This is very disorientating and I was glad of the Instrument Flying expertise. I just put my head down and ignored the lights, albeit with difficulty. On trip No.17, to Stettin, we got two visuals on what looked like a Ju 88 but lost it in cloud. No.18 to Bremen was uneventful, but No.19 on 26/27 August to the same target resulted in the destruction of a Ju 88.

Took off from Great Massingham at 22.35 hours in Mosquito T, setting course immediately over base, crossing English and Enemy coasts on ETA. Nothing of note occurred until we reached position approx. 5300N 0800E at 23.45 at 20,000 ft where considerable searchlight activity was observed to port. It was apparent there were obviously aircraft of some sort concerned as we decided to investigate and forthwith 'mucked-in' with a Hun searchlight co-op exercise. Occasional fleeting, AI contacts were obtained all showing hard above and from this, the position of the cone, and the firing of apparent colours of the day, it was assumed that there were some aircraft, possibly single-engined, at about 25,000 ft which made chances of interception very slim with a Mosquito VI. Having ourselves been coned on two occasions, and discretion being obviously the better part of valour, we proceeded to leave that area and attempt to reach our scheduled patrol area.

At 00.30, nothing further having been seen, we turned on a reciprocal westerly course, and after about 20 minutes flying, obtained at 20,000 ft, a forward AI contact at maximum range. Target appeared to be crossing port to starboard on estimated course of 030 degrees. We chased for approx. 5 mins reducing height to 14,000 ft where target was held in dead ahead position at 1,000-ft range. A visual was obtained and range reduced to 500' where aircraft was positively identified as a Ju 88. We allowed target to pull away to 1,000' range when we opened fire, the port engine immediately bursting into flames. Target turned gently starboard into a diving turn, leaving a long spiral of grey smoke. We followed, firing intermittently, observing strikes all over the fuselage. A tremendous flash was seen as aircraft hit the ground. A westerly course was set for base, which was reached at 02.25 hours without further incident.

Turner and Francis' victim, which was brought down by 480 rounds of cannon fire, was Ju88G-1 710542 D5+BR of 7./NJG3, flown by *Leutnant* Achim Woeste. He and *Unteroffizier* Anton Albrecht were KIA. *Unteroffizier* Heinz Trippe and *Gefreiter* Karl Walkenberger, who were both wounded in the action, baled out. The aircraft crashed near Mulsum, forty-two kilometres east of Bremen. Turner adds:

The large number of cannon rounds used was, in the main, due I fear to a feeling of extreme anger at the time. Just before take off I had read the Press reports of the discovery of the extermination ovens at Lübeck and I was so incensed that I was determined that any Nazi within range was not going to aid that war effort.

Trip No.20 to Darmstadt was notable for a near miss from flak.

I remember that the smoke from the explosion curled over the starboard wing and I nearly baled out the navigator! No.21 to Mannheim needed 3 hr 15 mins on instruments in dense cloud. We got plenty of practice on those occasions. On No.22 we saw our first V-2. It came up from the Dutch coast and I thought it was flak at first – then a V-1 – and I turned towards it, at which point it passed us going up and up and up...! At debriefing the Intelligence Officer was most interested in the report. Trips 23 to 25, to Emden, Frankfurt and Munster produced some chases, but no results. Trip No.26 was to have been a low level Ranger patrol. We landed in France for refuelling but shortly after crossing into enemy territory the weather closed in and, if I am honest, we got completely lost. So I aborted the patrol and came home. Nothing much happened on trips 27 to 30. We got contacts and fleeting visuals on, we believe, other Mosquitoes and a chase but no visual near Mannheim. No.31 took us to Stuttgart – a rather long haul without result.

Between 6–7 and 12–13 September, eight more German night fighters fell to 100 Group Mosquitoes. On 13–14 September Flight Lieutenant Bill House and Flight Sergeant Dennis McKinnon of 85 Squadron patrolled Germany looking for a ninth victim to add to the tally. 85 Squadron had been short of navigators when McKinnon had been posted to the squadron straight from training and he had never been to Night Flying Training School. In fact he had never been in an aircraft that had occasion to fire any guns. McKinnon recalls: 'I guided Bill onto a Me 110 near Koblenz and managed to get behind it without the crew being aware of us. Bill opened fire and I thought it was us who were being attacked. The noise, to me, was terrifying but to the enemy it must have been terrible. The whole plane just blew up in front of our eyes.' Their victim was Bf110G-4 440384 G9+EN of *5./NJG1* piloted by *Oberleutnant* Gottfried Hanneck. Hanneck was a very experienced pilot who served with various *Luftwaffe* units flying forty different aircraft types for five years before he joined *5./NJG1* at Deelen in April 1944. On his fourth operational sortie, on the night of 11 May 1944 he shot down his first RAF night bomber and had gone on to claim another five '4-Mots'. He recalls:

After the successful invasion by the Allied Armies in the summer of 1944, the second Gruppe of NJG1 was posted from Deelen to

Düsseldorf airfield at the end of August 1944. The big problem of our night fighter controllers at this time was the loss of the radar stations in France and along the coast of the Canal. Thus, the preparations by the RAF for incursions over the Reich could not be established in time and effective countermeasures could not be prepared anymore. Instead, our leadership, suspecting a RAF raid, had to scramble a number of night fighter crews and keep them in the air in case a raid developed.

Thus, on 13 September 1944 me and my crew of Unteroffizier Erich Sacher, radar/radio op, and Unteroffizier Willi Wurschitz, who on this mission served as air gunner but normally was a radar operator, were ordered to take off and fly to a radio beacon in the Frankfurt area and await further developments. We took off at 22.34 in our Me 110 G9+EN. Once we had arrived at the radio beacon, we flew around in wide circles and listened to the messages from our controllers on the radio frequency relating the developments in the air.

Then my radar operator reported a blip on his SN-2 radar set – he could not quite determine it but gave me courses to steer to the target. The target flew in a Westerly direction at a distance of about 6,000 metres. It could be a homebound enemy aircraft. I followed it and tried to reduce the distance by increasing my airspeed. The blip on the radar screen however did not become clearer, and since we had been chasing it for about 20 minutes and by now had probably arrived over the frontline, we had to turn around and return to the radio beacon.

At this very instant we were fired upon and I saw many hits striking in the wings of my aircraft. The control column was shaking, a clear indication that the controls were heavily damaged, and I ordered my crew to 'prepare to bail out'. At this time, the intercom was still functioning and my crew was not injured. After I told my crew to prepare to bale out, we received another burst of gunfire and the 110 immediately caught fire in both wings and the pressure on my control column was completely gone. The aircraft was plunging down out of control! There was only one option left to save our lives: the parachute. I counted for 4 or 5 seconds to give my crew the opportunity to 'hit the silk', and then I opened the roof of my cockpit and jumped out through the ball of fire. Again, I counted for several seconds before I pulled the chord of my parachute, for fear of colliding with my crashing plane. The canopy unfolded and I floated down towards the dark earth. In order to be able to estimate my height, I fired off a Verey light towards the ground. It fell into a meadow, and I swung to and fro three or four more times before I hit the ground. I glanced at my watch and saw it was 23.35 hours. I had come down East of Pruem in the Eifel. I had suffered second and third degrees burns to my head and hands, and stayed in cover at the edge of a small wood for the remaining hours of darkness, as I did not want to walk into the arms of enemy soldiers. At the break of dawn, I sneaked to the East, and soon I ran into German soldiers.

My crew had been killed in the crash. In this way, a RAF long-range night fighter 'revenged' my six night kills of four-engined bombers. [The 110 crashed at Birresborn in the Eifel at 23.35 hours].

On 17–18 September *11./NJG1* lost Bf110 G-4 740358 G9+MY when it was shot down east of Arnhem by Ginger Owen and Flying Officer McAllister DFM of 85 Squadron. Walter Sjuts, *Unteroffizier* Herbert Schmidt and *Unteroffizier* Ernst Fischer, were all killed. The same RAF crew also shot down Bf110G-4 740757 G9+GZ of *12./NJG1* in the same area. *Unteroffizier* Heinz Gesse, Josef Kaschub and *Obergefreiter* Josef Limberg were all killed. By the end of September 100 Group Mosquitoes had claimed fourteen aircraft destroyed and in October another seventeen were claimed.

Bob Symon of 85 Squadron recalls:

The 12th of September 1944 was a frustrating night's work. I found two sitting duck targets, a Ju 88 and a Me 110, for the first one the gun-sight suddenly flared up and wrecked Michael's (Miller) night vision. We fired some rounds waving our nose around hopefully but saw no strikes. The second sitting duck was equally fortunate – gunsight dead. The 15th of September the trip to Kiel was short on targets for us but we found that we were an excellent target for them. I have never felt so embarrassingly naked as I did on top of that searchlight cone. Like taking over from Eros in Piccadilly Circus on boat-race night with all the car headlights trained on me. I was thankful that Michael had done two tours in Wellingtons and was quite at home taking evasive action. This was my first experience of this treatment: at one moment one is being pushed through the bottom of the aircraft and the next one is picking up pencils, bits of paper, a bar of chocolate and whatever is floating around in the cockpit. To give the Germans their due I confess that they were pretty good with their heavy metal. When one can hear the shell explode over the engine noise it must be pretty close.

On 27 September 1944 we did an Intruder patrol to Ober-Olm. Nothing seen. Very thundery. This was my last flight with Michael and his last too. He had done two tours in Wellingtons, and I think that this was his third tour with night fighters. He was sent to see the MO after we came back from this flight and was sent to hospital for examination. They found he had diabetes. When one considers the work he had done since the beginning of the war it is a wonder he lasted that long. Capt Svein Heglund of the Norwegian Air Force came to the Squadron at the beginning of October. He had no Nav/Rad waiting for him and I was asked to show him around until his Nav/Rad turned up. After a couple of flights we got on so well that I went to the CO and asked him to let me have him permanently.

We flew our first op on 14 October, a bomber support run to Brunswick. We had one chase but it was one of ours. We did four more Ops in October, all of them different. The first was hunting for Heinkels, which launched flying bombs from over the North Sea. This involved flying at less than 500 ft. on a bumpy windy night. We never found anything, but I was mightily impressed by the way Svein handled the Mossie. The next one was supporting our mine layers in the Kattegat. We had one chase but it was, again, one of our own. The next was a low level ranger patrol to Vechta/Diepholz, which we didn't reach as the radar set gave up and died. It was a bright night so we stayed low and kept our eyes open for a likely target on the ground. At one point we were shot at by light flak which seemed to cover the ground for miles around. Tracer was coming from all sides and I wondered how we were going to get out of this mess. My unflappable Norwegian put our nose down and all was peace. I said, 'Thank God we are clear of that horrible place.' – 'Not Yet', said Svein, 'but at this height if they shoot at us they will shoot each other.' At this point my breathing got back to normal and the adrenaline took over. Hedge hopping by moonlight! We had a pot shot at a train and missed, I think we had more luck with a car, we hoped it was full of Gestapo agents. As we turned away a pair of cooling towers faced us: no room to climb over, so go between. Svein had to bank a bit to get through.

This brought us to a small town. I looked up at the church clock as we passed – it was just after 10pm. I did some research with the map and decided that we had passed over Meppen. I don't think I want to do that over again. The final op on the 31st was a bomber support run to Frankfurt.

On 16 November 1944 we were airborne 00.10 hours a bomber support ops for the Dortmund raid. No reaction, no searchlights, no gunfire. The met briefing before we left warned us that Swannington probably would be clamped down on return. When we were over the sea on the way back all our electrics went out, no radio, no blind flying panel. We were above cloud at around 10,000ft. Svein reckoned that our only way out was to fly until we were sure of being over land, pointing our Mossie towards the sea and making a jump for it. I wonder who has tried this one? I recall one peculiar event coming back one night from a bomber escort trip to Dortmund. The weather forecast was for cloud over the east of England with a base of 500ft and a ceiling of 10,000ft odd. We were just short of the coast when all the electrics quit on us: no instruments, no radio. Without the blind flying panel there was not much future in flying down through the cloud. I suggested to my pilot that our Mark X AI (which has its own generator and was functioning) could give me a good enough clue as to whether we were nose up or nose down or which wing was up or down. A short check on my claim satisfied us that a controlled downward spiral was possible and we proceeded to do so until the ground return suggested that we were at about 3,000ft. At this point the tube told me that we were in a straight steep dive. I protested but was calmly informed that there was a hole with a light beyond and he was going for it. And so we landed at Coltishall.

On 6–7 October Ju88G-1 710639 D5+EV of *10./NJG3* was shot down by Flight Lieutenant Gallacher and Pilot Officer McLean of 141 Squadron. It crashed near Groningen. *Oberleutnant* Walter Briegleb, pilot, *Unteroffizier* Brandt, flight engineer, and *Unteroffizier* Braeunlich, air gunner, were WIA. *Feldwebel* Paul Kowalewski, radar operator, was killed. On 7–8 October, Flight Lieutenant Jimmy Mathews and Warrant Officer Alan 'Penny' Penrose of 157 Squadron picked up a contact at six miles range west of Neumünster while on a high level support sortie. Mathews narrowed the range and as they got a visual at 1,000 yards the target straightened out. It was recognized as a Me410 with long range tanks. Mathews opened fire with a short burst from 100 yards dead behind. Strikes were seen and a small explosion occurred in the starboard engine. Another burst and the starboard engine caught fire. It dived burning to the ground and exploded. Flight Lieutenant Paul Mellows and Flight Lieutenant Dickie Drew of 169 Squadron meanwhile, sought targets at Egmond on a Serrate patrol. Mellows reported:

Mosquito arrived in Patrol area at 2005 hours, flying at 15,000 ft. Two beacons flashing were observed near two airfields 15 miles to the North, so we proceeded to the area to investigate. At 2022 hours an AI contact was obtained hard port at maximum range, our height being 14,000ft. Mosquito closed to 7,000ft when target commenced hard turns to port through a number of orbits. Enemy aircraft then straightened out and climbed at low IAS and we closed to 100ft to identify enemy aircraft as Ju88. In climbing at 140 IAS to attack, we dropped back and opened fire at 500ft. Time, 2037 hours. Strikes being observed between the starboard engine and fuselage. Enemy aircraft immediately peeled off to port and visual was lost, but contact was held at 10,000ft range and we closed again losing height to 14,000ft and obtained another visual while in hard starboard turn, at 500ft on enemy aircraft which was losing height and turning starboard. However visual could not be held and no further AI contact was obtained on enemy aircraft, which was inside minimum range.

We continued to patrol the area, where three aerodromes were now lit, until 2120 hours at heights ranging between 7,000 and 15,000ft, numerous sisters were seen to be fired mostly well below but no further contacts were obtained. Course was then set for base.

On the night of 19–20 October Squadron Leader 'Dolly' Doleman and Flight Lieutenant 'Bunny' Bunch DFC of 157 Squadron were airborne from Swannington at 19.24 hours on a High Level Support Patrol to Nuremburg. Their patrol was uneventful until at 21.02 hours a contact was obtained head-on, same height, at four miles range at Beacon *Fritz*. Doleman reported:

Turned round on to a target at approximately the same height. Closing in with visuals at 2,000' when we went through search-light cone. Target pooped off some colours, about six stars, mixed green and white, illuminating us. Searchlights doused. Target on course of 310, which seemed very 'phoney', so closed to 400 ft. and identified as a Ju 88. Dropped back to about 800 ft, and in spite of having a screened sight, when I put spot on him he disappeared. Had a squirt and missed. Target continued straight and level. Repeated process with strikes all along fuselage from dead astern. Target just seemed to drop straight down and went into 10/10ths cloud at 8,000ft, contact disappearing from C scope on –15 with extreme speed.

Fanned around, then did a reciprocal at about 11,000–12,000 ft. Contact obtained port, turning port at 4 miles. Closed at full boost and revs and identified another Ju.88 with night glasses at 14,000 ft. about 600 ft range. Had a squirt with no results, and target peeled off port down to 10,000 ft. Followed on A.I. and closed into 800ft on target, climbing port. It levelled off again at 14,000 ft so had another squirt. Target again peeled off to port to 10,000 ft, and again contact held. Climbed and closed to about 800 ft at 12,000 ft. squirted once more with mass of strikes on port wing root, and thereabouts. Target slowed down very quickly and in spite of throttling right back overshot to starboard, as he dived to port. Inaccurate traces came from dorsal position. Much profanity as we thought he had got away, but when he was below at about 7,000 ft. range on Monica, he caught fire, and went down burning though not fully alight, in a 45 degree dive, the flames spreading quite nicely until he hit the deck, somewhere near a steady searchlight. No more joy so set course for base at 2200 hrs. Flight Lieutenant Bunch was 'wizard' on the infernal machine, never making a mistake.

Doleman and Bunch's possible victim was Ju88G-1 714510 27+CM of 4./NJG6 which crashed at Murrhard south-east of Heilbronn, Germany. *Unteroffizier* Georg Haberer, pilot and *Unteroffizier* Ernst Dressel, radar operator, were both KIA.

Warrant Officer Les Turner and Flight Sergeant Freddie Francis of 169 Squadron meanwhile, had been piling up their ops and on 22–23 October they flew their 32nd trip, a Serrate patrol to Denmark. It was to prove eventful, as Les Turner confirmed in his combat report:

Took off from Great Massingham at 1744 hours in Mosquito Y reaching Patrol area at 1915 hours, without event. At 1920 hours

120

whilst on course West of Nissun Fiord height 15,000 ft, contact was obtained at maximum range showing hard starboard and below. Pursuit action was immediately taken and for the next five minutes we indulged in tight turns eventually reducing range to 2,000 ft where a visual was obtained of an aircraft believed to be a Ju 88 standing on its port wing, also tight turning. The enemy aircraft must have seen Mosquito and peeled off whereat we lost some range. Contact was held and after a further three minutes of hectic dog-fighting range was once again closed to 2,000 ft where aircraft was identified as a Ju 88 travelling at about 150 mph. We throttled back and put down full flap opening fire at about 400 yards observing large strike on port wing root. Enemy aircraft peeled off starboard and an ineffective burst was fired leaving Mosquito in an awkward position at about 145-mph – full flap and being curiously knocked about by slipstream from the Ju 88. We followed down on AI to about 4,000-ft height where contact was lost in ground returns. We patrolled off the coast for another thirty minutes with no further joy. Course was set for home at 2005 hours and reached without further event at 2120 hours.

Though they could only claim a 'damaged' Turner was convinced this aircraft crashed subsequently as there was a fire on the ground some ten minutes after the attack. He adds, 'I am fairly certain that the R/T listening group known as the "Y Service" monitored the German R/T and confirmed this combat. For security, there was no mention of this on the paper. I am also fairly certain that this aircraft crashed subsequently. There was fire on the ground some ten minutes after the attack. On a personal level, I was commissioned. Frank was promoted to warrant officer and we were awarded the DFC and DFM respectively. These awards were effective before my commission and Franks' promotion, hence the DFM rather than DFC.'

Trip number thirty-three for Turner and Francis was to Osnabrück. Turner recalls:

I obtained a visual on a Mosquito on which, in a fit of bravado, I formated for a minute or two! This was not the way to fly over enemy territory. This was an occasion when we were diverted else-where because of bad weather at base. We then had a couple of days at Fulbeck on Lancaster affiliation – giving their gunners training by making mock attacks on them. Trip No.34 was a long haul to Munich having refueled at Ford. Nothing happened! Trip 35 was to the Ruhr and No.36 to Düsseldorf. On the last one we had an inconclusive 'dogfight' but I can recall nothing but a feeling of pleasure that we had reached the end of the tour unscathed. After Christmas at home I was posted to the BSDU at Great Massingham.

On 4–5 November two more Bf110s which were shot down probably fell to 100 Group Mosquito crews. Bf110 of *II./NJG1* was shot down at 19.00 hours at a height of 20,000 feet. *Unteroffizier* Gustav Sario, pilot, was injured and baled out. *Unteroffizier* Heinrich Conrads, the radar operator, and *Obergefreiter* Roman Talarowski, air gunner, were both killed. Another Bf110 of *II./NJG1* was shot down by Squadron Leader Branse Burbridge DSO* DFC* and Flight Lieutenant F. S. Skelton DSO* DFC* of 85 Squadron into the River Rhine near Hangelar airfield at 21.50 hours. *Oberleutnant* Ernst Runze, pilot, was killed and *Obergefreiter* Karl Heinz Bendfield, radar operator, baled out safely. Two other Bf110s were also shot down this night. Bf110G-4 440648 G9+RS of *8./NJG1* was possibly shot down by a Mosquito night fighter. It crashed at Bersenbrueck, thirty kilometres north of Osnabruck, Germany. *Feldwebel* Willi Ruge, pilot, was wounded and baled out. *Unteroffizier* Helmut Kreibohm, radar operator, and *Obergefreiter* Anton Weiss, air gunner, were both killed. Also shot down this night by a Mosquito was *Leutnant* Heinz Rolland, the twenty-six-year-old pilot of *IV./NJG1*, who had fifteen victories at night. Rolland, *Feldwebel* Heinz Krueger, twenty-five-year-old radar operator, and *Unteroffizier* Karl Berger, twenty-two-year-old air gunner, were all killed when their Bf110 crashed south-west of Wezel, Germany.

On 6–7 November, two Ju88G-6 aircraft were lost. 620396 R4+KR of *Stab/IV./NJG3* was shot down by a Mosquito and crashed at Marienburg, Germany. *Hauptmann* Ernst Schneider, pilot, was killed. *Oberfeldwebel* Mittwoch, radar operator, and *Unteroffizier* Kaase, both baled out safely. 620583 R4+TS of *11./NJG3* was shot down in air combat and crashed south-west of Paderborn. *Oberleutnant* Josef Foerster, pilot, survived. *Feldwebel* Werner Moraing, radar operator, and *Feldwebel* Heinz Wickardt were both wounded. This same night Squadron Leader Dolly Doleman and Flight Lieutenant 'Bunny' Bunch DFC of 157 Squadron were airborne from Swannington at 17.34 hours in their NFXIX. Doleman recalls:

Before reaching our patrol point we obtained a contact to starboard just by the Rhine. Chased and obtained a visual on exhausts like a Mosquito, but on closing in to identify definitely, aircraft did steep turn to port. Chased on AI on target, which was taking evasive action, and obtained a second contact head-on, which we chased and got a visual on a Me 110 going west. The position and time are somewhat uncertain after the first chase. Minimum range on weapon was poor, but opened fire on a visually estimated range of 500–600 ft with a short burst. Strikes and explosion occurred instantaneously and poor Hans went straight down in flames.

Contacts were obtained on bags more, Mosquitoes and the odd bomber throwing out Window, and also on two aircraft (at different times) going North West at very high speed. Mosquito flat out but contacts drew steadily away. One visual obtained on two pairs of exhausts, one of these at 6,000-ft range. Do not know what they were but most certainly they were not Mosquitoes on one engine.

Returned from these chases towards Koblenz, and was followed by some crab in a friendly for about 15 minutes, in spite of 'G' band, Type 'F' and calling on Command Guard. At 2040 hours set course for base as supplies of chewing gum were running low. Saw one beacon lit up. No contacts obtained and Monica was u/s by then anyway. Near Brussels was challenged by an American on Channel C and put navigational lights on as second American was advising our chum to 'shoot the basket down' – only he didn't say 'basket'. Landed base with nasty smell of burning in cockpit at 2155 hours. Claim 1 Me.110 destroyed.

As a result of large-scale use of the Mosquito late in 1944, the German night fighter defences were made to change their tactics and this seriously reduced their efficiency. One *Geschwader*, with a strength of about 100 crews, lost, in three months, twenty-four crews killed, ten missing and fifteen wounded. It was at around this time that the real '*Moskitopanik*' started and from then on all the normal run of crashes through natural causes were attributed to the Mosquito. The Mosquito's increased reputation heightened the German night fighter crews' despondency and their demoralization was complete late in 1944 when they had to resort to throwing out *Düppel* (Window) as a routine, to mislead and distract the Mosquito night fighters. *Hauptmann* Heinz-Wolfgang Schnauffer, the top scoring German night fighter pilot, with 121 victories, attributed his continued survival to the fact that he did not only weave but actually carried out what he described as 'steep turns' from take off to landing. He even continued to weave when in AI contact with a bomber. His impression was that none of the top German night fighter pilots dared to climb until the last moment and all remained very low, or at '*Ritterkreuz Height*', as if they flew higher they would never survive to receive the decoration. Schnauffer recalled that the only time that they felt at all free from RAF fighters was in the bomber stream but he said because of the threat of Mosquito intruders, 'it was impossible to relax even then.'

Hauptmann Hans Krause, with twenty-eight destroyed, quoted an instance in the Ruhr when he was intercepted in the target area and pursued for forty-five minutes having frequent visuals on a Mosquito as it came into range. He took violent evasive action in azimuth and height and by going through cloud but this failed to shake off the fighter. He finally succeeded in evading only by flying to a district in the Ardennes that he knew really well, flying, as he said, 'Down a valley below the level of the hills.' This confirmed in his mind the exceptional standard of the British AI radar. German night-fighter crews now flew at tree top height to the beacons. This caused many accidents and German night fighters often flew into the ground. An alternative technique of returning to base, provided the pilot could come straight in and land, was to approach straight from 10,000 feet. When possible, Krause preferred to do this for as he said, 'It had the added advantage that if you were shot down by a Mosquito you had plenty of time to bale out.'

'*Moskitopanik*' reached a peak during December 1944 when thirty-six enemy night fighters were shot down. On 2–3 December Captain Weisteen of 85 Squadron shot down Bf110G-4 180382 of *12./NJG4*, which had taken off from Bonninhardt at 20.47 hours. It crashed at 21.45 near Lippborg near Hamm. *Leutnant* Heinz-Joachim Sclage, pilot, survived, but the other two were killed. Flight Lieutenant W. Taylor and Flying Officer J. N. Edwards of 157 Squadron shot down a German night fighter, possibly Ju88 714819 3C+WL of *3./NJG4*, which crashed at Rheine. *Oberfuehrer* Erhard Pfisterhammer, pilot, *Unteroffizier* Wolfgang Sode, radar operator and the air gunner, were all WIA.

On the night of 4–5 December there was a spoof on Dortmund while the main force attacked Heilbronn and Karlsruhe. German night fighters were sent to the spoof and they waited in the area for about fifteen minutes for the attack to start. However, they found nothing but high intruders and their losses were high. On this night 100 Group Mosquitoes shot down five and probably destroyed another. Flight Lieutenant R. T. 'Dickie' Goucher and Flight Lieutenant C. H. 'Tiny' Bulloch of 85 Squadron destroyed two of them, while Flying Officer Ginger Owen and Flying Officer J. S. V. McAllister, also of 85 Squadron, scored the squadron's 100th victory when they shot down Ju88G-1 714152 of 6./NJG4, which crashed near Krefeld. *Unteroffizier* Wilhelm Schlutter, pilot, was wounded and *Unteroffizier* Friedrich Heerwagen, radar operator and *Gefreiter* Friedrich Herbeck, air gunner, were both killed. Captain S. Heglund DFC * and Flying Officer Robert O. Symon of 85 Squadron were airborne from Swannington this night on a High Level Support Patrol in the Karlsruhe area. On reaching patrol at 18.55 hours, contacts were obtained on bombers and later two targets, with violent evasion, were chased eastwards. At 20.05, Schwabish Hall airfield was seen lit and several fleeting contacts appeared well below. The Mosquito went down to 2,500 feet to investigate but all lighting was doused. The Mosquito regained height and, at 20.15 hours, north-east of Heilbronn, Symon obtained a contact.

Heglund reported:

We had just regained height at 10,000 ft, after investigating Schwabish Hall airfield and were flying on about 260° when, at 2015 hours, my N/R said he had contact and told me to turn 100° port. Our position then was about 10 miles N.E. of Heilbronn. Contact was then obtained 6 miles ahead and well below. The aircraft was doing a mild corkscrew on an easterly course and we came in behind at 4,000 ft (about 2,500 ft. above the ground). The aircraft being chased was travelling very slowly – 190 – 200 IAS – and we overshot, recognising it as an ME.110 by its square wingtip and 2 fins and rudders, as we pulled away to starboard 400 ft. away. Contact and visual were momentarily lost but contact regained and maintained to bring a further visual at 400 ft. we were still overtaking and I lost the visual in making further S turns to lose speed, and remained behind the enemy aircraft. Contact was maintained the whole time and finally the visual was obtained at 400 ft. and held steady. I fired a 1-second burst obtaining strikes immediately on the starboard engine and wing root. The enemy aircraft burst into flames, lighting up the crosses on wings and fuselage and showing up the Radar aerial display on the nose. Enemy aircraft sideslipped into the ground near Rothenburg where it exploded. Time 2025.

At 20.26 Heglund and Symon set course for base via the Frankfurt area where several airfields were seen active but their fuel was low and Heglund had to put down at Brussels, where they arrived at 22.00 hours. After refueling, the Mosquito took off again at 23.20 and landed back at Swannington at 00.10 hours. Heglund had expended just forty rounds to bring down the Bf110. Robert Symon adds, 'Captain S. Heglund DFC * who joined 85 Squadron (and his fellow group of Norwegians) in October 1944, was a delightful and modest young man, who, I found later, was Norway's Ace. As a point of interest check the number of rounds it took my friend to bring down three 110s compared with the number of rounds fired to bring down No.1. I can only assume that this was the first for Swannington and he was going to be sure that it would never fly again.'

On 6–7 December Flight Lieutenant J. O. Mathews DFC and Warrant Officer A. Penrose DFC of 157 Squadron destroyed a Bf110 and a Ju88 (712268 of *I./NJG4*, which crashed near Giessen killing the air gunner, *Gefreiter* Alfred Graefer). Squadron Leader Dolly Doleman and Flight Lieutenant Bunny Bunch DFC of 157 Squadron were also airborne from Swannington at 18.35 hours in what Doleman described as 'my plywood pantechnicon'. He and Bunch set course for patrol but got hung up in the bomber stream west of the Rhine and saw the flares being laid on Biesson. Doleman continues:

We saw bags of four or five-star reds being fired from the Frankfurt searchlight belt so bogged off to have a look. No joy so returned to Giessen, which was being inundated with incendiaries (wizard alliteration) and saw lashings of Lancs flying across the target. We stayed overhead to see if we could pick off someone trying to pick off a Lanc, but nothing happened so went NW to clear the bomber stream. We had just arrived, at 2030 hours, when we picked up an almost head-on contact at 15,000 ft at six miles, same level. Target dived to 11,000 ft on bomber withdrawal route then did a figure of eight and stooged off eastwards. Closed in and identified as a Me 110 and shot it down at 2040 hours in Kitzingen area. Night glasses were used to advantage. We had a persistent Monica

126

contact before and after the happy event and as he wouldn't close to less than 8,000 ft we had to turn and try to catch him. He must have seen what we were trying to do, for he had no forward contact but saw the Hun colours fired in the direction he should have been, but out of range. Looked in at an aerodrome near Zelhausen and later at Bonn, but no bon, as they say, so returned to base, where we landed at 2320 hours – the landing as usual, being the most exciting thing of the evening for Bunny. Claim 1 Me 110 destroyed.

Flight Lieutenant Edward R. Hedgecoe DFC and Pilot Officer J. R. Whitham, who were attached to the Fighter Interception Unit, destroyed a Bf110 west of Munster, possibly Bf110G-4 740078 G9+HZ of *12./NJG1*, which crashed ten kilometres north-west of Handorf. This aircraft was flown by *Hauptmann* Hans-Heinz Augenstein, *Staffel Kapitän*, *12./NJG1*, who was killed, along with *Feldwebel* Günther Stems, his radar operator. Augenstein had forty-six night victories, including forty-five RAF night bombers and had been awarded the Knight's Cross on 9 June 1944. *Unteroffizier* Kurt Schmidt, *Bordschütze*, who was WIA, baled out successfully. Hedgecoe and Whitham destroyed two more Bf110s on the night of 12–13 December, when 100 Group shot down five more German night fighters, Squadron Leader Branse Burbridge DSO* DFC* and Flight Lieutenant F. S. Skelton DSO* DFC* of 85 Squadron added a Ju88 and a Bf110 to their rising score. The Ju88 G-1 714530 of *6./NJG4*, crashed at Gütersloh airfield. *Unteroffizier* Heinrich Brune, pilot, *Unteroffizier* Emil Hoffharth, radar operator, and *Unteroffizier* Wolfgang Rautert, air gunner, were all killed. Wing Commander Beauchamp, DSO, DFC, CO 157 Squadron, flying with Flight Lieutenant Scholefield, was airborne from Swannington at 17.03 hours and went on patrol in support of Bomber Command attacks on Essen. Their patrol was uneventful until 20.10 hours, when a contact was obtained in the area south-east of the Ruhr and chased to Aschaffenburg, where it was attacked and damaged. An airfield was active in Aschaffenburg area, and several other contacts were obtained during and after the combat, suggesting enemy fighter activity. Beauchamp reported:

I patrolled uneventfully until bombing commenced. At 1925 hrs the markers were seen on Essen and Osnabruck. At 2010 hrs Flight Lieutenant Scholefield got a contact at 6 miles range, 30 degrees to starboard and going away to starboard. I turned after it, and abased for 25 minutes, first on course 120 and then on 150, and descending during chase to 10,000 ft., just above cloud tops. At 2035 hrs the target did a port orbit over a lit airfield, believed to be Aschaffenburg. I closed to 200 ft below and on the quarter, and identified it as a Me.110 with long range tanks, and burning an orange light inboard of the starboard engine. Identification was checked by Flight Lieutenant Scholefield using night binoculars. I dropped back to 600 ft. astern and fired two short bursts at 2037 hrs., 10,000 ft. Saw strikes on the starboard wing and there were two large showers of sparks. Immediately after this, visual was lost, and as the AI had been upset by firing the guns, contact was also lost. I patrolled in the area hoping to regain contact. We had had two forward Monica contacts during the chase and got another AI contact at 2040 hrs, which was followed down to 5,000 ft. and lost in violent manoeuvres. I claim 1Me.110 damaged.

Three Bf110s were destroyed on the night of 17–18 December. On 18–19 December, Flight Lieutenant William Taylor and Flying Officer J. N. Edwards destroyed He219A-O 190229 G9+GH of 1./NJG1. The *Uhu* (Owl) crashed at Suedlohn killing *Unteroffizier* Günther Heinze, radar operator. *Unteroffizier* Scheürlein, pilot, baled out safely. (Edwards was killed on 22 December during landing back at Swannington with Taylor).

On the night of 21–22 December 1944 Wing Commander K. H. P. Beauchamp DSO DFC and Flight Lieutenant L. Scholefield DFC of 157 Squadron in a NFXIX flew in support of Bomber Command operations against Bonn and Cologne. Beauchamp returned to report:

We had completed our patrol uneventfully at 1852 hrs and were on the way home at 12,000 ft, just west of Koblenz when my navigator got a contact 60 degrees to port at 5 miles range, going port. This was chased on an initial heading of 150 degrees, turning port slowing on to 060 degrees. We were losing height and eventually overtook him at 4,000 ft having been flying at 300 mph for most of the time. A visual was obtained at 2,500 ft and was identified as a Ju 88 in the light of a half-moon from 200 ft on his starboard quarter below. I dropped back to 200 ft dead astern and fired a short burst, causing strikes. Enemy aircraft immediately peeled off port and went down on to the top of some stratus cloud, which appeared to be just above ground level. I thought he had dived right through this as I had lost visual contact, but as there was no resultant explosion I followed down and regained a visual on him as he was weaving away violently just above cloud. I closed in on his port quarter and slightly above, opening fire at about 600 yards, as I was anxious to inflict further damage before he could make good his escape. Strikes were obtained from this burst and from two more, the last of which set his port engine on fire. I pulled up and did a port orbit over him watching the fire increase until the enemy aircraft flew into the ground in a shallow dive and exploded ... in view of the length of time of the combat and his final behaviour of the enemy aircraft it seems likely that the crew had time to escape by parachute.

On the night of 22–23 December Swannington celebrated in huge style when 85 Squadron's Burbridge and Skelton shot down a Bf110 and Ginger Owen and Flying Officer McAllister scored a hat trick of victories, with two Ju88s and a Bf110. Ju88 621441 27+HK of II./NJG6 crashed at Landstuhl killing *Oberfeldwebel* Max Hausser, pilot, *Oberfeldwebel* Fritz Steube, radar operator, and *Feldwebel* Ernst Beisswenger, air gunner. Ju88G-6 621436 2Z+DC also of II./NJG6, crashed at Lebach, north of Saarbrücken. *Unteroffizier* Werner Karau survived while the other two crew were killed. Squadron Leader Dolly Doleman and his navigator Flight Lieutenant Bunny Bunch also returned to the Norfolk station with news of a kill. They had taken off in their NFXIX at 17.06 hours on a High Level patrol in support of Bomber Command operation against Koblenz and Bingen. The Mosquito remained in his patrol area until the bombing of Bingen commenced, and then flew toward the target, and a contact was obtained north at Bingen at 18.35 hours. Doleman continues:

We were at 15,000 ft and chased it up to 20,000 ft, just north of Bingen. As staggering up the last few thousand feet a Monica contact whistled in, and position became so uncomfortable, we had to leave the original contact and try to catch the other type. As we turned to port the Monica, which had been frantically jammed, cleared (we think the first contact might have been a Dinah Mosquito) and we saw the type behind showing IFF. After several conversations on the R/T, starting with 'Please go away' and finishing '——— off, you silly ———'. We neared the bomber stream and dived into a cloud of Window where we lost him. This had wasted about 20 minutes of valuable time, and as bombing had finished we went along north of Frankfurt to have a look at Limburg. This proved a good bet, as we obtained a contact at 10 miles range and well below. We were at 15,000 ft and time 1925 hrs. We closed range and descended to 8,000 ft and obtained visual at 3,000 ft; the target by this time was doing a hardish port turn. Identified at 1,500 ft from below in the turn as a Ju 88 then the silly clot slackened his turn and we were able to close in nicely to 500 ft and prang him with only ½-ring deflection. The fuselage and port engine burst into flames. We hung behind just to make sure, but he dived straight in 5 miles west of Limburg at 1935 hrs. We wished him a Merry Christmas on the way down – literally cooking his goose for him.

No more joy, so left patrol at 1949 hrs. Saw a buzz bomb in Malmedy area on way back. Just getting nicely in position when some brown job opened up with one solitary gun, missed the buzz bomb and frightened us away. I hope it landed on their headquarters. Landed base 2107 hrs. Claim 1 Ju 88 destroyed.

On Christmas Eve 100 Group supported two raids by 104 Lancasters of 3 Group on Hangelar airfield near Bonn, losing one aircraft, and ninety-seven Lancasters and five Mosquitoes of 1 and 8 Groups on the marshalling yards at Cologne/Nippes. At Cologne good Oboe marking resulted in an extremely accurate bombing raid. Railway tracks were severely damaged and an ammunition train was blown up. The nearby Butzweilerhof airfield was also damaged. Eighteen civilians and one soldier were killed, probably when houses near the railway yards were hit. Losses were five Lancasters shot down during the raid and two more crashed in England. *Hauptmann* Baake of I./NJG1 claimed one Lancaster over Cologne. In support of these two raids, forty-two RCM sorties were flown and forty-two Mosquitoes of 100 Group patrolled the *Luftwaffe* night fighter bases and radio beacons along the route taken by the heavies. These Mosquitoes claimed four Me110s and one Ju88 shot down. (2nd TAF was also active on the same night, with 139 Mosquitoes being dispatched on bombing attacks on targets in north and south-west Germany; one Mosquito was lost. Also, thirty-seven Mossies of the 2nd TAF patrolled the areas of Aachen, Arnhem and the Dutch Frisian Islands, and flew 'close support' sorties over the front lines. None of these Mosquitoes was lost and they shot down two Ju87s, two Ju188s, one Ju88 and one Me110. In addition they 'bagged' fifty trucks and six trains). Some eighteen German aircraft were shot down, five of them by four Mosquito crews of 100 Group.

In 157 Squadron, Squadron Leader James Benson DFC* and Flight Lieutenant Lewis Brandon DFC* destroyed a Bf110 to take their score to nine. Lewis Brandon recalls:

We decided to have our Christmas dinner on Christmas Eve. As a maximum effort had been asked for from the station for the night's operations, we were very pleased that we all had an early time for takeoff. It was arranged that dinner would be held back until we returned, giving us something to look forward to. We left Swannington at 16.30 hours on our way to Limburg. We had put in quite a lot of flying time in that area during the past few weeks and considered ourselves rather as specialists around Frankfurt – a couple of Frankfurters almost.

We had been on patrol at 14,000 ft for about half an hour when we obtained a contact. We were just north of Limburg and the aircraft was well below us. Down we went pretty smartly to 8,000 ft after a target that was flying level at that height but weaving quite violently. As we closed in, Ben had fleeting visuals two or three times. Each time, however, he could not hold on to them nor could he identify the aircraft. We continued to follow him on AI, and he turned through two complete orbits before settling down on a northwesterly course. Shortly afterwards we saw some target indicators go down ahead of us. We had closed in on the aircraft and Ben got a visual on a Messerschmitt 110 at a range of two thousand feet, silhouetted against the light of the target indicators.

'Okay. I can see him all right now', said Ben. 'Just look at that. No wonder we've taken such a while to close in.'

As I looked up, I saw the Messerschmitt go across us from starboard to port. It went a fair way out to port, then went right up on one wing and came back in front of us, crossing the other way in this violent weave. Ben followed it through several of these weaves, fairly well throttled back and far more gently than the Messerschmitt. Then, from about 150 yards he gave it two short sharp bursts, firing at the exhaust flames. The second burst set the port engine and the whole of the port side of the fuselage alight.

We dived under some large pieces of debris that came flying back and heard them swoosh above the cockpit. The Messerschmitt was well alight now and going over to our starboard. We saw it hit the ground and explode near a small town by the name of Dottesfeld, where we could see it burning brightly.

'About bloody time we shot one down again,' remarked Ben. 'Look at it burning. I wonder if the camera gun would pick that up?'

'Why not have a go?' I suggested. So we did.

We had a good look around to see that there was no high ground and Ben did two runs right down to within a few hundred feet of the burning aircraft. All in vain though, nothing appeared on the film when it was developed.

We landed back at Swannington at five minutes to nine. Dinner had been laid on for half past so after a pretty rapid debriefing we set off for the mess. We were fortified with the news that, in addition to our Messerschmitt, Jimmy Matthews and Penrose had destroyed a Junkers 88 [Flight Lieutenant Jimmy Mathews and Warrant Officer A. 'Penny' Penrose of 157 Squadron chased the Ju 88 and shot down with a 1½ second burst, which resulted in the starboard engine bursting into flames. As it turned to port, three parachutes came out in quick succession and three bodies sailed to earth. The aircraft then spun down and crashed 3 miles SW of Cologne]. As can be imagined, this gave the squadron something to celebrate. Four enemy aircraft destroyed in one night was by no means a record, but this had been accomplished on Christmas Eve, just before a party.

At Swannington 85 Squadron was not to be outdone. Squadron Leader Dolly Doleman and Flight Lieutenant Bunny Bunch DFC and Captain Svein Heglund DFC and Flying Officer Robert C. Symon also had reason to celebrate. Doleman and Bunch had taken off on their High Level Support Patrol for the Bomber Command attacks on Cologne and Hangelar at 16.26. Doleman reported:

We reached patrol area and saw an aircraft hit the deck dead below us near Siegen. Things seemed pretty dead, so went towards Cologne and just as we arrived, obtained a contact: range 6 miles well below. Overhauled fairly quickly and just managed to slow down into an ideal position, where we identified an Me 110 doing

132

an orbit at 9,000 ft. I think the crew must have been full of the festive spirit as we were directly up moon at 600 ft when we opened fire with a very long burst. The pride of the Luftwaffe caught fire immediately but we gave them another burst just for fun, and he went down and pranged just west of Cologne at 1905. We immediately had another contact at 10 miles' range, well above. Chased this at full bore and luckily the tyke dived down and we closed in very rapdily, eventually slightly overshooting. About 50 yards to port, having a wizard view of another Me 110. We did a hard port orbit and picked him up at 3 miles – by this time we were at 8,000 ft, going NW slap across the Ruhr – closed in and identified again and opened fire from about 500 ft with long burst. He caught fire and pieces of debris fell off including one quite large piece. He continued flying evenly so we gave him three more bursts, when he went down in the Duisburg area at 1921 hours. We headed west, as we could not fix on Gee and found ourselves near Krefeld so flew straight home. Cannot write any more as there is a party on in the mess. Claim 2 Me 110s destroyed. Aircraft landed at base 2024 hours.

One of their victims was Bf110G-4 740162 G9+OT of 9./NJG1, flown by *Hauptmann* Heinz Strüning, *Ritterkreuz mit Eichenlaub* (Knight's Cross with Oak leaves), fifty-six night victories. He was shot down at 22.00 hours and crashed at Bergisch Gladbach/Rheinland. The *Bordfunker* and *Bordschütze* baled out safely but Strüning was killed when he hit the tail of his 110. His body was found two months later. *Luftwaffe* losses included Bf110 of 7/NJG1, which crashed near Roermond killing the crew and one Ju88 of 5/NJG2, which crashed near Roermond; one of the crew was killed, three became POWs. This may have been the aircraft claimed by Mathews and Penrose of 157 Squadron. A Ju88 of 5/LG1 crashed south of Afferden (one KIA, two MIA, one POW).

Captain Svein Heglund DFC and Flying Officer Robert C. Symon meanwhile, had downed a Bf110 north of Frankfurt on their High Level Support Patrol for the Bomber Command attacks on Cologne and Hangelar. Heglund reported:

We were flying in a South Easterly course away from target area and towards a visual beacon in Wiesbaden area when we obtained a contact head on and below at 6 miles range. We turned port and dived, leveling out at 14,000 ft. coming in behind an aircraft doing a mild corkscrew, range 1½ miles. We chased rapidly to 3,000 ft. and aircraft climbed rapidly to 14,000 ft. weaving all the time. A visual was obtained at 2,000 ft, on a faint outline and a dim white light inboard of the starboard engine. Following the white light through several turns range was closed to 150 ft. when aircraft was recognised as a Me.110 by twin fins and rudders, general outline and large drop tanks. We dropped back to 600 ft. and fired a ½ second burst, obtained strikes on starboard wing root. Aircraft exploded immediately and we dived hard to avoid flaming debris which showered back over us. The Me.110 was seen to hit the ground.

We once again turned on original South easterly course and almost immediately obtained another contact dead ahead at 6 miles, height being 15,000 ft, travelling on the same course as ourselves. We increased speed and went into a shallow dive slowly overhauling the aircraft which was travelling at about 300 mph IAS. Shortly before arriving at the beacon and when we had closed range to 2,500 ft. aircraft dived hard to starboard then climbed hard, contact being lost for some seconds. Contact was regained and aircraft dived hard again turning as it did so. Contact was finally lost. During the last part of the chase the port engine was getting very rough, cutting intermittently and vibrating.

It was Heglund's fourteenth victory of the war having scored twelve and one third kills flying Spitfires with No.331 Squadron.

The last of thirty-nine *Luftwaffe* aircraft to fall to 100 Group in December were two Ju88s and a He219 *Uhu* on New Year's Eve. On this night Flight Lieutenant Paul Mellows and Flight Lieutenant S. L. Dickie Drew of 169 Squadron, who were attached to 85 Squadron at Swannington to try interceptions with AI Mk X, took off at 16.54 hours on a High Level Support Patrol west of the Ruhr. Their patrol was reached at 17.58 hours and at 18.08 hours a contact was obtained. Mellows reported:

AI contact was obtained at 6 miles range and ceased turning slowly port and climbing from 15,000 ft to 18,000 ft. While this contact was still well above another came in at 3 miles range from the west nearly head on. This was found to be at our height so we turned starboard as it passed us and came in 4,000 ft. behind. A visual was

134

obtained at 2,000 ft. on four white exhausts and on closing to 400 ft. twin tail fins were seen, and shortly after black crosses on the blue undersurface of the wings were seen in the light of a search-light. On the strength of this I fired a 2-second burst from slightly below causing debris to fly off and a small fire in the fuselage. Another 2-second burst caused an explosion by the light of which Flight Lieutenant Drew clearly saw the dihedral and slanting fins of a He.219, which I confirmed. A further short burst set him well alight and from 1,000 ft to starboard we saw him climb for a few seconds before plunging to earth, where he exploded with a bright orange flash at 1824 hrs in the Koln area, Throughout the combat the He. 219 was flying straight and level and appeared to have no knowledge of our presence.

He 219A-2 290194 G9+KL of 3./NJG1 crashed at Schleiden, fifty kilometres south-west of Cologne. *Oberleutnant* Heinz Oloff, pilot, and *Feldwebel* Helmut Fischer, radar operator, who were WIA, both bailed out and survived. The Mosquito landed at Manston at 20.05 hours and the crew returned to base 11.45.

Sixteen aircraft were claimed shot down by 100 Group Mosquitoes in January 1945. Dickie Goucher and Tiny Bulloch of 85 Squadron got the month off to a flying start with two aircraft destroyed on 1–2 January. A Ju188 was claimed ten miles north of Münster, while Ju88G-6 621364 27+CP of 5./NJG6, crashed at Dortmund. *Oberleutnant* Hans Steffen, pilot, *Unteroffizier* Josef Knon, *Unteroffizier* Helmut Uttler and *Unteroffizier* Friedrich Krebber, were all killed. Another top scoring team, Flight Lieutenant Ben Benson and Flight Lieutenant Brandy Brandon, notched their ninth combined victory on 5–6 January, shooting down He219A-0 190188 G9+CK of 2./NJG1. It crashed at five kilometres south of Wesendorf. *Oberfeldwebel* Josef Stroelein, pilot, was killed. *Unteroffizier* Kenne, radar operator, bailed out safely. Ju88 620513 R4+CD of III./NJG2 is possibly the aircraft shot down by Flight Lieutenant A. S. Briggs and Flying Officer Rothwell of 515 Squadron. It crashed at Jagel airfield. *Oberleutnant* Bruno Heilig, pilot, *Unteroffizier* Günther Kulas, radar operator, *Gefreiter* Johan Goliasch, flight engineer, and *Obergefreiter* Horst Jauernig, were all killed. This same night Captain Svein Heglund DFC of 85 Squadron went in search of his fifteenth victory of the war with Flying Officer Bob Symon as his navigator. They were airborne from Swannington at 19.55 hours for a High Level Support Patrol north of Osnabruck. Heglund reported:

After having patrolled beacon in Munster/Osnabruck area without any contact we set course for Hanover and arrived just as the target indicators were sent out. We got contact, which we chased in a westerly direction for 20 minutes with everything pushed forward. We just got a visual of exhaust flames which looked like a Mosquito and took it for one of the pathfinder force and turned back towards target.

At 2223 hrs. we got another head-on contact north of Osnabruck and turned in behind it. It was slightly above and we closed in to about 2,000 ft. when my operator lost contact owing to scanner trouble. We made one orbit and picked up contact again at 4 miles' range. We closed in again and got visual of Me.110 recognising square wings and twin fins and rudders. As we were slightly over-shooting I weaved underneath enemy aircraft keeping visual contact all the time. At 500 ft. range I pulled up behind it and gave it is a short burst, which caused an explosion in fuselage. Lots of smoke and debris was flying off and enemy aircraft continued flying straight and level. I rather think the crew was killed right away. I fired another burst which missed and noticed small explosions going on all the time. The third burst put enemy aircraft we'll on fire and it crashed on the ground with a large explosion at 2230 hrs. We got two more contacts afterwards, which turned out to be Mosquitoes and then set course for base.

It was Heglund's fifteenth and final victory of the war. He finished the war as the top scoring Norwegian pilot with fifteen and one third victories.

Flight Lieutenant K. D. Vaughan and Flight Lieutenant R. D. McKinnon of 85 Squadron shot down two enemy aircraft during January 1945, the first of these on the night of 14–15 January. Vaughan wrote:

Whilst on High level Patrol supporting attack on Merseburg at 2125 hrs on last leg of patrol navigator reported contact 4½ miles 11 o'clock port side crossing starboard to port, above. Our height 15,000-ft. Chased target flying straight in South westerly direction gradually losing height. Closed in on target to identify. At range of

136

100ft directly beneath, identified target as Ju 188 by pointed wings, underslung engines, no protruding leading edge between engines and fuselage and no exhausts. I increased range to 600ft and fired a 1-second burst dead astern, which produced a large explosion from starboard engine. I pulled away to starboard, but seeing no further results followed again on AI and closed in to 900ft firing a 2-second burst which produced no strikes. Closed in to 600 ft on target now rather rapidly losing height and decided to make certain this time. I fired a 1-second burst, range 500-ft, producing strikes and explosion again in starboard engine with pieces flying off past Mosquito. Target then disappeared straight down to explode on ground right beneath us at 2143 hrs lighting up countryside and cockpit of Mosquito with large orange glow. We orbitted fire on ground. I claim 1 Ju 188 destroyed. Mosquito landed base 2315 hrs.

Their victim was possibly Ju88G-1 710818 05+EP of *Stab/NJG3*, which crashed three kilometres south-east of Friedberg, north of Frankfurt. *Oberfeldwebel* Johann Eels, pilot, *Unteroffizier* Richard Zimmer, radar operator and *Gefreiter* Werner Hecht, *Bordschütze*, were killed.

Vaughan and McKinnon went looking for their next victim on the night of 16–17 January during a High Level Support patrol in the Frankfurt area. Vaughan reported:

We had completed uneventful patrol East of Frankfurt supporting raid on Zeitz and set course for base at 21.40 hrs. At 21.45 hrs, on vector 290° navigator reported contact 3½ miles range crossing starboard to port. We closed in on target, losing height to 10,000 ft. IAS. 260. At 4,000-ft range two pairs of brilliant white exhausts could be seen. We closed to 150 ft below and astern and identified target as He.219 by twin fins and rudders, narrow wings with marked tapor on trailing edge outboard of engines, long nose and those brilliant exhausts. Confirmation was obtained as to target's identity from my navigator using night glasses.

I dropped back to 600-ft range astern and fired a 2-second burst between the pairs of exhausts but no strikes were seen. Closed in to 400 ft. range and fired another 2-second burst and immediately a large explosion occurred in the port engine and we pulled up to starboard to avoid debris, which was coming back at us, and passed over enemy aircraft which went down to port with port engine on fire. We did a quick starboard orbit and saw burning fragments of aircraft falling and small fires starting on ground suggesting it had disintegrated in the air.

One of the new arrivals in 100 Group at about this time was John Beeching. He recalls:

I started out flying Beaufighter Mk.Is and 6s at No. 51 OTU at Cranfield, Bedfordshire and at a satellite field at Twinwoods Farm. Beaufighters were brutes of things; great big powerful monsters and very tricky to take-off and land, being very prone to swing either way. We had 32 accidents in a month during our operational training, many of them fatal. Most flying was done at night. We didn't need the Germans to scare us; we were mostly terrified of the equipment we had. However, I liked the old Beaus. Sitting up there in the nose, with a big Hercules engine purring away on either side gives a 21 year old an enormous sense of satisfaction and power. Hercules engines were sleeve-valved and very quiet. Then came the great day when I converted to Mosquitoes. They were so easy and nice to fly that I had only 30 minutes dual instruction on a Mk 3, the only dual instruction mark there was. I went on to fly Pathfinder Mosquitoes and altogether I flew over 50 different individual aircraft of different Mosquito marks and 25 different Beaufighters.

Fred Herbert my navigator and I flew our first operation as a night fighter patrol over the German night fighter bases at Egmond-Leeuwarden-Oldenburg. On this operation, we saw one of the early V2 (A5) rockets launched. We had no idea what it was and as it was launched from almost directly below us, we thought it was some diabolical invention designed to knock high flying (25,000') Mosquitoes out of the sky. This great bright light got closer and closer (there seemed little point in turning one way or the other, because of relative distances) so we were greatly relieved to see this oversized shell go hurtling past us quite a distance away leaving a very disturbed vapour trail. It was soon out of sight. At this particular time the Ijsselmeer had been deliberately flooded and the whole area was a great sheet of ice. This operation was flown in a Mark VI equipped with Mk.IV radar, which was pretty good but relied on altitude for its range. These Mk VIs were pretty heavily overloaded. We carried 716 gallons of fuel (we had 100 gallon drop tanks on each wing), a ton of radar and about 800 rounds of 20 mm cannon ammunition. The second speed of the Merlins' superchargers were controlled by an automatic barometric switch and would not kick in until about 13,000 ft had been reached. By 12,000 ft our rate of climb had fallen off to about 50 ft per minute. The rate-of-climb indicator needle was about a line thickness above 'straight and level' by this time and it was just a matter of wallowing slowly upward until the second speed of the superchargers came in with a great surge of power and away we soared up to our operational height. The Mosquito was not quite the most superior fighter at any height. Fortunately we never had any occasion to worry as nothing ever seemed to happen around that altitude. We normally liked to fly a few thousand feet higher than the main bomber stream. That way, we could see the main stream on our radar screen and any interloper could be more easily picked out. More often than not, any odd signals were usually one of our own people and identification could be a real problem. Anything that was as fast as us would normally be another Mosquito.

We did quite a few operations in Mk.VIs and on 14 January 1945 Fred and I flew over to Swannington, in Norfolk and collected MM46, the first of the Mark 19's. The Mk.19 was fitted with Mk.10 American built (but British developed) radar which was infinitely superior to the old Mk.IV. I was initially somewhat nonplussed by this great long nose sticking out the front which housed the radar scanner and made landing and taxying, until one got used to it, rather difficult. Our radar sets carried the original cavity magnetrons, virtually identical with the present day microwave units, located in front of our knees and blasted away with no ill effect for hours on end. It was referred to then as the High Frequency Unit, and as far as I know carried no protective screening. The original cavity magnetron body, which was made of copper, resembled a revolver magazine because a revolver chamber-drilling jig was used to make them. It just happened to be available and was of the right configuration.

I was never involved with Serrate, although most of the Mk.VIs on 169 Squadron were equipped with the gear. No Mk.19's were fitted. Some of our 19's were fitted with Monica tail warning radar, which was of mixed value, as the Germans could home on to it –

a sort of Serrate in reverse. We carried all kinds of peculiar gear towards the end of the war – like infrared telescopes, which could pick up engine exhausts and the like. 169 also carried out some low-level Ranger operations. In the early part of 1945 we tried to creep up on one or two German training airfields. They could be seen from afar at night because of that long, single string of lights with crossbars they used to illuminate their final approaches, but somehow they always heard us coming as the lights went out long before we ever got near them. Actually, Fred and I were never very involved with enemy aircraft in the air and I like to think that we were instrumental in keeping them on the ground. We did one or two 'Spoof' bombing raids, marking decoy targets to confound the German ARP defences.

On the night of 28–29 January 1945 Paul Mellows and Dickie Drew tried to score another victory using Mk X AI while on their sojourn at Swannington. At 20.50 hours they took off for a high-level support patrol to Stüttgart for some 'beacon bashing'. Mellows reported:

> Shortly after completing patrol on Beacon Fritz a single white flare was observed to the North West, presumably over Darmstadt. We proceeded in that direction and Biblis airfield was seen to be lit and had a canopy of four searchlights 2 miles to the West. From 6,000 ft three single-engined aircraft on the airfield were soon outlined against the snow. As there were no signs of airborne activity and time was short it was decided to make an attack. The airfield was approached from the South-West and one single-engined aircraft, believed to be Fw190, was attacked with two 3-second bursts from height of 1,500 ft. to 1,000 ft. No results were observed, from first burst, but strikes were seen on and around fuselage from second burst. Defences opened up when we were over the centre of the airfield, but without results.

In February ten German aircraft were destroyed by Mosquitoes of 100 Group, plus a probable on 1–2 February. This night *Oberleutnant* Gottfried Hanneck of *5./NJG1*, who had been shot down by House and McKinnon on 13–14 September 1944, returned to Bf110 operations, with a new crew of *Feldwebel* Pean, radio/radar operator, and *Unteroffizier* Gloeckner, air gunner:

After seven practice flights in January we arrived at Düsseldorf airfield on 1 February to fly on operations again. By this time, the night fighter control organization was experiencing severe problems when trying to assess the plans of the enemy, as we had lost the complete advanced defence line (Holland, Belgium and France were already occupied by the enemy). Therefore, on this day a number of crews were ordered to fly to several night fighter beacons, and wait there at the height at which the bombers were expected to fly in. I received orders to take-off [in Bf110G-4 730262 G9+CN] at 1945 hours, proceed to a beacon in the Frankfurt area and wait for any reports of enemy aircraft movements. Thus, we were flying around in wide circles and figures of eight in the prescribed area and waited for the enemy reports. These however, did not reach us, but something else did – the enemy in the shape of a Mosquito (which we were expecting because who else would have come?), which completely by surprise gave us a short burst of fire. We were hit. The intercom was put out of action, and the landing light in the wing came on. I stood the aircraft on its nose to avoid a second attack and to find shelter in a layer of clouds beneath us. My crew, who couldn't contact me any more, must have assumed I was hit as I was slumped over the control column. They baled out – and landed safely.

I was now alone in the machine. I safely reached the layer of clouds and was now confronted with the question: should I bail out or attempt a crash-landing? There was no question that I should continue with my flight without any radio contact and with the light on. I decided to crash-land. I could only switch off the light by stopping both engines and glide towards the ground in an aircraft which weighed several tons. But where should I land? Fortunately, I could distinguish between the dark forest and the snow-white fields and I steered towards such a field where I let the tail unit touch the ground first (to avoid nosing over) and then with retracted undercarriage, slid over the ground on the motor gondolas. I had come down 2 kms west of Kettershausen in the Westerwald. The time was 2110 hours. My face slightly hit the gun sights but I was able to scramble out of my seat and withdraw from the machine through the snow and shouted for help. A farmer 'collected' me on his horse-drawn sleigh and took me to the nearest Army post. There I received first-aid, and large quantities of Cognac as a remedy for the shock and pain. Then I was transported

141

to the nearest hospital which was at Wissen on the Sieg. (It is believed that Hanneck's adversary was either a 157 or 239 Squadron Mosquito. Squadron Leader Ryall and Pilot Officer Mulroy of 157 Squadron claimed a Bf110 'probable' at Oberolm, while Wing Commander Walter Gibb DSO DFC and Flying Officer R. C. Kendall DFC of 239 Squadron destroyed a Bf110 at Mannheim.)

Also on 1–2 February meanwhile, Flight Lieutenant Paul Mellows and Flight Lieutenant Dickie Drew of 169 Squadron, who were still operating with 85 Squadron at Swannington, had taken off at 17.00 hours for a High Level Support Patrol at Stüttgart, scene of their eventful night intruder operation a month earlier. Mellows reported:

> We arrived at our patrol point at 1845 hrs, and after 10 minutes proceeded in a north-westerly direction. A Red star cartridge was soon to be fired some way off to the north so we proceeded to investigate, losing height to 10,000 ft. A head-on contact was obtained and after being once lost was converted to an intermittent visual on a blue light at 2,000 ft range, height then being 11,000 ft. We closed on AI to 1,000 ft where navigator identified it as a Me.110 with the aid of night glasses. Target was climbing and weaving 30° each side of course. We closed to 200 ft to confirm and opened fire at 300 ft. from slightly below with a 2-second burst from which a small explosion sent debris flying back. A second burst resulted in a very large explosion and for a few moments the Mosquito was enveloped in flame, the heat of which was felt in the cockpit. We broke to starboard and watched enemy aircraft flying straight but losing height with starboard engine well on fire, in the light of which a black cross and all details of the aircraft were plainly visible. A further explosion occurred whilst it was going down, and enemy aircraft eventually exploded on the ground at 1910 hours. As combat had affected rudder control, the patrol was terminated.

Mellows fired seventy-two rounds of SAPI and sixty-eight rounds of HEI to down the Bf110, probably Bf110 730370 2Z+EL of 3./NJG6, which crashed twenty-five kilometres south of Stuttgart. *Oberleutnant* Willy Rathmann, pilot, *Feldwebel* Erich Berndt, radar operator and *Obergefreiter* Alfred Obry, air gunner were killed.

Warrant Officer Les Turner who, it will be remembered, had finished his tour just before Christmas and had transferred to BSDU at Great Massingham, had become fed up 'flying Ansons loaded with pupil navigators learning ASH radar'. He had teamed up with his original navigator, now Flight Lieutenant Jimmy Wheldon, who was there as an instructor also, and they had agreed to rejoin 169 Squadron, then equipped with NFXIXs with Mk.X radar, for a second tour. Turner recalls:

Jimmy had served in another 100 Group squadron as the Wing Commander's navigator and I was quite flattered that he wished to fly with me again! Needless to say, he was an excellent radar operator and I always felt safe in his hands. We trained throughout the second half of January 1945 and did our first op on 2 February. This was to the Ruhr and the logbook records one chase without results. Trip No.2 was another 'Beacon' patrol, where German night fighters were supposed to assemble, but we had no contacts. Jimmy then took some leave to complete his studies for and sit his LLB Finals. He was an intellectual throughout and after the war attained a high position in the Civil Service. To keep me occupied I was attached to Massingham's Gunnery Flight and it was there that I experienced my second incident of engine failure, only this time, rather unnervingly, as passenger. I must confess that I had less than 100% faith in the pilot's ability but, by leaving him to control the flying and with me dealing with undercarriage and flaps and keeping up a running commentary on our approach speed, we landed without incident. Jimmy and I 'squeezed in' trip No.3 to Mannheim on 13 February and then it was back to the Gunnery Flight. I didn't distinguish myself particularly at practice air-to-air firing, although I once shot the drogue off, having 'led' too much with the sight!

Trip No.4 on 8 March was to Kassel and here a radar contact led us to a visual on one of 100 Group's radio-RCM Fortresses. We were most surprised! Trip No.5 was a Ranger patrol between Hanover and Berlin. We had some more success than on earlier occasion and attacked two trains. On one of these we must have clipped the top of a tree because they found twigs etc in the radiator intakes. We didn't notice this at the time but I have a vivid memory of flying down the railway line on ahead-on attack on the train and seeing a signal gantry almost level with our starboard wing tip. The rate at which I hastily pulled G must have given a high G-loading to the aircraft!

239 Squadron crews were prominent on the night of 7–8 February when the main force targets was Cleve and Hussum. Flight Lieutenant O. A. O. Cather DFM and Flight Sergeant L. J. S. Spicer BEM shot down Bf110G-4 730322 G9+HR of 7./*NJG1*, which crashed west of Soest in the Ruhr. *Feldwebel* Heinz Amsberg, pilot, and *Unteroffizier* Matthias Oengs, radar operator, were killed, while *Gefreiter* Karl Kopperberg, air gunner, who was WIA, baled out. Flight Lieutenant A. J. Holderness and Flight Lieutenant Walter Rowley DFC meanwhile, had taken off from West Raynham at 20.25 hours for a patrol in the Dressel area. Holderness reported:

We carried out the first part of our patrol quite uneventfully, before and while Cleve and Hussum were being bombed. Towards the end of the bombing we moved closer in to the targets and were doing a short 'square search' patrol when, at 13,000 ft we got a contact at 2240 hrs at about 6 miles range. It was only slightly above but difficult to close, as it was taking what appeared to be precautionary evasive action, diving and climbing through a series of steep turns. Throughout this part of the chase our altimeter was reading anything from 11,000 to 15,000 ft. Several times I caught sight of the exhausts glow, but was unable against the starlit sky to hold them for more than a few seconds at a time. After about ten minutes of this, when we had closed to 1,000 ft we suddenly found ourselves overshooting very fast and some way above, and had to turn 60° to port, then back onto our original course to recover the blip. This time the contact was headed away from the target, flying on an easterly course and at a height of about 12,000 ft. The pilot must have thought either that there was no longer any need to evade, or that he had shaken us off because he was flying straight and level. We closed in fairly fast and from only about 200 ft below and behind identified as Me 110. I dropped back to about 250 yards and opened fire. Quite a lot of debris flew back past us and the port engine immediately caught fire. Then the nose came up and he went into steep climb, which I tried to follow, still firing. Although I throttled right back we were rapidly overtaking him and had to pull away quickly to starboard. Just then he seemed to stall and flick over to port. I turned as slightly as our low airspeed

144

would allow and saw him diving very steeply with the port engine now a mass of flame. My navigator could still see burning pieces coming off when he went into the cloud. Almost simultaneously there was a terrific white flash which lit up the clouds. We followed through about 3,000 ft of cloud to come out at 4,000 ft on the altimeter, and there it was, burning immediately beneath us.

While serving in 239 Squadron at West Raynham Flight Lieutenant Donald R. 'Podge' Howard DFC had destroyed three aircraft, June–October 1944. Howard joined 239 Squadron on 2 May 1944 and completed thirty-two operational sorties by 9 November. On 27 June 1944 he and Flying Officer 'Sticky' Clay DFC had destroyed a Ju88 over Belgium. His own aircraft being damaged by flying debris from the Ju88, Howard flew back to RAF Manston on one engine where he landed without causing further damage to the aircraft. On 14 October 1944 Howard shot down a Fw190 over Holland after a considerable dog fight and, on 29 October 1944, he destroyed a He111 which was flying very low and very slowly over north-west Germany. During four other sorties he damaged eight trains in Holland and Germany. He was awarded the DFC on 9 November 1944. Now, in February 1945 attached to the BSDU at Swanton Morley, Howard and Clay were evaluating AI Mk X and Serrate IV with a lowered frequency band of 80 m/cs. On 13–14 February when the bombers' targets were Dresden and Leipzig, Howard and Clay had a very eventful night patroling beacons *Kolibri, Ida, Elster, Nachtigall* and *Otto*. Howard reported:

Beacon Kolibri was reached at 2011 hours (6 minutes after start of Mandrel Screen) and proceeded to Ida where at 2015 signals were ahead of Serrate IV (77.5 m/cs). The D/F on this low frequency was very suspect and we were not surprised when we found we could not D/F these signals. It was however an indication that Huns were around. We then set course in an easterly direction and the signals strength increased. We obtained a Mark X contact about 5 miles 30 degrees to port and down. We turned after it and lost height and eventually discovered it was in a climbing port orbit and the range closed fast. The A/C did not show Type F and by now the George box [George Baillie] was trilling furiously (still in dashes) and A/C apparently levelled out. A visual was obtained on an A/C at 1,000 ft and at 600 ft in a rate 1–1½ turn to port the A/C was recognised as a Me 110. At a range of about 600 ft with a ¼ ring deflection a short burst was fired but no strikes seen. Increased deflection and fired another burst which caused strikes all over starboard engine, wing root and starboard side of cockpit. A fire started in starboard wing root and the Me 110 turned over to port burning well and dived straight down and entered cloud; shortly after there was a vivid white explosion on the ground at 2033 hours, our height being 12,000 ft. Claim – 1 Me 110 destroyed.

Two minutes after this type had bought it, another Mark X contact appeared crossing starboard to port and above range 12,000. Turned after it and range closed fast and after turning about rate 1 for about two complete circles and got visual on an A/C at 1,000 ft with George box still pushing out its very loud Hun note. At 600 ft this A/C was identified as another Me 110 in a port turn. Opened fire at 600 ft and missed and the Hun promptly rolled into a starboard bank during which he presented no deflection and he received a 1 second burst which caused strikes on the cockpit fuselage and port wing root. The type then dived away to starboard and we gave him another burst, which set his port engine on fire and caused bits to fly off. He then dived vertically into cloud, burning very well. We had to pull up and out of our dive and we didn't see it hit the deck but as the cloud was only about 5,000 ft and he was well on fire this is claimed as a Me 110 destroyed. At 2040 hours, 5,000 ft we obtained yet another Mark X contact almost at once but although we chased him in an easterly direction for about 20 minutes at full bore we could not overtake him so we decided he was very fortunate and returned to our patrol area and came back to base via Kolibri and West Kappelle.

Howard had fired eighty rounds of HEI and eighty rounds of SAPI on the sortie. One of the downed aircraft, Bf110 480164 C9+ of *5./NJG5*, crashed near Bodenbach in the Frankfurt area. *Feldwebel* Heinrich Schmidt, pilot, *Unteroffizier* Erich Wohlan, radar operator, and *Unteroffizier* Adam Zunker, air gunner, were killed.

Chapter Seven

Carthage

Throughout January-March 1945 138 and 140 Wings along with all the other Allied tactical squadrons, continued the offensive on most nights with attacks on German road and rail transport when possible, and bombing rail junctions on Gee when bad weather prevented visual sightings. On 29 January 1945 21 Squadron had flown from Thorney Island to Fersfield Suffolk for a secret briefing on an attack on the *Gestapo* HQ in Copenhagen but the weather deteriorated and was unsuitable for low flying over the sea, so the operation was postponed for twenty-four hours. On 31 January the raid was again postponed for a further twenty-four hours, and next morning, 1 February, AVM Embry announced that he could not afford to have his aircraft hanging around doing nothing for any longer. The operation would have to take place at a later date.

In 1934 Ove Kampmann, a young Danish engineer, had worked on the construction of one of Copenhagen's largest new office buildings. Each floor was made of steel-framed reinforced concrete. To Kampmann, looking at the finished building, it was no more than *Shellhaus*, the new headquarters of the famous international oil company (A/S Dansk Shell). He would have been incredulous had he been told that ten years later he would occupy a tiny cell in the attic, which he would share with a Danish Nazi informer. Kampmann's crime was hiding refugees and passing them through the escape routes to freedom in Sweden. Later he began to act as a liaison contact between the Copenhagen military groups and the communications systems. The SD (*Gestapo*) came for him early in the morning of 24 February 1945. He was dragged from bed and taken to *Shellhaus*. For forty-eight hours, almost without a break, he was whipped and beaten. The SD knew that he was due to attend an important meeting at 09.00 on the following Monday morning to exchange information with a number of resistance leaders. Again and again the same question was repeated: 'Where is the meeting to be held?' He had never considered himself a brave man but if he could hold out until after 09.00 he could then tell them what they wanted to know. If he did not arrive within five minutes of the appointed time, the other resistance members would realize that something was wrong and they would not wait. By 09.15 they would have scattered and the meeting place would not be used again. Kampmann's iron will conquered. He painfully watched as the hands of the clock moved passed the time of the meeting. At last with triumphant relief he told them what they wanted. The beating stopped, he was untied and dragged to his cell. His interrogators had done a better job than he knew. During the night, while he was unconscious, they had altered the clock. Unwittingly he had given the *Gestapo* the location of the meeting with time enough for them to arrange an ambush. More arrests were made.

Ove Kampmann was put into cell 13, which he shared with an informer. He tried to warn his two comrades in the next cell by pushing a note through a crack in the partition. However, they had already guessed the worst and immediately pushed the message back to him. Kampmann was one of twenty-six Danish prisoners imprisoned on the sixth floor of the *Shellhaus*. The *Gestapo* had managed to capture several members of the Freedom Council – the underground movement. Not only was this a blow to the efficiency of this organization, it was also a great threat to Danish resistance and the SOE organization in Denmark. At the same time the *Gestapo* records within *Shellhaus* had become the key to wholesale discrimination of the resistance movement. Ove Gessø Pedersen was arrested by the *Gestapo* in February 1945 as a suspected member of the resistance group *'Frit Danmark'* (Free Denmark). He was immediately imprisoned on the sixth floor of *Shellhaus* along with twenty-three other prominent members of the underground. At first he shared cell 14 with Professor Brandt Rehberg. He was later moved into No. 9, one of the so-called 'arrest' cells, together with Lars Hansen Christiansen, who was arrested early in February 1945 for his part in a sabotage group.

Not only was the capture of several key members of the Freedom Council a blow to the efficiency of this organization, it was also a serious threat to Danish Resistance and the SOE organization in

Denmark. Telephone taps on the lines between German High Command in Copenhagen and Berlin, had revealed plans to wind up the resistance movement in Copenhagen conclusively – the consequences of which would have allowed the release of 100,000 German troops to bolster the Battle of the Rhine. Such an event could have caused a major Allied defeat.

Signals to England requesting the bombing of *Gestapo* HQ were being received on an almost daily basis by the middle of January 1945. Normal procedure required that a special attack of this kind, which was to take place in friendly occupied territory, had to be sanctioned by the Air Board. Studies revealed the great risks involved in hitting a single target in a city centre. Civilian casualties were estimated at 300 and the percentage of aircraft losses could be considerably high. The Air Board passed responsibility for the final decision to AVM Basil Embry DSO** DFC* AFC, CIC 2 Group, whose 140 Wing 2nd Tactical Air Force, sometimes known as the 'Gestapo Hunters' would be the ones to carry out such a daring pin-point raid. Embry in turn insisted that the final decision should come from someone on the spot. This person would have full possession of the facts from both sides and up-to-date knowledge on the requirements of the Resistance. Furthermore, realistic estimates of casualties and possible damage had to be determined. The modern reinforced concrete building had been turned into a veritable fortress. As a deterrent against air attack, the building had been camouflaged with green and brown stripes. In fact, as it turned out, the stripes proved to be an added recognition aid as the building was the only one the city to be camouflaged! As a further 'defence' the *Gestapo* had converted the top storey into a twenty-two-cell prison where the prominent Danish prisoners were placed. It was thought that with this human shield, the *Gestapo* would be immune to air attack.

Ole Lippmann, Chief of Operations in the field and Allied representative of the Freedom Council (Danish Resistance) was the only man qualified to assess the risks and in February 1945 he was sent back to Denmark to make an appraisal and, consequently, the final decision for the attack on *Shellhaus*. Lippmann discovered that the situation was so critical that he urgently requested that 'Carthage be destroyed'. Carthage was the code he was briefed to use. On 15 March 1945 he repeated the request and the following message was received: 'Military leaders arrested and plans in German hands. Situation never before so desperate. Remaining leaders known by Hun. We are re-grouping but need help. Bombing of SD Copenhagen will give us breathing space. If any importance at all to Danish resistance you must help us irrespective cost. We will never forget RAF and you if you come.' Despite the risk of civilian casualties and heavy defences, the raid was finally sanctioned, although Embry admitted that he was horrified by the thought. Nevertheless, as the request had come from 'The Field', the raid would take place, the actual date and time were closely guarded secrets.

In the months leading up to the raid, Special Operations Executive (SOE) worked closely with the Danish Resistance and British Intelligence to gather an enormous amount of material. Most of this came from the staff under the command of Major Sven Truelsen Chief of Danish Military Intelligence. From this they were able to construct a highly detailed relief scale model, depicting a square mile of Copenhagen city centre. Meanwhile, time was fast running out for the Danes imprisoned in *Shellhaus*.

Ebbe Wolfhagen, a Commander in the Royal Danish Navy, had scuttled his ship in Copenhagen harbour, and he had joined the resistance organization, *Holger Dansker,* a sabotage group. On the afternoon of 21 February 1945 Wolfhagen and another resistance member were apprehended walking down a street in Copenhagen. Imprisoned in *Shellhaus* Wolfhagen's interrogations started with a broken nose and a black eye, then a beating and questioning for sixteen hours without a break. He had a feeling that the situation was not very favourable and he waited each day in his cell to be told of the hour of his execution. On 19 March 1945 he had been taken down to the interrogation rooms again. The *Gestapo* placed some papers in front of him, covered except for one small space at the foot of the final page. They ordered him to sign. He refused, saying that he could not put his signature to any document that he had not read. After some argument he was allowed to read his 'confession'. Throughout his interrogations he had refused an interpreter and had answered all questions himself in German. He had decided upon this as a precaution against being forced or tricked into revealing secret information, as he could always plead that he had not understood the question and had therefore answered it incorrectly or untruthfully. With this as his excuse, he insisted upon the deletion of all the most incriminating evidence. He was then sent back to his cell and on the following day a new typescript was presented for him to sign. Although not all of the incriminating material had been removed, he signed. The *Gestapo* officers were friendly and congratulated him on his good sense. His interrogator then asked him one final question:

'How many murders have you committed?'

Wolfhagen truthfully answered, 'None'.

'Not even one little one just before you were arrested?'

His reply firmly and in all honesty was, 'I am unable to distinguish between little murders and big murders. I have not committed murder of any kind.'

At 03.00 in the morning of 21 March Ebbe Wolfhagen was moved from *Shellhaus* to Vestre Prison, a move that may have saved his life.

A day earlier eighteen FBVIs from 140 Wing (21 RAF, 464 RAAF and 487 RNZAF Squadrons), plus two FPU (Film Production Unit) specially modified Mosquito BIVs were detached from their base at Rosières-en-Senterre in France to RAF Fersfield in Norfolk. The move was made so that the route over the North Sea to Denmark would avoid flying over enemy-held territory with all the attendant risk of flak and radar detection. However, this stretched the Mosquitoes' range to the limit of endurance, a total flight time of over five hours. Group Captain R. N. 'Bob' Bateson DSO DFC AFC and Squadron Leader Ted Sismore DSO DFC, the leading tactical navigator in R5570, would lead the operation. AVM Embry alias 'Wing Commander Smith', would fly in PZ222, a Mosquito loaned by 107 Squadron, in the first wave, with Squadron Leader Peter Clapham as his navigator. The crews were briefed intensely on 20 March and before take-off the next day, and kept in a confined and closely guarded area away from the other personnel on the base.

Nineteen Mosquitoes would attack at minimum altitude, in three waves of seven, six and six aircraft respectively. Included in this total was one FPU Mosquito IV (DZ414/O) flown by Flight Lieutenant Ken Greenwood and Flying Officer E. Moore of 487 Squadron, which carried two 500lb HE and two 500 lb M.76 incendiaries, and was to fly with and bomb with the first wave. The second FPU Mosquito IV (DZ383/Q-*Query*) was flown by Flying Officer R. E. Bob Kirkpatrick of 21 Squadron and Sergeant R. Hearne of 4 FPU. Kirkpatrick, an American from Cleveland, Ohio, had joined 21 Squadron in August 1944 after completing training in Canada and flying Beaufighters in a Coastal Command OTU. His first attempt to start his military career on 8 December 1941 had been rebuffed at the US Marines recruiting office when he was told that he had a heart murmur. Bob crossed the border to Windsor, Ontario and upon questioning his physical condition, he was told, 'If you can see lightning and hear thunder you can be a pilot!' He would probably see more than his share of both on Carthage because he and Hearne had the unenviable task of flying behind the third and last wave to film the results. In total the nineteen Mosquitoes carried a lethal load of forty-four 500lb bombs. Because of the very low levels flown, to prevent damage to aircraft following, the leading aircraft of each wave had thirty-second delayed action bombs and the remainder, eleven-second delayed action bombs. A proportion of the first and third waves carried M76 incendiaries.

At Fersfield the Mosquito crews were joined by thirty-one Mustang pilots from 64, 126 and 234 Squadrons (11 Group Fighter Command) which flew in from RAF Bentwaters. The fighters, who were to escort the Mosquitoes and eliminate flak positions in the target area, were led by their Belgian Wing Commander (later Lieutenant General) Avier Mike Donnet CVO DFC CG. Born of Belgian parents in Richmond, England in 1917, Donnet had escaped to England on 5 August 1941 after Belgium had capitulated, in a two-seater Stampe biplane with a fellow officer.

Twelve Mustangs of 126 Squadron would escort the first wave; six from 64 Squadron and two from 126 Squadron would escort the second wave and eight Mustangs of 64 Squadron, the third wave. Three Mustangs from 234 Squadron would sweep from ten miles north (Værløse air base) towards Copenhagen.

At 08.55 hours on 12 March the formation was airborne, forming up over Fersfield. Five minutes later it crossed the English coastline north-east of Norwich, with a direct course for the first checkpoint some 375 miles away at Hvide Sand in Denmark. The weather was stormy, with surface winds gusting at fifty knots, making it difficult to control the aircraft. After crossing the North Sea at fifty feet to avoid radar detection, the windshields had become coated with salt spray which reduced visibility – some pilots tried slowing down so that they could clear patches of their screens with gloves or cloths.

The checkpoint was dead-on with the force making landfall at Hvide Sand at 10.20 hours. Three Mustangs were forced to turn back due to bird-strike damage. Over Jutland, the aircraft, still flying at minimum height, began to attract the attention of Danes and Germans alike. The *Jagdfliegerfuhrer* (German Fighter Control) received continuous reports as they flew across Denmark. The formation flew on by way of Give and along the northern side of Vejle Fjord to Juelsminde and then across the Great Belt. On the island of

152

Zealand the checkpoint was Tissø, an almost circular lake chosen as an easy landmark. Here the formation split into the three wave formations ready to be escorted by the Mustangs. The first wave, lead by Group Captain Bateson, set course for Copenhagen at minimum altitude with an escort of eleven Mustangs, one having been forced to return due to bird strike damage. Flying on Bateson's port side was AVM Embry and Peter Clapham in PZ222/H. The remaining aircraft carried out 'rate-one turns' (orbits) of the lake, once for the second wave, twice for third and three times for the remaining FPU Mossie. This gave a distance of approximately nine miles between each wave, an interval of approximately two minutes flying time.

On the outskirts of Copenhagen the first wave began to pick out the details of the target area. Despite the bumpy conditions Ted Sismore identified the target by the green and brown stripes and Bateson led his force over the rooftops. The aircraft began to move into attack formation, bomb doors were opened, bombs fused and speed was increased to 300 mph. The escorting Mustangs increased speed and began to seek out their targets – the flak positions – most being unmanned at the time. The first wave continued their run-in towards the final checkpoint when 800 yards from the target tragedy struck. The leading aircraft of the second flight (SZ977, the fourth Mosquito in the first wave, behind Bateson/Sismore, Carlisle/Ingram (PZ306) and Embry/Clapham (PZ222), collided with a 130 feet high floodlight pylon in the marshalling yards and went into a vertical dive. The pilot, Wing Commander Peter Kleboe DSO DFC AFC, aged twenty-eight, was the newly appointed CO of 21 Squadron. (On 2 February 'Daddy' Dale and Hackett, his navigator, went missing on a night patrol. On 6 February the squadron transferred to Rosières-en-Santerre and shortly afterwards Wing Commander V. R. Oates took over command. He failed to return from a sortie on 12 March and Peter Kleboe arrived to take over the squadron). His navigator was Canadian Flying Officer Reg Hall aged thirty. Flight Lieutenant T. M. 'Mac' Hetherington RCAF and Flight Lieutenant J. K. Bell, in HR162, were flying No.6 on the starboard side of, and slightly behind, Kleboe's aircraft. Hetherington observed:

We watched each other and attempted to follow the leader by 'biting hard into his tail' and at the same time, staying clear of his slipstream. We followed each other like shadows. We were altogether; some twelve feet lower than the first three aircraft. We knew that we had to turn, but apparently Wing Commander Kleboe had not seen the pylon or had reacted too slowly. Suddenly, through the side window I observed Kleboe's aircraft climb at a very steep angle and fall off to port. Squadron Leader A. C. Henderson [in LR388, the 5th Mosquito] and I instinctively threw our aircraft to starboard and continued on towards the target.

Flight Lieutenant Ken Greenwood, in DZ414/O, flying on the port side of Kleboe's aircraft, was just twenty-five feet away on Kleboe's port side. He adds:

Some 10–15 seconds before the accident, bomb doors had been opened, copying the leader. Kleboe's aircraft lost height, some 15 ft, and I suppose by peripheral vision I saw the pylon and realised that he was going to fly into it. As the aircraft struck the pylon, part of the port engine was damaged. The Mosquito rose almost vertically and then rapidly to port. I had to take violent evasive action to prevent a mid-air collision and swung too hard to port.

Kleboe's two bombs struck a building in Sdr Boulevard (one, a dud, failed to explode) and eight civilians were killed. The Mosquito was observed waggling its wings and trailing smoke before it crashed into a garage on *Frederiksberg Allé* adjacent to the Jeanne d'Arc School. The force of the explosion from the fuel created a huge pall of black smoke. Kleboe and Reg Hall were both killed. They were later buried in Bispebjerg Churchyard. The remaining aircraft of the first wave continued over the target area. Group Captain Bateson was the first to attack with his bombs going in between the second and third floors of the west wing at 11.15 – right on schedule.

AVM Embry and Squadron Leader Peter Clapham, and Squadron Leader Tony Carlisle and Flight Lieutenant N. J. 'Rex' Ingram got their bombs away. Carlisle followed with Embry directly behind and observed the AVM's bombs strike the building at street level. Henderson, and 'Mac' Hetherington, each put their two bombs through the roof of the *Shellhaus*. Embry moved into Henderson's flight path, which forced him to go over Embry. Henderson's navigator, Bill Moore, said, 'Look, the old man's going sightseeing!' After getting their bombs away, the first wave scattered and exited Copenhagen at roof top height in a north-westerly direction over the city and made for home. Until now, the Germans had not sounded the air-raid warning. The Danish Civil Air Defence had also followed the path of the aircraft. Realizing the danger to the city it tried to persuade the Germans to sound the alarm. By the time the Germans took action, bombs were already smashing into the *Shellhaus*. Official records have revealed that the German officers responsible for this negligence were court-martialled.

As the Mustangs crossed the target area, the second loss of the day occurred. Flak tracer shells bracketed Flight Lieutenant David Drew DFC's Mustang, the aircraft had sustained a hit – evident by a thin black line of smoke appearing from the underside of the aircraft. Drew banked his Mustang and turned north. It disappeared over the rooftops and crashed in Fælled Park. Drew was killed, he was later buried at Bispebjerg Churchyard together with Kleboe and Hall.

As the attack started and the first bombs exploded, tiles began to fall down leaving a hole in the roof of the *Shellhaus*. In a panic reaction, Ove Kampmann, one of the twenty-six Danish prisoners imprisoned on the sixth floor, laid himself down on the bed with a blanket over his head. The sound of banging on doors was heard. Shortly after, Christian Lyst Hansen (cell 6) opened the door with the keys he had wrestled from a panic-stricken SS guard. Together with the other surviving prisoners, Kampmann made his way across the empty attic area on the east side of the building. The stairs were slippery with blood from the dead and dying and it was almost impossible for the prisoners to find space for their feet. When they reached the first floor level they saw that the carnage was even more appalling; every stair was piled high with bodies. Stumbling and slipping over the dead Germans, they made their way to the ground floor and the main entrance. There was not a guard in sight. The men split into pairs or went off alone. Together with Poul Brandt Rehberg, Kampmann made his way to a safe house before escaping to Sweden.

Ove Gessø Pedersen in No.9, one of the so-called 'arrest' cells, with Lars Hansen Christiansen, recalls: 'After the first bombs had struck the building I was possessed with only one thought, to get out.' Upon hearing the sound of aircraft engines, Christiansen's first thought was that they were German, 'then we (Gessø Pedersen) heard the first bombs exploded and the building seemed to lift itself up. Dust and debris fell from the ceiling covering us from head to toe. After discovering that three rather weak hinges supported the numerous locks the *Gestapo* had put in the door, we tried to break the door down.'

Pedersen continues: 'First I tried to smash the door with a folding chair but this fell to pieces. Then I tried with a stool, which proved to be stronger, with this, I was successful in smashing the door.'

Christiansen got out onto the corridor and turned right towards the empty attic area.

> I ran across to the east stairway where I had to climb over the dead and wounded lying on the stairs. Nobody tried to stop me. I ran out onto the street still covered in white dust, and over to Vestersøhus (an apartment building next to *Shellhaus*). I rang a number of door bells, the people opened up their doors and asked where I came from. When I replied from *Shellhaus*, nobody would take the chance of hiding a fugitive from the Gestapo, so the doors shut in my face. Eventually I got into an apartment at number 42 where, over a glass of brandy, I sat back and watched *Shellhaus* burn.

Meanwhile, in the corridor outside cell No.9 Pedersen noticed a single SS guard, rooted to the spot, covered in dust and shaking with fear:

> Close by was huge gaping hole cut by the first bombs and a marvellous view over the rooftops of Copenhagen. As I stood outside the cell, I realised that I had forgotten a coat that my brother had lent to me. Feeling rather embarrassed, I ran back to collect the coat. I returned to the corridor and swung myself down through the hole by means of a thick length of insulated electrical wiring. I then made my way to the second floor. I had to push my way through a crowd of panic-struck people on the stairs and came out into the street where I jumped over the barbed wire. I made my way towards Svineryggen (Street) by the lakes. From this point I managed to see the aircraft from the second wave of Mosquitoes attack the *Shellhaus*, I then ran off down the street.

The second wave of six Mosquitoes of 464 Squadron RAAF led by Wing Commander Bob Iredale DSC DFC RAAF and Flying Officer B. J. Standish in SZ968 arrived over Copenhagen some two minutes behind the first. By this time the sky over Copenhagen was being crisscrossed by flak. The leading three crews were distracted by the smoke coming from Kleboe's wrecked aircraft as this was greater than that coming from the *Shellhaus*. Confusion reigned and the force was split into two. A split-second decision had to be made. Iredale broke off his attack and circled to come in again. At the same time the three remaining Mosquitoes of 'Blue Section' led by Flight Lieutenant Archie Smith DFC and Flight Sergeant E. L. Green in PZ309, had realized the mistake and located the target slightly to the right of their track. Smith made two orbits of the target area before bombing. His bombs struck the outside of the east wing, destroying a pillbox situated on the corner. In the confusion it appears that one aircraft bombed the school by mistake, the remainder (together with the Mustang escort) began to circle the area to clarify their position. In the first manoeuvre some Mosquitoes were too far left of the target and only those aircraft closest to *Shellhaus* were able to bomb. Both Iredale, who got his bombs away on the east end of the *Shellhaus*, and Smith, who also attacked a flak position at Hundested, managed to bomb *Shellhaus*.

During his orbit, Flight Lieutenant W. Knowle Shrimpton DFC and Flying Officer Peter R. Lake RAAF in PZ353 in the No.2 position behind Iredale in the second wave, came into conflict with the incoming third wave. Shrimpton explains:

We came up to the lake where we would drop our wing tanks. I had to keep the Mosquito level and straight during this part of the operation, no skidding, so that the tanks would fall away cleanly without rolling into the tailplane. This was no easy task due to the extremely high turbulence. Peter was then concentrating more on map reading whilst I concentrated on accurate flying. I prayed that he had memorized the track. Then on the outskirts of the city I recognized the first landmark shown on the briefing model. Flying became precise; height 50 ft, engine revs, and boost. We wanted 320 mph but settled for 305 to 310, which was about all we could get. I set the bomb fuses and opened the bomb bay doors. We were getting close. Flak was looping over the target from the right with not much room over *Shellhaus*.

The next event was a shock. Peter yelled, 'Don't bomb, smoke to port!' He signalled to me that something was wrong. Were we on target? This all took place some 10–15 seconds from what we believed to be the target. Enough time to see that the building in question was not damaged but not enough to evaluate all the facts. Therefore, I aborted the attack, cleared the building and closed the bomb doors. Throttling back and keeping low, I commenced a left-hand orbit. After a moment we had left the Flak area and I reduced the rate of turn. We then had the opportunity to assess the situation and make a plan. The building which we were confident was the target was not damaged, no fire or smoke. We decided that the preceding aircraft had probably bombed the wrong target. Was the fire a decoy?

We decided to get ourselves into position for another run up to the target. Then, realizing that we were alone without orientation of our position, we commenced another orbit. After about 325° we both became re-orientated, first by Peter's recognition of the run up track and as a result of that, my identification of the target. Here we determined that *Shellhaus* had been hit. We could see dust and smoke. I continued to turn on the run-up and as we came in we both agreed that the job had been done. We observed heavy damage to the base of the building and lots of dust and smoke. More bombs might have unnecessarily endangered the Danes in the building so we aborted the attack. Later, on the long flight home, there was a distinct sense of failure or at least disappointment that we still had our bombs.

Two of the Mosquitoes from 'Blue Section' in the second wave were hit by flak over the north of Zealand on the return flight. SZ999 crewed by Flying Officer R. G. Shorty Dawson RAAF and Flying Officer F. T. Murray, ditched near Lisleje Strand. RS609 crewed by Flying Officer J. H. Spike Palmer RAAF and Sub Lieutenant H. H. Becker, a Norwegian, ditched in Samsø Belt. There were no survivors from either aircraft.

The third wave consisting of the six 487 Squadron FBVIs, led by Wing Commander F. H. Denton DFC*, a New Zealander, and his Australian navigator, Flying Officer A. J. Coe, in PZ402 had navigation problems. They approached Copenhagen from the north-east; a completely different direction from the planned flight path. This wave had been observed in front of the returning aircraft from the first wave as they left the target area. Delayed by some minutes they were caught up by DZ383 *Q-Query*, flown by Flying Officer R. E. Bob Kirkpatrick with Sergeant R. Hearne that had departed the Lake Tissø area two minutes behind the other six Mosquitoes. By mistake, four crews in the third wave bombed the area around the school. Denton and Coe, who located *Shellhaus*, saw so much damage already that the pilot aborted his attack and jettisoned their bombs in the sea. Flak tore away the starboard flap and knocked out the hydraulic system but Denton managed to nurse his flak-damaged FBVI back and belly-landed in England. (Coe was killed in a flying accident on 6 April 1945). Squadron Leader W. P. Kemp RNZAF and Flight Lieutenant R. Peel in PZ339, and New Zealanders Flying Officers G. L. Peet and L. A. Graham in SZ985 returned safely. Flight Lieutenant R. J. Dempsey and Flight Sergeant E. J. Paige RAAF in PZ462 had one engine damaged by a single bullet in the coolant system over the west coast of Jutland and flew 400 miles home with the engine feathered. *Q-Query* also limped home after taking a flak hit over the target. Kirkpatrick recalls:

As we approached the city I could see a huge pall of black smoke dead ahead, and, at the same time, some Mossies in a tight left turn. Our courses were converging. As they straightened out towards the smoke I had only a second to decide to join them close enough to avoid the 11 second delay bombs, rather than risk a right turn with the cruddy windshield [which had become coated with salt spray low over the North Sea]. The Mossies levelled off on track and I tucked in close, just as their bomb doors opened. I opened mine and saw their bombs drop just before we entered the smoke. I dropped my bomb load, then we got a pretty good wallop in the smoke and after breaking out I lost contact with the other Mosquitoes.

On the outskirts of the city, I saw two Mossies at about 3 o'clock on a northerly heading. I joined up with them only to see that one was smoking badly from the starboard engine. [NT123, Flight Lieutenant D. V. Pattison and Flight Sergeant F. Pygram's Mosquito had been hit by flak from the cruiser *Nürnburg* moored in the harbour]. The escorting Mosquito waved me off, as without guns, I would be just a burden and their course was not towards England. I turned back west just in time to see a sandbagged gun pit with two guns firing at the three of us. We had inadvertently got close to a large barracks, a fenced area with several low build-ings. The best and quickest evasion was to go straight towards the gun pit and dive. I opened the bomb doors to get their attention and spoil their aim. As the doors opened the gunners abandoned their guns and ducked down. We were gone in a flash, right over them.' [Pattison broke R/T silence with the message 'Z-Zebra-Christmas' the code for a forced landing in Sweden. The aircraft

159

had been hit on the port engine, which began to burn fiercely. Flying towards the Oresound, with hopes of making it across the water to neutral Sweden, the aircraft lost height rapidly and control was difficult. The Mosquito was last seen as it ditched in Oresound one kilometre east-south-east of the Swedish Hveen Island. The crew was spotted standing on the wing, but the weather conditions made it impossible to launch a rescue boat. Both men were posted as missing believed killed in action – no bodies were ever recovered. The wreck of the Mosquito has since been precisely located at a depth of 115 feet].

Kirkpatrick concludes:

On the return trip we sweated fuel for over an hour. When we spotted the English coast, and, not too far inland, an air base. I went straight in. I got the wheels down, but nothing for flaps or brakes, so I coasted to a stop on the grass by the runway. We had found a B-24 base [Rackheath] near Norwich. Hearne and I were escorted by MPs to the control tower to explain our presence.

Pilot Officer R. C. Hamilton RAAF's Mustang in 64 Squadron sustained damage over the target area and he lost oil pressure before being forced to ditch in Ringkøbing Fiord near Tarm, Jutland. Hamilton survived to be taken prisoner and he was later sent to *Stalag Luft I* at Barth in Germany. In all, four Mosquitoes and two Mustangs failed to return, for the loss of nine aircrew.

Ebbe Wolfhagen imprisoned in Vestre prison heard the explosions in the distance. 'My first reaction that day was of shock. Later I asked a guard for a pencil and paper so that I could write a note to *Shellhaus* to ask for permission to smoke and read. The guard replied, "You can forget that: *Shellhaus* is in flames". I was at that time very concerned about my colleagues' fate, were they dead or had they survived?'

Of the twenty-six prisoners on the sixth floor, eighteen escaped. The remaining prisoners died in the building. Some of those that had survived the attack were injured or killed by jumping from the fifth floor into the street below. If the entire Mosquitoes' bombs had been dropped on *Shellhaus* it is doubtful that anyone would have survived. Tragically at the Jeanne D' Arc School eighty-six children were killed and sixty-seven wounded, sixteen adults also lost their lives with thirty-five more injured. Several other people were killed elsewhere as a direct result of the attack. Had the air-raid warning been sounded on time, civilian casualties may have been much less. The *Gestapo* lost their precious archive material and their Headquarters. The total number of dead was seventy-two, with twenty-six members of the *Gestapo* and some thirty being Danish collaborators. The remainder were innocent Danes. An official number has never been revealed. The escape of so many Danish patriots provided the Resistance with the much-needed breathing space. The tragedy at the Jeanne d'Arc School marred this success, as one can never balance the lives of innocent children against those of resistance fighters, nevertheless there has never been any retribution shown towards the RAF for this costly operation. After the war, a fitting memorial was raised to the children and adults killed at the Jeanne d'Arc School. Likewise, at the new *Shellhaus* building there is a memorial to the Resistance members that lost their lives. Today at *Shellhaus*, there is a memorial to the nine aircrew members that laid down their lives in the fight for Denmark's freedom.

140 Wing had one more low-level pinpoint raid to fly. On 17 April six FBVIs of 140 Wing, led by Group Captain Bob Bateson DSO DFC** AFC and Ted Sismore, taxied out for a daylight strike on a school building on the outskirts of Odense, which was being used by the *Gestapo* as a HQ. AVM Basil Embry went along, as usual. The six Mosquitoes destroyed the *Gestapo* HQ and eighteen days later Denmark was free. During April the retreat by the *Wehrmacht* had left medium bombers far to the rear of the battlefront, so at the end of the month 138 Wing advanced to Achmer.

Chapter Eight

End Game

During March 1945 100 Group Mosquitoes shot down thirteen aircraft. The first two, both Ju88s, occurred on the night of 5–6 March, and both are credited to Wing Commander Walter Frame Gibb DSO DFC and Flying Officer R. C. Kendall DFC. Ju88G-6 622319 C9+GA of *Stab/NJG5* which crashed near Altenburg, twenty-five kilometres north-west of Chemnitz was piloted by *Oberst* Walter Borchers, Knight's Cross (29 October 1944), *Kommodore, NJG5*, a fifty-nine victory ace of which sixteen had been scored by day and forty-three by night. Borchers, and his radar operator, *Leutnant* Friedrich Reul, were killed. The second Ju88 to fall to Gibb's guns was Ju88G-6 622318 C9+NL of *3./NJG5*, which also crashed near Chemnitz. *Unteroffizier* Hans Dorminger, pilot, *Unteroffizier* Max Bartsch, *Obergefreiter* Franz Wohlschloegel and *Unteroffizier* Eriedrich Rullman, were all killed.

On the night of 7–8 March Flying Officer E. L. Heath and Flight Sergeant Thompson of 23 Squadron took off from Little Snoring at 20.44 hours and arrived in their patrol area at 22.25 hrs. Heath reported:

> Ten minutes later both Burg and Stendal lit up A/F flarepath and perimeter lights. Two green Vereys and two flares were fired from each airfield as Mosquito approached. Mosquito continued patrol and each time the airfields were approached the green vereys and white flares were fired. At 2325 hours an enemy aircraft was observed taking off from Stendal, burning navigation and downward recognition lights. Mosquito was then about ten miles south of Stendal at the time, 'going through the gate', reached airfield as

162

enemy aircraft was just airborne. Mosquito gave two 2 seconds bursts at enemy aircraft at 600-ft height, 1½ rings deflection, 250 yards range, but no strikes seen. Mosquito overshot and enemy aircraft turned port climbing rapidly making left-hand circuit of airfield. Mosquito turned quickly inside enemy aircraft and came in astern. Enemy aircraft was still burning all lights which made recognition difficult (downward recognition light was very bright). Closing into 150 yards, same height, half ring deflection, Mosquito fired a 2 seconds burst. Strikes seen on port wing, root and fuselage and identified as Fw190. Immediate flash and enemy aircraft peeled off to port from 1,200 ft, exploding on the ground six miles south of airfield three seconds later and 2330 hours. Mosquito immediately left patrol area with enemy aircraft still burning.

Heath claimed a Fw190 destroyed.

On 12–13 March when the heavies bombed Lutzkendorf Flight Lieutenant J. W. Welford and Flying Officer R. H. Phillips of 410 Squadron in a NFXXX, claimed a Ju88 'probable' in the Dunkirk area. In 100 Group meanwhile, Squadron Leader Dolly Doleman and Flight Lieutenant Bunny Bunch DFC of 157 Squadron had taken off from Swannington at 18.47 hours only to find that their Gee apparatus was u/s. Doleman however decided to carry on because:

We dared not change aircraft as Bunny had just given a lecture saying that Gee was merely an aid to navigation. We D/R'd onwards and checked position with a prang at Zweibrucken and picked up the 5 Group bombers shortly after. We escorted them uneventfully, looking for the odd airfield, but none were lit.
'We were investigating a small Squadron Leader line pointing from somewhere near Nurnburg to the target when contact was obtained, 6 miles head-on 20 degrees to port. We closed to 1,500 ft. at 10–11,000 from a violently moving target, orbiting and climbing and diving. Unfortunately all this was taking place in the darkest patch of sky over the whole of the continent. After sitting behind him in formation for about 15 minutes we pulled up very close and identified as a Ju 88G by the square top of the fin and elevators set forward. Pulled up and target became an indistinct blur. Had a crack at that from short range even closer. Strikes were seen, but impossible to say whereabouts they were. We were within

163

minimum Mk.X range and Bunny obtained his next contact about 2,000 ft, 90 degrees starboard. We whipped around but he must have gone down on the deck, as no further contact was obtained. Bags of blasphemy. Went on to target but no further joy, so set course base and landed base 0055 hrs, brassed off to hell.

On 18–19 March, Wing Commander Gibb and Kendall shot down a He219 *Uhu* at Witten to take their score while with the squadron to five. *Hauptmann* Baake, pilot and *Kommandeur* of *I./NJG1*, and his radar operator, *Unteroffizier* Bettaque, baled out safely. A third He219 was brought down during the last 100 Group victories of the month, on 20–21 March, during an eventful patrol north-west of Kassel by Flight Lieutenant G. C. Chapman and Flight Sergeant J. Stockley of 85 Squadron who were on high level escort of bombers to Bohlen. Their NFXXX was equipped with Perfectos, which was instrumental in their success as Chapman reported:

At 0255 hours just after passing Hamm on the way in to escort the bomber stream, we got a Perfectos contact at 12 miles range – height 12,000'. Range was closed to 1 mile but no AI contact was obtained and the range started to increase again, so deciding that the contact must be below, we did a hard diving turn to port, down to 9,000'. We finally D/F'd on to the target's course at 7 miles range. We closed in to 6 miles range on a course of 120°M and an AI contact was obtained at 6 o'clock 10°. The target was climbing and we closed in rapidly and obtained a visual at 900' – height 13,000'. The target was still climbing straight ahead and was identified with the night glasses as a Me.110. It had a pale blue light between starboard nacelle and fuselage. I closed in to 600' and pulled up to dead astern when the Hun started to turn to port. I gave it ½ ring deflection and a 3 second burst, whereupon the E/A exploded in the port engine in a most satisfying manner, with debris flying back. It exploded on the ground at 0305hrs 25/30 miles N.W. of Kassel. All this excitement was too much for the Perfectos which went u/s unfortunately, so we set course for the rendezvous with the bomber stream reaching there at 0322 hours.

The patrol with the bomber stream was uneventful until leaving the target when at 0400 hrs I noticed to port and 15 miles south a ball of yellowish flame take off from Plauen airfield and climb very rapidly. I thought it was a flare or a V2 until it started emitting a meteor tail several hundred foot long. We turned port towards it and lost height to 7,000' that being the height of this phenomenon as far as I could judge, and continued watching. It travelled in a NW direction very fast and suddenly to our astonishment fired off some R.P's (4 single and 1 pair) in the general direction of the departing bomber stream. We were pretty amazed at all this and decided that it must be a Me 163. I continued turning port and got behind it. It was vectoring 275°M by this time and doing about 260 IAS. Using the AI to check range we closed in to 1,000' and visually identified a twin engined A/C with rocket apparatus slung under the fuselage – a He 219. Considerable quantities of flames and sparks were flying back preventing me from identifying the tail unit, so I decided to open fire at that range.

I gave it several longish bursts as two of the cannon had stoppages and was gratified to see an explosion take place somewhere in the fuselage and debris fly back. The E/A nosed straight down through the patchy cloud and at 0408 hrs exploded on the ground with a tremendous glare. An interesting point about all this was that we could see plainly when the pilot opened up his rocket apparatus by the tremendous increase in size of the meteor tail. The E/A appeared to have a phenomenal rate of climb. [Their victim was He219V-14 190014, of *3./NJG1*, flown by *Oberleutnant* Heinz Oloff, *Staffel Kapitän, 3./NJG1*.]

Three more victories were recorded on the night of the 21–22nd and they went to 2nd TAF Mosquito crews. A 604 Squadron NFXIII crew dispatched a Bf110 in the Dhunn area, and Flying Officer R. I. E. Britten DFC RCAF and Flight Lieutenant L. E. Fownes DFC of 409 Squadron in a NFXIII, shot down a Bf110. The third victory of the night, a Bf110, went to Flying Officer K. Fleming and Flying Officer K. L. Nagle of 488 Squadron. On the night of 24–25 March 604, 605 and 410 Squadron crews shot down four more enemy aircraft. On the night of 25–26 March crews in 409 and 264 dispatched two Bf110s and a Ju88 plus one 'probable'. There was a great deal of activity on 26–27 March with raids concentrated on the Rhine bridgehead at Emmerich and as a result, the *Luftwaffe* was forced up into the night sky, but with disastrous results. Flying Officer T. R. Wood and Flying Officer R. Leafe of 604 Squadron, in NFXIII MM497, shot down a Ju88, while Flying Officer Reed and Flying Officer Bricker of 219 Squadron, flying a NFXXX, downed a Ju188, and Flight Lieutenant

B. E. Plumer DFC and Flight Lieutenant Bradford of 410 Squadron, flying a NFXXX, destroyed a Bf110.

Flight Lieutenant Al Gabitas of 488 RNZAF Squadron recalls:

At this stage of the war the Germans were feeling the effects of the Allied bombing on their synthetic petrol plants and were obviously trying to conserve fuel. This meant that their night flying activity tended to be concentrated on to particular nights, with long intervals of inactivity. The night of 26/27 March was to be a busy one with raids against the Rhine bridgehead at Emmerich. Flight Lieutenant Johnny Hall DFC, an Englishman on the Squadron, and his navigator Pilot Officer Taylor, contacted a Junkers 88 and brought it down 20 miles north of Emmerich after several bursts of cannon fire. But the Mosquito itself was damaged by flying debris and burst into flames as it landed on its belly at Gilze Rijn in Holland. Fortunately the top hatch slid back easily and the crew escaped unhurt.

Chunky Stewart and Bill Brumby were also on patrol over the bridge-head, in NFXXX NT263. About eight miles north-west of Bocholt they intercepted a Bf110, which, after a short burst, hit the ground with a brilliant explosion. Their radar set then became partially useless but even so, Brumby managed to pick up a contact, which turned out to be a He111. Stewart gave the Heinkel a quick couple of bursts and it went into a steep dive. At the same time Stewart realized that he was being chased by a German night fighter and he had to break off the engagement.

Flight Lieutenant Al Gabitas adds:

Following these successes there were many hours of patient patrolling and sky-searching and it was well into April [the night of 7–8] before Chunky and Bill were directed to a 'Bogey' over the Ruhr. In the long chase that followed the rear gunner on the Me 110 opened fire on the Mosquito several times but Chunky was not able to get his sights on to the enemy or fire his guns. Presently a small fire started in the tail of the Messerschmitt and then grew larger until it dived into the ground and exploded. Although their guns were not fired, Chunky and Bill were credited with one enemy aircraft destroyed. The enemy had shot off his own tail. Thus Chunky, in a comparatively short time had brought his score up to

166

five enemy aircraft destroyed and 1 damaged. Recognition of this achievement was to come with the award of DFCs to both Chunky and Bill. Unfortunately the paper work for the awards was rather slow and they were not announced until after the Squadron had been disbanded and left the Continent. I did not see Chunky again until 1949, by which time he was a full partner in his legal firm in Dunedin and making a name for himself in the profession. Sadly, he lived for only a few short years after the war and died suddenly in his home town from a massive coronary. All those who knew him were profoundly shocked at the death in times of peace of one so apparently fit and comparatively young.

For Les 'Dutch' Holland, a pilot in 515 Squadron, 100 Group at Little Snoring, 4 April 1945 was his twenty-third operation of the war. He recalls:

Night intruding and 'Bomber Support Special Duties' was a solitary business and only twice did I see another aircraft of our squadron or Group. I did an interception of a Halifax over Norway and on 27 February 1945 an escort for Liberators to Wilhelmshaven, two anti-flak efforts on minelaying and an attack with others on Westerland, Sylt. We saw the Libs OK all the way. When we returned they phoned and said, 'Where the hell were you?' I'm glad they didn't see us. On the other efforts I didn't actually see other aircraft I saw enemy aircraft on the ground and in the air a couple of times but all at night of course.

My aircraft was 'C' and my navigator was Flight Sergeant (later Warrant Officer) Robert Young. My assignment was a straightforward intruder patrol of the airfield at Plauen, about 40 miles SW of Chemnitz. As a rule we were pretty good at low level contact navigation but there was a lot of haze that night and it is 550 miles to Plauen from Little Snoring (direct). We confidently believed that our fuselage bay contained flares. It did not. We were certainly carrying 2 x 50-gallon wing tanks so our fuel load was 553 gallons and normal cruise consumption was 100 gall/hr.

So having arrived in the area and being unable to identify Plauen, we scouted around a bit and made out a large railway yard, which we reckoned was Pilsen. Hopeful that flares dropped on the ground – we were at about 1,000 ft – would help, we duly released the 'flares' from about 500-ft. Two hefty thumps told us that the flares were 250lb bombs. However, at low level we could see quite a lot of what was going on, so we used our cannon on the water towers etc., taking a good half-hour generally active in the area.

On the return journey, a place which had obviously been bombed passed beneath us where it had no business to be. A German airfield obligingly lit up for us when we should have been well past the front line. Our first reliable pm point showed that we were much further east than our reckoning, probably due to strengthening westerly winds. The appearance of the Friesian Islands showed that we were as far from known friendly airfields to the south as we were from Norfolk and had better start doing some sums. Halfway across the North Sea, judging by the fuel gauges (which were about 1" diameter with a pointer about 3/16ths wide) there wasn't much left. I remember alarming Bob by saying, 'I'm not sure whether we should press on or be ready for ditching'.

On the Norfolk coast was a 'Diver belt' which was a series of anti-aircraft batteries whom I had previously observed shooting down V1 flying bombs (Divers) with extreme accuracy. We had enough problems without tempting fate and so I sent out a Mayday to be let through the Diver-belt on a direct approach to Coltishall where we landed long after the fuel low pressure warning lights had come on. The engines stopped after we turned off the runway. We had been airborne for 5hrs 50 min. which would account for 553 galls of fuel-plus a bit more.

What everybody else was doing on that night I do not know but they must have been busy.

They were. On 4–5 April Squadron Leader Tim Woodman and Flight Lieutenant Neville, who were serving at BSDU, destroyed a Bf109 west of Magdeburg (Woodman's seventh confirmed victory of the war). Flight Lieutenant C. W. Topsy Turner and Flight Sergeant George Jock Honeyman of A Flight, 85 Squadron meanwhile, claimed a Ju188 destroyed west of Magdeburg at 22.44 hours during a High Level escort of the Window force. Turner reported:

While en route to target at 2238 hrs a Mk.X contact was obtained at 3½ miles range, crossing starboard to port, slightly above, 19,000 ft. We turned after him and closed in to 1½ miles when target ran into acres of Window. We 'pressed on regardless' and closed range to 1,000 ft when visual was obtained on a gently weaving target. There was no Type F response and we closed in to 100 ft and identified target as Ju 188 by pointed wing tips and tail assembly. Whilst dropping back to open fire, a black object – single engined aircraft (?) – whistled across our bows at about 100 ft causing both of us to duck smartly. After multiple curses and bags of brow-mopping we saw our quarry still ahead and opened fire from 20 yards astern with 5 degrees deflection, obtaining strikes on port engine. Two more short bursts made the Hun burn nicely. It spun and crashed, burning fiercely on the ground, West of Magdeburg at 2244 hours. Claim 1 Ju 188 destroyed. Aircraft landed base at 0130 hours.

On 9–10 April Wing Commander Howard Kelsey DFC* and Flight Lieutenant E. M. Smith DFC DFM, destroyed a Ju188 south-east of Hamburg for their fifth victory while with 100 Group (and Kelsey's eighth overall, plus three aircraft destroyed on the ground).

On the night of 13–14 April 515 Squadron flew their first Master Bomber sortie, dropping target indicators followed by bombs and incendiaries by the Mosquito force while 100 Group Mosquitoes made 'spoofing' raids on enemy airfields and cities. Flight Lieutenants Vaughan and McKinnon of 85 Squadron flew an Intruder patrol. Vaughan reported:

We planned to cross the enemy coast at Westerhever at 2320 hours mid then proceed to a point 20 miles SW of Kiel, which was the target for the main bomber force. We had originally intended to cover the bomber route out from the target area to the enemy coast-line for a period of 35 minutes. We were then aiming to do a free lance patrol in the Luneburg area. After being on patrol for 40 minutes we were still getting groups of bomber contacts. As there was apparent ground activity with searchlights and ground flashes on the bomber route which were definitely not gun flashes but some sort of indicating aid to the Hun nightfighters, we decided to continue patrolling the same area. However, this area quietened down considerably and after many alterations of height etc, on patrol, at 2020 hours, height 18,000 ft, just when our time limit on patrol had expired, my navigator obtained a crossing starboard to port contact at 5 miles range 35 degrees above. We chased our target in a port turn on to a southerly vector with the range rapidly reducing to 9,000ft and the target losing height at a rather low air speed, 220–230 IAS. The target kept up a continuous weave but settled down at about 10,000 ft. We closed range to 1,000 ft but experienced difficulty in getting behind him owing to his weaving activities. I got a visual on a pale blue light. But the aircraft did a peel off to port and range went out to 5,000 ft. We followed on AI, which incidentally was very ropey, in turns. Again we closed on the hard weaving target. I got fleeting visuals on bright exhausts at one stage, at about 2,000ft range, but still could not get comfortably settled astern. Three times we closed in to 1,000ft, the target peeling off on every occasion. The blue light was visible on most of these occasions from just astern but I was unable to follow visually owing to the target's activities.

We could identify target as a twin-engined aircraft on our very few opportunities. On one occasion, my navigator confirmed this with night glasses. On the third occasion that we closed range to 1,000ft, the target, to me anyway, appeared to catch fire underneath the fuselage. I got my navigator's head out of the box to confirm this and very quickly and brightly he yelled 'That's his jet', which jolted me out of my fire theory very quickly. The Target again started one of his routine turns and I immediately pushed the throttles fully open +12 and already using 28,000 revs, and gave a ½ second deflection shot on his jet at about 900ft range. However, this burst produced no strikes, so I got dead astern in the turn and at 700ft range, fired another burst, which caused a large explosion and strikes on his starboard side. I gave him another burst for luck and another explosion appeared on the port side and the E/A burned from wing tip to wing tip, going down in a spin to starboard and hit the deck at 0031. From its general appearance and behaviour, particularly the two of a jet we consider this A/C was a He 219, and we claim it as destroyed. We then set course for base. No Perfectos throughout patrol. The Hun did not seem to have any tail warning device but was apparently carrying out the usual evasive action. CLAIM: 1 He. 219 destroyed. A/c landed Swannington 0211 hours.

On the night of 14–15 April five Mosquitoes of 141 Squadron fitted with 100-gallon Napalmgel drop tanks, carried out the first of thirteen Firebash raids, on night fighter airfields at Neuruppin and Juterbog near Potsdam and Berlin. By 17–18 April, the last month of the war in which 100 Group victories were recorded, eleven aircraft had been shot down by day and night Mosquito intruders of 100 Group. During the remainder of April no less than twenty-three *Luftwaffe* aircraft, including a He177, Ju88Gs and 188s, Ju52s, a He111, and two Ju290s, were claimed shot down by NFXIIIs and NFXXXs of 219, 410, 264, 488, 409, and 406 Squadrons. April proved to be a magnificent month for 264 Squadron. After a slow start a Ju88 at rooftop height, just west of Berlin, was destroyed on 20–21 April by Flying Officers P. N. Lee and R. Thomas and on the 21st–22nd 264 Squadron claimed three and a probable. Two of these were Ju290s destroyed by Flying Officer J. Daber and Warrant Officer J. A. Heathcote. It was hoped that they were carrying a large number of high-ranking *Nazis*. The *Luftwaffe* continued to attempt to escape at night from doomed Berlin and 264 Squadron destroyed a Ju88 on the 22–23rd, a He111 on the 23–24th and a Fw190 on the 25–26th. (These were the last *Luftwaffe* aircraft the squadron destroyed, although difficult targets such as Bf108s and Fiesler Storchs were seen later). On the 26th the advance party moved into Germany to Rheine. The air party moved to Gilze Rijen, where they watched the war gently peter out. The Squadron score of 148 enemy aircraft destroyed was a fitting conclusion to a magnificent European record.

On 19–20 April Flight Lieutenant D. P. Podge Howard DFC and Flying Officer W. Sticky Clay DFC of BSDU claimed a Ju88 destroyed during a patrol to South Denmark and Island of Fyn airfields in their NFXXX. The bombers' target was a point in Kiel area. Howard wrote:

Aircraft BSDU/B was airborne Swanton Morley 2043 hours to carry out a low-level patrol of South Denmark and airfields on the Island of Fyn. The aircraft was equipped with Mk.X AI, Serrate IVA and Wolf. Landfall was made at 2204 hours, height 15,000 ft. from there, height was lost to Bogense where we arrived at 2216 hours, height 3,000 ft. a patrol of the Fyn Island was carried out for an hour, during which time only one airfield was observed at Boldringe. At 2305 hrs an attack parallel to the runway was made on a dispersed barrack site with two bursts of two seconds each. Strikes were seen. The airfield was not lit and no flak was experienced. Many small convoys were seen on roads. At 2316 hours course was set from the island at 2,000ft. At 2324 hours a

Mk.X contact crossing starboard to port, range 4 miles and above, our height being 2,000 ft. At 2324 hours, position 55°48N 09°11E, a Mk.X. contact crossing starboard to port, range 4 miles and above, our height being 2,000 ft. We turned behind the contact at 5,000-ft range when a visual was obtained on an aircraft heading on a course of 175°. A Ju 88 was identified with the aid of glasses at 1,500-ft range, height 3,000 ft, speed 240 IAS. A short burst from dead astern at 250 yards, which caused the outer half of the port wing to fall away. The e/a rolled on its back, hit the ground at 2328 hours, spread over a wide area and caused a large number of small fires. Course was set for base, crossing out at Farne at 2340 hours, and landed at base 0104 hours. Claim: – 1 Ju88 destroyed Cat. 1A.

On 24–25 April 456 and 151 RAAF Squadrons flew their last operation when four Mosquitoes of 456 and six of 151, flew Night Rangers, while 141 Squadron carried out a Napalm attack on Munich-Neubiberg airfield again. The final victory awarded to 100 Group went to the CO of 515 Squadron, Wing Commander Howard Kelsey DSO DFC* and his navigation leader, Flight Lieutenant E. M. Smith DFC* DFM.

Right up until the German surrender, Mosquitoes, Mitchells and Bostons of 2 Group continued operations against rail and road targets. On the night of 2 May, for instance, forty-two aircraft attacked troop transports with 500lb bombs, flares and cannon, and machine-gun fire, leaving nine trains burning furiously.

Life had not been dull for Warrant Officer Les Turner and Flight Lieutenant Jimmy Wheldon in 169 Squadron, as Turner recalled:

On Trip No.6 to Brandenburg we had a 20-minute radar chase, only to find another Mosquito as the target! Trip No.7 was to Traumunde north of Lubeck and was uneventful. By then, the war was moving to a close and there were few German night fighters airborne, so on Trip No.8 they loaded us with two 500lb bombs and 100 gallons of incendiary fluid (Napalm) and we carried out an attack on the aerodrome at Flensburg. I made a diving attack and said to Jimmy that if anything went wrong I would pull up hard and he was to bale out. Fortunately, nothing went wrong!

The last trip of the war (No.9) was on 2 May 1945 and was another 'bombing' raid, this time with 200 gallons of Napalm. The target was the airfield at Jagel. [Turner's was one of twelve Mosquito crews who went to Jagel when Bomber Command brought down the curtain with raids by 8 and 100 Groups on North German targets. In the last operation of the war a record 106 100 Group aircraft took part. Some 126 Mosquitoes from 8 Group followed in the wake of sixteen Mosquitoes of 8 Group and thirty-seven Mosquitoes of Nos. 23, 169, 141 and 515 Squadrons in 100 Group in Firebash attacks on airfields at Flensburg, Hohn, Westerland/Sylt and Schleswig/Jagel. Hohn and Flensburg airfields were bombed with Napalm and incendiaries directed by Master Bomber, Squadron Leader Griffiths of 515 Squadron]. By then I had enough of destruction and, while I could see the surrounding buildings, I decided to drop the Napalm on the airfield. The war was obviously not going to last much longer. The opposition was quite intense and as I followed Keith Miller (later to become famous as an Australian Test cricketer) the light flak aimed at him was passing worryingly close to us. One of Keith's drop-tanks hung up and slewed him to starboard. But for this he reckoned that he would have got caught in the flak. As it was we regrettably lost one of our crews – such a waste so near the end. On the day before VE Day [At 08.00 hours on 8 May the ceasefire in Germany came into effect and VE Day was declared] we did a sight-seeing tour covering Aachen, Cologne, Dusseldorf, the Möhne Dam, Dortmund and Duisburg. The destruction was appalling and a sense of the terrible waste hung over a number of us over the Victory celebration days. We repeated the trip a week later – it was for the (?) benefit of ground crews who had, of course, seen nothing of this.

During 25 June-7 July 1945 Exercise Post Mortem was carried out to evaluate the effectiveness of RAF jamming and spoof operations on the German early warning radar system. Simulated attacks were made by aircraft from four RAF groups, the early warning radar being manned by American and British personnel on this occasion. Post Mortem proved conclusively that the countermeasures had been a great success. The success achieved by the RAF on night and day operations over the Third Reich 1942–45 owed much to the incomparable Mosquito fighters and fighter bombers. Radar equipped, they proved the scourge of the *Nachtjagd*.

Moskitopanik was their proud legacy.

Appendix One

MOSQUITO AIR-TO-AIR VICTORIES 1942-APRIL 1945

Date	Type Serial Sqn Enemy A/c details	Pilot-Navigator/Radar Op
29/30.5.42	II W4099 157 Sqn Do217E-4 S of Dover.	S/L C. Ashfield.
29/30.5.42	II DD608 151 Sqn Do217E-4 (Prob) North Sea	P/O J. A. Wain-F/Sgt T. S. G. Grieve.
28/29.6.42	II 264 Sqn Do217E-2 over Creil	F/O Hodgkinson (Uffz Rudolf Blankenburg, KG2).
24/25.6.42	II W4097 151 Sqn 2 x Do217E-4 The Wash	W/C I. S. Smith DFC-F/L Kernon-Sheppard.
25/26.6.42	II DD61 6 151 Sqn He111 H-6 North Sea.	P/O J. A. Wain-F/Sgt T. S. G. Grieve.
26/27.6.42	II DD609 151 Sqn Do217E-4 North Sea.	F/L Moody-P/O Marsh.
6/7.7.42	II DD670 'S' 23 Sqn Do217 16m E Chartres.	W/C B. R. O' B. Hoare DFC*-P/O S. J. Cornes.
8/9.7.42	II DD670 'S' 23 Sqn Do217 Etampes/ He111 Evreux.	S/L K. H. Salisbury-Hughes.
21/22.7.42	II W4090 151 Sqn Do217E-4 off Spurn Head	P/O Fisher (Ofw Heinrich Wolpers and crew, Do217E-4 U5+IH 3./KG2).
27/28.7.42	IIs DD629 & DD608 151 Sqn 2xDo217E-4 North Sea	S/L Pennington & Pilot Officer Fielding. (Fw Richard Stumpf of I/KG2 and Lt Hans-Joachim Mohring of 3./KG2).
27/28.7.42	II W4099 157 Sqn He111 North Sea	S/L G. Ashfield.

Date	Aircraft	Crew
29/30.7.42	II DD669 151 Sqn Do217E-4 North Sea	F/O A. l. McRitchie-F/Sgt E. S. James (Do217E-4 U5+GV, flown by Ofw. Artur Hartwig of II/KG2).
30/31.7.42	II DD670 'S' 23 Sqn UEA Orleans.	W/C B R. O'B. Hoare DFC*-W/O J.F. Potter.
30/31.7.42	II DD639 264 Sqn Ju88A-4 N Malvern Wells	S/L C. A. Cook-P/O R. E. MacPherson ((KüiFlGr 106).
22/23.8.42	II DD612 157 Sqn Do217E-4 Worlingworth	W/C Gordon Slade-P/O P. V. Truscott (Do217E-4 U5+LP of 6./KG2, flown by 29-year-old ex-Lufthansa pilot Oblt. Hans Walter Wolff, Deputy Staffelkapitän).
8/9.9.42	II DD669 151 Sqn Do217E-4 Orwell, Cambs	F/O A. l. McRitchie-F/Sgt E. S. James (Do217E-4 F8+AP, on loan to 3./KG2 and piloted by Fw. Alfred Witting).
10/11.9.42	II 'B' 23 Sqn UEA 12m S Enschede	W/C B. R. O'B. Hoare DFC*-W/O J. F. Potter.
17/18.9.42	II DD610 151 Sqn Do217E-4 Cr. Docking	F/L H. E. Bodien DFC-Sgt G. B. Brooker. (U5+UR of 7./KG2 piloted by Fw Franz Elias) cr. at Fring and all four crew were taken prisoner.
30.9.42	II DD607 157 Sqn Ju88A-4 30m off Dutch coast	W/C R. F. H. Clerke.
26.10.42	II DD716 157 Sqn Ju88D-1 off Beachy Head	F/O E. H. Cave.
15/16.1.43	II DD609 151 Sqn Do217E-4 Cr. Boothby Graffoe	Sgt E. A. Knight RCAF-Sgt W. I. L. Roberts (Do217E-4 U5+KR of 7./KG2. Lt. Günter Wolf, pilot, Uffz. Helmut Knorr, Uffz. Kurt Semitschka, dorsal gunner, & Ogfr. Karl-Heinz Krusewitz) all KIA.
17/18.1.43	II VY-V 85 Sqn Ju88A-14 SE England	W/C C. G. L. Raphael DFC*-W/O W. N. Addison DFM (Ju88A-14 of IV.KG3 or III/KG6).
22.1.43	II HJ929 410 Sqn Do2l7E-1 (Prob)	W/C P. G. Wykeham-Barnes DSO DFC*-F/O G. E. Palmer DFC.
18/19.43	II W4099 157 Sqn Ju88A-14 off Harwich	F/O G. Deakin-P/O de Costa.
18/19.3.43	II HK936 410 Sqn Do217E8-4 King's Lynn	F/O D. Williams-P/O P. Dalton (Do217 U5+AH W/Nr. 5523) I/KG2 flown by Uffz. Horst Toifel, Uffz. Heinrich

Date	Type Serial Sqn Enemy A/c details	Pilot-Navigator/Radar Op
28/29.3.43	II W4079 157 Sqn Do217E-4 off Southwold	Peter, gunner, Ludwig Petzold radio operator, Ogfr. Georg Riedel, observer. F/O J. R. Beckett-F/Sgt Phillips (Do217E-4 U5+NM (W/Nr. 4375) of 4./KG2, flown by Fw. Paul Huth. Uffz. Werner Hans Burschel, dorsal gunner, Oblt. Gottfried Thorley, observer, and Uffz. Konrad Schuller, radio operator, all KIA. Victory shared with a 68 Squadron Beaufighter piloted by F/O Vopalecky with F/Sgt Husar; both Czech).
30.3.43	II 264 Sqn He111 8m N Redon	S/L M. H. Constable-Maxwell.
13/14.4.43	II DZ243 157 Sqn Do217E-4.	
14/15.4.43	XII VY-F 85 Sqn Do217E-4 Clacton-on-Sea	S/L W. P. Green-F/Sgt A. R. Grimstone (Do217E-4 F8+AM of 4./KG40).
14/15.4.43	XII VY-G 85 Sqn Do217E-4 Clacton-on-Sea	F/L G. L. Howitt-F/O G. Irving (Do217E-4 U5+DP of 6./KG2 flown by Uffz. Franz Tannenberger).
14/15.4.43	II DD730 157 Sqn Do217E-4 SW Colchester	F/L J. G. Benson DFC-F/L L. Brandon DFC (Do217E-4 U5+KP flown by Uffz. Walter Schmurr of 6./KG2. Uffz. Franz Witte, radio operator-gunner KIA. Schmurr, Lt Karl-Heinrich Hertam, observer and Uffz. Martin Sehwarz, gunner, baled out. Witte's body was found in the wreckage).
24/25.4.43	XII 85 Sqn Ju88 nr Bromley, Kent	F/O J. P. M. Lintott -Sgt G. G. Gilling-Lax (Ju88A-14 3E+HS of 8./KG6 disintegrated in the air and the wreckage fell in Bromley, Kent).
4/5.5.43	II 605 Sqn Do217K1 x 2 Eindhoven	F/O B. Williams-P/O D. Moore (Do217K-1 U5+AA (W/Nr. 4415) of 6./KG2. Lt Ernst Andres, pilot, seriously injured, Maj. Walter Bradel, Kommodore of KG2 KIA

13/14.5.43 — II 157 Sqn Do217E4 10m NE Colchester — Sgt R. L. Watts-Sgt J. Whewell (157 Squadron shot down two Do217E-4s of *KG2* piloted by Lt. Stefan Szamek and Lt. Gerd Strufe). A Do217E-4 of *II/KG2* was intercepted by a Mosquito NF.II of 157 Squadron from Hunsdon, flown by Sgt R. L. Watts with Sgt J. Whewell, and shot down after an exchange of fire. A fire started in the Dornier's starboard engine and it crashed about 10 miles NE of Colchester at 02.07 hrs. Near Norwich, a Do217K-1 of *4./KG2* flown by Uffz. Erhard Corty was claimed at about 02.50 hrs).

16/17.5.43 — XII 'A' 85 Sqn Fw190A-4/U-8 nr Dover — S/L W. P. Green-F/Sgt A. Grimstone.

16/17.5.43 — XII 'G' 85 Sqn Fw190A-4/U-8 15m S. Hastings — F/L G. L. Howitt-F/O G. Irving.

16/17.5.43 — XII 'L' 85 Sqn Fw190A-4/U-8 Dover Straits Fw190A-4/U-8 *(Prob)* — F/O B. J. Thwaites-P/O W. P. Clemo DFM*.
F/O B. J. Thwaites-P/O W. P. Clemo DFM*.

16/17.5.43 — XII 'D' 85 Sqn Fw190A-4/U-8 off Gravesend — F/O J. D. Shaw-P/O A. C. Lowton.

18/19.5.43 — XII 'Z' 85 Sqn Fw190A-5 Kent — F/O J. P. M. Lintott-Sgt G. G. Gilling-Lax.

21/22.5.43 — XII 'V' 85 Sqn Fw190A 25m NW Hardelot — S/L E. Crew DFC*-F/O F. French.

29/30.5.43 — XII 'S' 85 Sqn Ju88S-1 Isfield nr Lewes — F/O J. P. M. Lintott -Sgt G. G. Gilling-Lax (3Z+SZ of *I/KG66*).

5.6.43 — XII 29 Sqn Ju88A-14 off Ostend. — F/O Burnett.

11.6.43 — XII 256 Sqn Do217 South of Ford — F/L J. Singleton-F/O W. G. Haslam.

11.6.43 — II 85 Sqn 25 Ju88 Bay of Biscay

in the crash at Landsmere, near Amsterdam. Flg. Wernerker also killed, although he may have died in the Mosquito attack, and rest of the crew injured. All recovered, Andres being promoted to Oblt and receiving the *Ritterkreuz* on 20 April 1944. He was killed with 5./NJG4 on 11 February 1945.

Date	Type Serial Sqn Enemy A/c details	Pilot-Navigator/Radar Op
12/13.6.43	XIX MM630 'E' 157 Sqn Ju188 Foret de Compeigne	F/L J.G. Benson DFC-F/L L. Brandon DSO DFC.
13/14.6.43	XII DZ302 'R' 85 Sqn Fw190A-5 Wrotham	W/C J. Cunningham DSO* DFC*-F/L C. F. Rawnsley DFC DFM* (W/C Cunningham, CO 85 Squadron, who had shot down 16 enemy aircraft while flying Beaufighters, pursued Fw190A-5 CO+LT of 3./SKG10 over his own airfield and shot it down. The Fw190, flown by Lt. Ullrich, crashed at Nettlefold Farm, Borough Green near Wrotham, but incredibly, the pilot had been catapulted through the canopy in the death dive of the aircraft and was taken prisoner).
14/15.6.43	XVII HK315 219 Sqn Ju88 Harwich area	F/L M. J. Gloster DFC-F/L J. F. Oswold DFC.
17/18.6.43	XII 85 Sqn Fw190 (Prob)	Lt Räd RNWAF.
19.6.43	II 151 Sqn Ju88 Bay of Biscay	F/L H. E. Bodien DFC.
21/22.6.43	XII 'E' 85 Sqn Fw190 River Medway	F/L W. McGuire-F/O W. D. Jones (Fw190 GP+LA of 2./SKG 10).
2/3.7.43	XII HK166 FIU Ju88D-1 45m S Bognor	W/C R. A. Chisholm DFC-F/O N. L. Bamford DFC.
3/4.7.43	II DD739 157 Sqn Do217 St Trond	F/L J.G. Benson DFC-F/L L. Brandon DSO DFC.
9.7.43	XII 'Z' 85 Sqn Fw190 nr Detling	F/O J. P. M. Lintott -Sgt G. G. Gilling-Lax (Lintott's 4th victory - Do217K-1 U5+FP, piloted by Oblt. Hermann Zink of 6./KG2. Zink and his crew were all KIA. The GCI controller who had put Lintott onto the raider saw two blips on his CRT merge and stay together for 7 minutes: then they had faded. 2 mls from where the Dornier fell the Mosquito crew were also found dead in the wreckage of their aircraft).
11/12.7.43	II HJ944 410 Sqn Do217 10m E Humber	S/L A. G. Lawrence DFC RCAF-F/Sgt H. J. Wilmer DFM.

Date	Squadron / Claim	Details
13/14.7.43	XII 'T' 85 Sqn Me410A-1 off Felixstowe	F/L E. N. Bunting-F/O F. French (Me410A-1 U5+KG flown by Fw. Franz Zwißler (pilot) and Ofw. Leo Raida (bordfunker) of 16/KG2. Bunting closed to within 200 yd, but the Mosquito got caught in the Germans' slipstream and he could not aim his guns. He dived below and closed in again before firing two short bursts. The Me410 burst into flames at once and fell into the sea 5 miles off Felixstowe. It was the first Me410 to be shot down over Britain.
13/14.7.43	II HJ944 410 Sqn (RCAF) Do217 off Humber Estuary	(Do217M-1, U5+EL of 3./KG2, flown by Uffz. Willy Spielmanns).
13/14.7.43	II 605 Sqn Do217M-1nr Eindhoven	F/O R. R Smart-F/O J. K. Sutcliffe (On Intruder over Holland, shot down Do217M-1 U5+CK of 2./KG2 Uffz. Hauck and his crew crashed in the vicinity of Eindhoven).
15/16.7.43	XII 'G' 85 Sqn Me410 A-1 off Dunkirk	F/L B. J. Thwaites- P/O W. P. Clemo DFM* (Me410 U5+CJ of V/KG2, flown by Hptm. Friederich-Wilhelm Methner and Uffz. Hubert Grube.)
18.7.43	XII 256 Sqn Fw190 Channel.	
25/26.7.43	II 605 Sqn Do217M-1 Soesterberg	F/L C. Knowles-F/O A. Eagling (Do217M-1 U5+KL, flown by Lt. Manfred Lieddert of 3./KG2.)
26/27.7.43	XII VY-A 85 Sqn Ju88 25m E Ramsgate	S/L W. P. Green DFC-F/Sgt A. R. Grimstone DFM.
29/30.7.43	XII 256 Sqn Me410A-1 20m S Beachy Head	W/C G. R. Park (Oblt. Helmut Biermann and Uffz. Willi Kroger in Me410A-1 U5+BJ. They fell into the sea 20 miles south of Beachy Head.)
July 43	XII 29 Sqn Ju88 NE of Foreness.	
15/16.8.43	XII 256 Sqn 2 x Do217M-1 30m SE Selsey	W/C G. R. Park (Uffz. Karl Morgenstern and Uffz. Franz Bundgens' Do217M-ls in the sea off Worthing.

179

Date	Type Serial Sqn Enemy A/c details	Pilot-Navigator/Radar Op
15/16.8.43	XII 256 Sqn 2 x Do217M-1 France	Park's third 'kill' of the night occurred when he shot down Uffz. Walter Kayser's Do217M-I).
15/16.8.43	VI HP849 410 Sqn Do217M 17m off Beachy Hd	F/Sgt Brearley (Fw. Theodor Esslinger fell near Evreux and Lt. Franz Bosbach crashed near St André.) P/O R. D. Schultz -F/O V. A. Williams (Do217M-1 U5+GT of 9./KG2 flown by Uffz. Josef Schultes and crew (all KIA).
17/18.8.43	VI 'O' 605 Sqn Bf109 E Schleswig	F/L D. H. Blomely DFC-F/O R. 'Jock' Birrel.
22/23.8.43	XII 'V' 85 Sqn Me410-A-1 Chelmondiston	S/L G. E. Howitt DFC-P/O J. C. O. Medworth (Me410A-1, U5+AF of 15./KG2 crewed by Fw. Walter Hartmann and Obgefr. Michael Meurer. Meurer baled out and came down at Stratton Hall, while Hartman's body was later found in a field, his parachute unopened.)
22/23.8.43	XII 'R' 85 Sqn Fw190 nr Dunkirk.	
22/23.8.43	XII HK197 29 Sqn Me410-A-1 E of Manston	
22/23.8.43	XII HK175 29 Sqn Me410 A-1nr Dunkirk.	F/L C. Kirkland-P/O R. C. Raspin.
22/23.8.43	XII HK164 29 Sqn Me410A-1 North of Knocke.	
23/24.8.43	XII DZ302 'R' 85 Sqn Fw190 off Dunkirk	W/C J. Cunningham DSO* DFC*-F/L C. F. Rawnsley DFC DFM*.
24/25.8.43	XII 'G' 85 Sqn Me410A-1	Capt J. Råd RNWAF-Capt L. Lövestad RNWAF DFM* (U5+EG, a Me410A-1 of 16./KG2, flown by Fw. Werner Benner with Uffz. Hermann Reimers). Victory was officially shared with W/C R. E. X. Mack DFC in a XII of 29 Sqn.
6/7.9.43	XII 'K' 85 Sqn Fw190A-5 France.	

180

Date	Aircraft	Crew / Notes
6/7.9.43	II 'V' 85 Sqn Fw190A-5 3m E Clacton	S/L G. E. Howitt DFC-F/L C. Irving DFC.
8/9.9.43	XV DZ302 'R' 85 Sqn Fw190A-5 off Aldborough	W/C J. Cunningham DSO* DFC*-F/L C. F. Rawnsley DFC DFM*.
8/9.43	XII 'L' 85 Sqn 2 x Fw190A-5 of I/SKG10 off N Foreland	F/L B. J. Thwaites-P/O W. P. Clemo DFM*.
11/12.9.43	XIX MM630 'E' 157 Sqn 2 x Ju188 Zeeland	F/L J. G. Benson DFC-F/L Brandon DSO DFC.
15/16.9.43	XII 'T'? 85 Sqn Ju88A-14 Tenterden	F/O E. R. Hedgecoe-P/O J. R. Whitham. Ju88A-14 3E+FP of 6./KG6. Mosquito was crippled by return fire, and the crew baled out, their aircraft crashing at Tenterden, Kent.
15/16.9.43	XII 'T'? 85 Sqn Ju88A-14 off Boulogne	F/L E. N. Bunting-F/O F. French (Ju88A-14 of II/KG6).
15/16.9.43	XII HK204 488 Sqn Do217M E of Foreness	F/L Watts (9./KG2 Do217M-1, flown by Ofw. Erich Mosler shot down into the sea SE of Ramsgate.)
15/16.9.43	XII HK203 488 Sqn He111 North of Bradwell.	F/O Jarris. (Ofw. Horst Muller and Uffz. Wolfgang Dose in Me410A-1 U5+AF of 15./KG2 off Beachy Head during a raid on Cambridge).
15/16.9.43	XII HK189 29 Sqn Me410 off Beachy Head	S/L D. H. Blomely DFC-F/O J. Birrel.
21.9.43	VI 'C' 605 Sqn 2 x Ju88 W Skaggerak	F/L W. A. Cybulski DFC-F/O H. H. Ladbrook DFC.
22.9.43	XI 85 Sqn Me410 off Orfordness.	W/C B. R. O'B Hoare DSO DFC*-W/O J. F. Potter.
26.9.43	II DZ757 410 Sqn Do217 Dutch coast	P/O T. Weisteen RNWAF-F/O F. French.
27/28.9.43	VI 'R' 605 Sqn Do217 Dedelsdorf	F/Sgt Robertson.
2/3.10.43	XII 85 Sqn 2 x Do217K off Humber Est.	F/L W. Maguire-Capt L. Lövestad RNWAF. Me410A flown by Fw. Georg Slodczyk and Uffz. Fritz Westrich of 16./KG2 Westrich's body was picked up off Dungeness on 13 October and buried at sea.
6.10.43	XII 488 Sqn Do217M-1 Canterbury.	
7/8.10.43	II DZ260 157 Sqn Me410A-1 (Dam?) off Shoeburyness	
7/8.10.43	XII 'E' 85 Sqn Me410A-1 15m off Hastings	

Date	Type Serial Sqn Enemy A/c details	Pilot-Navigator/Radar Op
7/8.10.43	XII 85 Sqn Me410A-1	F/L B. J. Thwaites-P/O W. P. Clemo. Me410A flown by Fw. Wilhelm Sohn and Uffz. Günther Keiser of 14./KG2, which crashed at Ghent.
8/9.10.43	XII 85 Sqn Ju88S-1 off Foulness	F/O S. V. Holloway-W/O Stanton (Ju88S-1 3E+US of 8./KG6).
8/9.10.43	XII 85 Sqn Ju88S-1 10m S Dover	F/L E. N. Bunting-F/O F. French (Ju88S-1 3E+NR of 7./KG6 into the sea 10 miles S of Dover at 20.20 hrs; Fw. W. Kaltwasser, Obgefr. J. Jakobsen and Uffz. J. Bartmuss were killed) .
12.10.43	XII 151 Sqn Me410 NE of Cromer.	
15/16.10.43	XII 'K' 85 Sqn Ju188E Birchington	F/O H. B. Thomas-W/O C. B. Hamilton.
15/16.10.43	XII 'E' 85 Sqn Ju188E-1 Hemley, Suffolk	F/L W. Maguire-F/O W. D. Jones .
	Ju188E-1 South of Clacton	Ju188E-1 3E+FL of 1./KG6, which went into the sea off Clacton and Ju188E-1 3E+RH, also of 1./KG6, which crashed at Hemley, Suffolk, to become the first Ju188 down on land in the UK.
17/18.10.43	XII 'V' 85 Sqn Me410A-1 Hornchurch/Little Warley	F/L E. N. Bunting-F/O F. French Me410 U5+LF of 15./KG2) flown by (pilot) Ofw. Lothar Bleich (k) and Uffz. Ernst Greiecker (inj).
20.10.43	XII 29 Sqn Fw190A-1 South of Beachy Head.	
20.10.43	XII 29 Sqn Me410A-1 over Channel.	
22.10.43	XII 29 Sqn Fw190A East of Beachy Head.	
20/21.10.43	XII HK163 29 Sqn Me210 (prob)	F/L R. C. Pargeter-F/L R. E. Fell. Dungeness-Ashford.
30/31.10.43	XII 'G' 85 Sqn Ju88S-1 20m SE of Rye	F/L R. L. T. Robb-F/O R. C. J. Bray. Ju88S of III./KG6 either W/Nr 1404853E+KS, or WNr 140585 3E+AS.
30/31.10.43	XII 'J' 85 Sqn Ju88S-I 20m S of Shoreham	F/O H. B. Thomas-W/O C. B. Hamilton.

Date	Aircraft / Squadron	Crew
1.11.43	XII 29 Sqn Ju88S-1? Nr Andover.	F/O E. R. Hedgecoe-P/O J. R. Witham.
2/3.11.43	XII 'K' 85 Sqn Fw190 S of Canvey Island	F/O C. F. Green-P/O E.G. White.
5/6.11.43	II HJ917 410 Sqn Me41010m S of Dungeness	
6/7.11.43	XII 'W' 85 Sqn Fw190A 2/3m S of Hastings.	
8/9.11.43	XII HK163 29 Sqn Me410A-1 nr Beachy Head	F/O Russell-Steward-F/O G. K. Main.
8/9.11.43	XII 'E' 85 Sqn Me410A-1 nr Eastbourne	S/L W. H. Maguire DFC-F/O W. D. Jones. W/Nr 10244 U5+BF of 15./KG2; Major Wilhelm Schmitter Knight's Cross with Oak leaves, and his *Bordfunker*, Uffz. Felix Hainzinger, both killed when the a/c crashed into Shinewater Marsh).
8/9.11.43	XIII HK367 488 Sqn Me410A-1 off Clacton	F/O Reed-P/O Bricker.
9.11.43	VI 'O' 605 Sqn Bf110 20m W Aalborg	F/L D. H. Blomely DFC.
18/19.11.43	II HJ705 FIU Bf110 Mannheim	W/C R. A. Chisholm DFC-F/L P. C. Clarke.
20.11.43	I 157 Sqn Ju290 8 mls N Estaca Point-	W/C Mackie-F/O L. Scholefield.
20.11.43	II 157 Sqn Ju88 (*prob*) 15-40 mls N Cape Ortegal-	F/L Dyke-W/O C. R. Aindow.
20/21.11.43	XIII HK4G3 29 Sqn Fw190 Broadbridge Heath	F/L R. C. Pargeter-F/L R. E. Fell.
20/21.11.43	XII HK177 151 Sqn Me410 off Esparto Point.	
22.11.43	II HJ651 307 Sqn Fw200 120m NE Shetlands	F/Sgt Jaworski.
25/26.11.43	XII HK22B 488 Sqn Me410 off Calais	F/L P. F. L. Hall-F/O R. D. Marriott.
9.12.43	II EW-R 307 Sqn Ju88D-1.	
10/11.12.43	II DZ29 410 Sqn 3 x Do217M-1 Clacton-Dunkirk	F/O R. D. Schultz-F/O V. A. Williams (Do217Ms of KG2).
10/11.12.43	II HJ944 410 Sqn Do217 nr Chelmsford	P/O D.N. Robinson RNZAF.
19/20.12.43	XIII HK457 488 Sqn Me410A-1 nr Rye	P/O J. T. Caine RCAF-P/O E. W. Boal RCAF.
20/21.12.43	VI 418 Sqn UEA Delune a/f nr Metz	

Date	Type Serial Sqn Enemy A/c details	Pilot-Navigator/Radar Op
22/23.12.43	VI HX812 'T' 418 Sqn UEA (Prob) Orleans a/f	F/L D. A. MacFadyen RCAF-F/L Wright.
23/24.12.43	VI 'H' 605 Sqn UEA Fassberg airfield	F/L A. D. Wagner DFC-P/O E. T. Orring.
2.1.44	XIII HK461 488 Sqn Me410 Straits of Dover.	
2/3.1.44	XIII HK374 85 Sqn Me410 Sandwich	W/C J. Cunningham DSO* DFC*-F/L C. F. Rawnsley DFC DFM*.
2/3.1.44	II 96 Sqn Fw190 Rye	F/O N. S. Head-F/O A. C. Andrews.
4/5.1.44	XII 85 Sqn Ju88 off Dieppe	F/O E. R. Hedgecoe-P/O J. R. Whitham DFM*.
4/5.1.44	XIII 96 Sqn Ju888-1 3m S of Hastings	W/C E. D. Crew DFC-W/O W. R. Croysdill.
10/11.1.44	VI 'E' 605 Sqn Ju188 4m E Chieves	W/C B. R. O'B Hoare DSO DFC*-W/O J. F. Potter.
15/16.1.44	XIII 96 Sqn Fw190 Dungeness	S/L A. Parker-Rees-F/O Bennett.
21/22.1.44	XII HK197 29 Sqn Fw190 S of Beachy Head	
21/22.1.44	XII HK168 29 Sqn Ju88 S of Beachy Head	
21/22.1.44	XII 'N' 85 Sqn Ju88 off Rye	
21/22.1.44	XIII HK414 96 Sqn Ju88 Paddock Wood Stn	Sub Lt J. A. Lawley-Wakelin-Sub Lt H. Williams.
21/22.1.44	XIII HK425 96 Sqn Ju88 Tonbridge.	
21/22.1.44	XIII HK372 96 Sqn 2xJu88 (Prob) S of Bexhill	F/L N. S. Head-F/O A. C. Andrews.
21/22.1.44	XII HK193 151 Sqn He177A-3 nr Hindhead	W/O H. K. Kemp-F/Sgt J. R. Maidment. The first He177 to be shot down over the British Isles, He177A-5 Werk Nr 15747 of I/KG40, crashing at Whitmore Vale, nr Hindhead, Surrey. Only the tail assembly about 3ft forward of the fin survived relatively undamaged.
21/22.1.44	XI 85 Sqn He177A-3 6m SE of Hastings	F/O C. K. Nowell-F/Sgt F. Randall (He177 of 2./KG40).
21/22.1.44	XIII HK380 'Y' 488 Sqn Do217M-1	F/L J. A. S. Hall-F/O J. P. W. Cairns 13m off Dungeness +Ju88A-14 Sellindge, Kent.

Date	Claim	Crew
21/22.1.44	VI 'D' 418 Sqn Bf110 20m SW Wunsdorf	1/Lt J. F. Luma US-F/O A. Eckert.
27.1.44	VI 418 Sqn Ju88 Clermont-Farrand a/f	F/L J. R.F. Johnson RCAF.
27.1.44	JuW34 x 2 10m SE Bourges	F/L J. R.F. Johnson RCAF.
27.1.44	VI418 Ju88 Clermont-Farrand a/f	P/O J. T. Caine RCAF-P/O E. W. Boal RCAF.
27.1.44	VI418 JuW34 x 2 10m SE Bourges	P/O J. T. Caine RCAF-P/O E. W. Boal RCAF.
27.1.44	VI 'R' 418 Sqn Fw200 SE Avord a/f	F/L C. C. Scherf RAAF.
28/29.1.44	XIII HK432 410 Sqn Ju88.	F/O S. A. Hibbert-F/O G. D. Moody.
28/29.1.44	XIII HK397 96 Sqn Ju88 nr Biddenden	F/O H. E. White DFC-F/O M. S. Allen DFC.
28/29.1.44	II HJ941 'X' 141 Bf109 nr Berlin	F/O N. Munro-F/O A R. Hurley.
28/29.1.44	II HJ644 239 Sqn Bf110 near Berlin	F/L G. J. Rice-F/O J. G. Rogerson.
30/31.1.44	II HJ712 141 Sqn Bf110 near Berlin	S/L J. A. H. Cooper-F/L R. D. Connolly. Bf110G-4
30/31.1.44	II HJ711 'P' 169 Sqn Bf110 Brandenburg area	W/Nr 740081 D5+LB of *Stab III/NJG3*, which crashed at Werneuchen, 20 kms E of Berlin. Oblt. Karl Loeffelmaan, pilot KIA. Fw. Karl Bareiss, radar op, and Ofw. Oscar Bickert, both WIA, baled out.
3/4.2.44	XIII 'P' 85 Sqn Do217 20m E The Naze	F/O H. B. Thomas-W/O C. B. Hamilton.
3/4.2.44	XIII 410 Sqn Do217	F/O E. S. P. Fox RCAF-F/O C. D. Sibett RCAF.
3/4.2.44	XIII HK463 410 Sqn Do217 off Orfordness.	
3/4.2.44	XIII HK367 488 Sqn Do217 off Foulness Pt	F/Sgt C. J. Vlotman-Sgt J. L. Wood.
4/5.2.44	VI 605 Sqn *UEA (Prob)* Chievres	W/C B. R. O'B Hoare DSO DFC*-W/O J. F. Potter.
5/6.2.44	II HJ707 'B' 169 Sqn Bf110 North Sea off England	P/O W.H. Miller-P/O F.C. Bone.
8.2.44	II 157 Sqn Bv.222 Lake Biscarosse	S/L H. E. Tappin DFC-F/O I. H. Thomas.
12.2.44	II 687 'A' 157 Sqn Fw200 *Instep* Criegal	F/O R. D. Doleman-F/L McAllister.
12/13.2.44	29 Sqn Me410 off Fecamp.	

185

Date	Type Serial Sqn Enemy A/c details	Pilot-Navigator/Radar Op
13.2.44	VI 'X' 418 Sqn He177 3m S Bordeaux	1/Lt J. F. Luma US-F/O C. Finlayson.
13/14.2.44	XIII HK426 96 Sqn Ju88 nr Whitstable	W/C E. D. Crew-W/O W. R. Croysdill.
13/14.2.44	XIII HK466 Ju88S-1 nr Romford	S/L J. D. Somerville-F/O G. D. Robinson. Ju88S-1 Z6+HH of I/KG66.
13/14.2.44	XIII HK429 410 Sqn Ju188 10-20m off E. Anglia	F/O R. D. Schultz-F/O V. A. Williams.
15/16.2.44	II DZ726 'Z' 141 Sqn He177 Berlin	F/O H. E. White-F/O M. Allen.
18/19.2.44	VI 'S' 605 Sqn Ju188 Brussels-Melsbroek	F/O l. Williams-F/O F Hogg.
18/19.2.44	VI 418 Sqn 2 x Me410 Juvincourt a/f	S/L R. A. Kipp DFC RCAF-F/L P. Huletsky RCAF.
19.2.44	II 157 Sqn 1 Ju290 on *Instep* patrol	F/L R. J. Coombs-F/O G. H. Scobie/F/L R. D. Doleman-F/L L. Scholefield.
19/20.2.44	XIII HK396 96 Sqn Me410 S of Dungeness.	
20/21.2.44	II DZ270 239 Sqn Bf110 near Stuttgart	F/O T. Knight-F/O D. P. Doyle.
20/21.2.44	XVII HK285 25 Sqn Ju188 E Essex.	P/O J. R. Brockbank-P/O D. McCausland. Ju188E-1 U5+LN flown by Lt. Ewald Bohe of 5/KG2. The Ju188E, blazing furiously, commenced a deep death dive through the clouds to crash at Park Farm, Wickham St. Paul, Essex. The time of the 'kill', 22.03 hrs, was logged; the first 'kill' attributed to a Mosquito NF.XVII. Bohe, Ofw. Karl Birtgen (BO), Uffz. Günther Güldner (BF) Uffz. Wilhelm Pyttel (BM) and Gftr. Hugo Schweitzer (BS) KIA.
20/21.2.44	XVII HK255 25 Sqn Do217K-10 50m E Lowestoft	F/L J. Singleton DFC-F/O W. G. Haslam. Victim either Do217K-1 U5+AR of 7./KG2, which was shot down at 22.36 hrs Oblt. Wolfgang Brendel, Fw. Bruno Preker, Ofw. Bruno Schneider and Uffz. Heinz Grudßus all posted as 'Missing'. Or, Do217M1 of 9.KG2. Uffz.

Date	Target	Crew
20/21.2.44	XVII 85 Sqn Ju188 (Prob) Lydd	Walter Schmidt, (pilot) Uffz. Fritz Frese, Ogefr. Siegfried Briesning and Ogefr. Heinz Bodzien (all KIA).
22/23.2.44	XVII HK285 25 Sqn He177A-3 nr Yoxford.	S/L B. J. Thwaites DFC-F/O W. P. Clemo DFM*. F/L W. Baillie-F/O Simpson. He177A-3 of 3./KG100. Ofw Wolfgang Ruppe (Flugzeugführer (pilot), Uffz. Ernst Werner Bordschutze (gunner), Uffz. Freidrich Beck, Bordfunker (radio operator) Uffz. Georg Lobenz, Kampf Beobachter (observer), Bordschutzen Obgefr. Georg Markgraf, & Obgefr. Bordwart (ground crew) KIA. Emil Imm, Heck Schutz (tail gunner) survived.
22/23.2.44	XVII 'Y' 85 Sqn Me410 off Dungeness	F/L B. Burbridge-F/L F. S. Skelton.
22/23.2.44	XVII 85 Sqn Me410 35m S Dungeness	F/O E. R. Hedgecoe-P/O J. R. Whitham.
22/23.2.44	XIII HK370 96 Sqn Me410 W Uckfield	S/L G. L. Caldwell- F/O Rawling.
22/23.2.44	XIII HK521 410 Sqn Ju88A-4 N Sea Ju188E-1 nr Rochford	S/L C. A. S. Anderson-F/Sgt C. F. A. Bodard. S/L C. A. S. Anderson-F/Sgt C. F. A. Bodard. Flt Off B. F. Miller USAAF-F/O J. C. Winlaw RCAF.
22/23.2.4	V/I 605 Sqn E/a Melsbroek	
23/24.2.4	XVII 25 Sqn Do217 off E. Anglia.	
23/24.2.44	XVII HK293 25 Sqn Ju188 off Yarmouth.	
23/24.2.44	XIII HK370 96 Sqn Me410 at Sea.	
23/24.2.44	XVII 'O' 85 Sqn Ju88 (Prob) Beachy Head	W/C J. Cunningham DSO* DFC*-F/O C. F. Rawnsley DFC DFM*.
23/24.2.44	VI 605 Sqn Ju88 Chievres airfield	F/O L. Williams-F/O F Hogg.
24/25.2.4	VI NS830 'G' 418 Sqn Me410 Würzburg a/f	F/L D. A. MacFadyen RCAF-F/L Wright.
24/25.2.44	VI 'R' 418 Sqn 2 x Ju88 Ansbach a/f	F/L C. C. Scherf RAAF.
24/25.2.44	XIII HK413 29 Sqn Do217M Dorking, Surrey	S/L C. Kirkland-F/O Raspin.
24/25.2.44	XIII HK515 29 Sqn Ju188E Framfield, Sussex	F/O W. W. Provan-W/O Nicol.

Date	Type Serial Sqn Enemy A/c details	Pilot-Navigator/Radar Op
24/25.2.44	XIII HK422 29 Sqn Ju88A-4+Ju188	F/L R. C. Pargeter-F/L R. L. Fell. Ju88A-4 of 8./KG6 was downed at Withyham, Sussex. Ju188 fell at Thame.
24/25.2.44	XII HK168 29 Sqn Do217M Willesborough, Kent Me4l0 (Prob)	F/O J. E. Barry-F/O G. Hopkins . F/O J. E. Barry-F/O G. Hopkins .
24/25.2.44	XII He177 30-35 mls S of Ford-Beachey Hd area	F/L E. Cox-W/O Kershaw.
24/25.2.44	XIII HK370 96 Sqn Me410 off Beachy Head	F/L D. L. Ward-F/L E. D. Eyles.
24/25.2.44	XIII HK415 96 Sqn He177 (probable) Sussex	S/L A. Parker-Rees-F/L Bennett.
24/25.2.44	XII HK228 488 Sqn He177A-3 Lamberhurst.	F/L P. F. L. Hall-F/O R. D. Marriott. He177A-3 of 3./KG).
24/25.2.44	FIU He177 at Sea (Prob)	
25/26.2.44	II DZ254 169 Sqn Bf110 SW Mannheim	F/L R. G. Woodman-F/O P. Kemmis.
25/26.2.44	XVII HK293 25 Sqn Ju188 off Yarmouth.	
26.2.44	VI 418 Sqn Go242 St Yan	S/L H. D. Cleveland RCAF-F/Sgt F. Day DFM.
26.2.44	VI 'F' 418 Sqn Go242/He111Z Dole/Tavaux a/f	F/L C. C. Scherf RAAF.
29.2/1.3.44	XVII 'S' 85 Sqn He177 English Channel.	
29.2/1.3.44	XIII HK469 96 Sqn Fw190 off Dieppe.	
?.44	VI 418 Sqn 4 x EA	F/L S. H. R. Cotterill DFC-F/L McKenna.
1/2.3.4	XIII HK499 96 Sqn Me410 50m SE Beachy Head	F/L W. J. Gough-F/L Matson.
1/2.3.44	XIII HK377 151 Sqn He177A-3 Cr. Hammer Wood	W/C G.H. Goodman-F/O W.F.E. Thomas.
1/2.3.44	XIII MM448 151 Sqn Ju188 at Sea	S/L Harrison.
1/2.3.44	XIII HK232 151 Sqn Ju88 at Sea	F/L Stevens.
5.3.44	VI LR364 'E' 613 He177 Chateaudun	W/C J. R. D. Braham DSO* DFC**-F/L W. J. Gregory DFC.
5.3.44	VI 515 He177 Bretigny? Melun	W/C E. F. F. Lambert-F/L E. W. M. Morgan

Date	Aircraft / Unit	Crew / Notes
5/6.3.44	VI 'J' 605 Sqn Fw190+2 Me410 Gardelegen a/f	DFM He177A-3 Wrk.Nr. 332214 5J+RL of 3./KG100 cr nr Chateaudun/France. Lt. Wilhelm Werner (pilot); Uffz. Kolemann Schoegl (WOp); Uffz. Gustav Birkebmaier (Flt.Eng); Uffz. Alfred Zwieselsberger (AG); Uffz. Josef Kerres (AG) all KIA.
6.3.44	VI 'Y' 418 Sqn Fw190 Pau	F/L A. D. Wagner DFC-F/O E. T. Orringe.
14/15.3.44	XIII HK406 96 Sqn Ju88A-4 Hildenborough Ju188 Channel	1/Lt J. F. Luma US-F/O C. Finlayson.
14/15.3.44	XIII HK466 410 Sqn Ju88 off East Coast.	F/L N. S. Head-F/O A. C. Andrews.
14/15.3.44	XIII HK521 410 Sqn Ju88A-4 Hildenborough	F/L N S Head-F/O A C Andrews .
14/15.3.44	XIII HK432 410 Sqn Ju88 off East Coast	1/Lt A. A. Harrington US-Sgt D. G. Tongue (Ju88A-14 B3+CK of 2./KG54.
14/15.3.44	XIII MM476 'V' 410 Sqn Ju188E-1	S/L E. N. Bunting DFC-F/L C. P. Reed DFC (Ju188E-l U5+BM, flown by Lt Horst Becker of 4./KG6 broke up in the air and crashed in flames at White House Farm, Great Leighs, nr Chelmsford. Becker, Uffz. G. Bartolain, Uffz. A. Lange, Uffz. G. Goecking and Ofw. H. Litschke, killed).
14/15.3.44	XIII 488 Sqn Ju188E-1.	S/L W. P. Green DFC-F/Sgt A. R. Grimstone DFM.
14/15.3.44	XIII NK523 410 Sqn Ju88	F/L J. Singleton DFC-W/O W. G. Haslam (Ju88 of KG30).
14/15.3.44	XVII HK255 25 Sqn Ju88 E Southwold	F/O H. E. White DFC-F/O M. S. Allen DFC.
18/19.3.44	II HJ710 'T' 141 Sqn 2 x Ju88 nr Frankfurt	F/O J. C. N. Forshaw-P/O F. S. Folley. Ju88C-6 Wr/Nr. 750014 R4+CS of 8./NJG2, shot down by Mosquito of 141 Squadron, cr at Arheilgen near Darmstadt, 2.5 kms
18/19.3.44	II DZ761 'C' 141 Sqn Ju88 nr Frankfurt	

Date	Type Serial Sqn Enemy A/c details	Pilot-Navigator/Radar Op
19/20.3.44	XVII HK255 25 Sqn 3 x Ju88 50m NNE Cromer	S of Frankfurt. Ofw. Otto Müller (pilot); Ogefr. Erhard Schimsal (radar op); Gefr. Gunter Hanke (AG) all KIA.
19/20.3.44	XVII HK278 25 Sqn Do217 NNW Cromer	F/O J. Singleton DFC-F/O W. G. Haslam.
	He177A-3 off Skegness	F/L D. H. Greaves DFC-F/O T. M. Robbins DFC.
19/20.3.44	XII HK119 'J' 307 He177 nr Humber Estuary	F/L D. H. Greaves DFC-F/O T. M. Robbins DFC.
19/20.3.44	XII 264 Sqn Do217M-1 Cr. Alford, Lincs	P/O J. Bruchoci-F/L Ziolkowski.
19/20.3.44	VI 'U' 418 Sqn JuW34+Ju52/3m Luxeuil a/f	F/O R. L. J. Barbour-F/O O. Paine.
21/22.3.44	XVII HK322 25 Sqn Ju188 35m SE Lowestoft	1/Lt J. F. Luma US -F/O C. Finlayson.
	Ju88 25m SE Lowestoft	F/L R.L. Davies-F/O B. Bent.
21/22.3.44	XIII HK456 410 Sqn Ju88A-4 Latchington, Essex	F/O S. B. Huppert-P/O J. S. Christie (Ju88A-4 of 4./KG30).
21/22.3.44	XIII HK365 488 Sqn Ju188 at Sea	F/Sgt C. J. Vlotman-Sgt J. E. Wood.
	Ju88 nr Herne Bay	F/Sgt C. J. Vlotman-Sgt J. E. Wood.
21/22.3.44	XIII HK380 'Y' 488 Sqn Ju88A-14	F/L J. A. S. Hall-F/O J.P.W. Cairns. Ju88A-14 3E+GS of 8./KG6 from Melsbroek fell on Earls Colne airfield where the aircraft and one of its 500-kg HE bombs exploded, damaging three B-26 Marauders of the 323rd BG, US 9th AF.
21/22.3.44	XIII MM476 488 Sqn Ju88A-4+Ju188E1	S/L E. Bunting DFC-F/L C. P. Reed DFC. Ju88A-4 4D+AT flown by Ofw. Nikolaus Mayer of 9./KG30 from Varélbusch. cr at Blacklands Hall, Cavendish, Suffolk where the bomber's fuel tanks exploded. Fw. K. Maser and Fw. Karl-Heinz Elmhorst had baled out and were taken prisoner. Mayer and Ofw. W. Szyska died in the crash. Ju188E-1 3E+BK of 2./KG6, flown by Lt. G.

Lahl hit the ground and exploded near Butlers Farm at Shopland, Essex shortly after 0110 hrs. Lahl, Uffz J. Fromm, Uffz R. Budrat and Obgefr Schiml were killed. Uffz E. Kosch baled out, injured, and was taken prisoner.

Date	Aircraft / Location	Crew
21/22.3.44	XVII HK359 456 Sqn Fw190 off S Coast.	F/L K. A. Roediger RAAF-F/L R. J. H. F. Dobson.
21/22.3.44	XVII HK297 'V' 456 Sqn Ju88 Rye	F/L J. C. Surman-F/Sgt C. E. Weston.
21/22.3.44	XIII 604 Sqn Ju88A-4 Chelmsford	S/L E. W. Kinchin-F/L D. Sellers.
22/23.3.44	II 239 Sqn Bf110 Frankfurt	F/L N. S. Head-F/O A. C. Andrews.
22/23.3.44	XIII MM451 96 Sqn Fw190 SE of Pevensey	W/C K. M. Hampshire DSO RAAF-F/L T. Condon.
22/23.3.44	XVII HK286 'A' 456 Sqn Ju88A-4 nr Arundel	S/L B. J. Thwaites DFC-F/O W. P. Clemo DFM*.
23/24.3.44	XII VY-R 85 Sqn Fw190 off Hastings	W/C J.R.D. Braham DSO* DFC**-S/L Robertson.
24.3.44	VI LR374 'W' 613 Sqn Ju52/3m 15m S Aalborg Ju64 6m S Aalborg	W/C J.R.D. Braham DSO* DFC**-S/L Robertson.
24/25.3.44	XVII HK293 25 Sqn Ju188E-1	F/L V. P. Luinthune DFC-F/O A. B. Cumbers DFC (Ju188E-1, U5+AN, flown by Uffz. Martin Hanf of 5./KG2. Hanf and his four crew died in a watery grave 45 miles SE of Lowestoft.
24/25.3.44	XII 'O' 85 Sqn Ju188 off Hastings	F/O E. R. Hedgecoe-F/O N. L. Bamford.
24/25.3.44	XVII 'M' 85 Sqn Do217+Ju88 Straits	F/L B. Burbridge-F/L F. S. Skelton.
24/25.3.44	XVII HK286 'A' 456 Sqn Ju88 Walberton, Sussex	W/C K. M. Hampshire DSO RAAF-F/L T. Condon.
24/25.3.44	II DD717 'M' 141 Sqn Fw190 Berlin	F/L H. C. Kelsey DFC*-F/O E. M. Smith DFC DFM.
24/25.3.44	VI 605 Sqn Bf109 Stendal-Burg	W/C B. R. O'B Hoare DSO DFC*-F/O Robert C. Muir.
27/28.3.44	XIII HK425 Sqn 96 Sqn Fw190 at Sea.	
27/28.3.44	XVII HK260 219 Sqn Ju88 Hestar Combe	S/L Ellis-F/L Craig.
27/28.3.44	XVII HK286 'A' 456 Sqn Ju88A-4 nr Beer	W/C K. M. Hampshire DSO RAAF-F/L T. Condon.

Date	Type Serial Sqn Enemy A/c details	Pilot-Navigator/Radar Op
	Ju88A-14 nr Ilminster	W/C K. M. Hampshire DSO RAAF-F/L T. Condon.
27/28.3.44	XVI HK323 Ju88 nr Beer	S/L B. Howard-F/O J. R. Ross.
30/31.3.44	II DZ661 239 Sqn Ju88 Nuremberg	F/Sgt J. Campbell DFM-F/Sgt R. Phillips. Ju88C-6 W/.Nr. 360272 D5+ of 4./NJG3, cr 10 kms SW of Bayreuth. Oblt. Ruprecht Panzer (pilot) WIA; radar op & AG baled out safely.
4.4.44	VI LR355 'H' 613 Sqn Bucker 131 St Jean-d'Angely	W/C J. R. D. Braham DSO* DFC**-F/L W. J. Gregory DFC.
5.4.44	VI 'F' 418 Sqn Bf110/Fw58 Lyon	F/L C. C. Scherf RAAF.
6.4.44	XIII MM448 151 Sqn Ju88 off St Nazaire	W/C G. H. Goodman-F/O W.F. Thomas DFM.
11/12.4.44	II DZ263 239 Sqn Do217 Aachen	S/L N. E. Reeves DFC DSO-W/O A. A. O'Leary DFC** DFM.
12.4.44	VI 418 Sqn Fw190 12m SE Verdun	F/L C. M. Jasper-F/L O. A. J. Martin.
13.4.44	VI LR313 'B' (613 Sqn) He111/Fw58 Esbjerg/Aalborg	W/C J. R. D Braham DSO*DFC** F/L W. J. Gregory DFC.
13/14.4.44	XIII MM497 96 Sqn Ju88 nr Le Touquet	P/O Allen? DFM.
13/14.4.44	XIII HK497 96 Sqn Ju88 off Dungeness	S/L A. Parker-Rees-F/L Bennett.
13/14.4.44	XIII HK415 96 Sqn Me410 at Sea	S/L A. Parker-Rees-F/L Bennett.
13/14.4.44	XIII Me410 off Dungeness	F/L D. L. Ward-F/L E. D. Eyles.
14.4.44	VI 418 Sqn 2 x Ju52/3m Kattegat	P/O J. T. Caine RCAF-P/O E. W. Boal RCAF.
14.4.44	VI 418 Sqn 2 x Ju52/3m Kattegat	S/L R. A. Kipp DFC RCAF-F/L P. Huletsky RCAF.
16.4.44	VI 418 Sqn Caudmon Goeland Luxeuil a/f	F/L C. M. Jasper-F/L O. A. J. Martin.
18/19.4.44	XVII 'B' 85 Sqn Ju88 Sandgate	F/L B. Burbridge-F/L F. S. Skelton.
18/19.4.44	XVII HK349 'R' 85 Sqn Ju188E-1 nr Dymchurch	W/C C. M. Miller DFC**- Capt L. Lövestad RNWAF

18/19.4.44	XIII MM499 96 Sqn Me410-1 Brighton	(5./KG2 Ju188E-1 U5+KN, piloted by Fw. Helmuth Richter).
		W/C E. D. Crew DFC*- W/O W. R. Croysdill. Me410A-1 of 1./KG51. Oblt. Richard Pohl (k) Fw. Wilhelm Schubert (k) KG2)?
18/19.4.44	XIII MM495 96 Sqn Ju884-4 nr Margate	S/L W. P. Green DFC-F/Sgt A. R. Grimstone DFM.
18/19.4.44	XIII 96 Sqn Ju88A-4 Cr. nr Cranbrook	P/O Allen-F/Sgt Patterson .
18/19.4.44	XIII MM551 'X' 488 Sqn Ju88 60m E Bradwell	F/L J. A. S. Hall-F/O J. P. W. Cairns.
18/19.4.44	XIII MM813 488 Sqn Ju88 at Sea	W/O R. F. D. Bourke.
18/19.4.44	XVII HK237 25 Sqn Me410 off Southwold	F/L R. M. Carr-F/L Saunderson (Ju188E-1 U5+DM of 4./KG2 flown by Hptm. Helmuth Eichbaum.
18/19.4.44	XIII MM456 'D' 410 Sqn He177	F/O S. B. Huppert-P/O J. S. Christie (He177 of 3./KG100 flown by Fw. Heinz Reis, which fell near Saffron Walden.
18/19.4.44	XIII 410 Sqn Ju88	F/O Snowdon-F/Sgt McLeod.
18/19.4.44	XVII 456 Sqn Me410-1 nr Horsham	F/L C. L. Brooks-W/O R. J. Forbes.
18/19.4.44	II DD799 169 Sqn Bf110 Compãigne	F/O R. G. Woodman-F/O P. Kemmis.
20.4.44	XVII HK354 25 Sqn Jul88 at Sea.	
20.4.44	XIII HK480 264 Sqn He17740m ENE Spurn Hd	F/O Corre-P/O C. A. Bines.
20.4.44	XIII MM446 'Q' 151 Sqn JuW34 N Biscarosse	W/C G. H. Goodman-F/O W.F. Thomas.
20/21.4.44	II DD732 'S' 141 Sqn Do217 N of Paris	F/L H. E. White DFC*-F/L M. S. Allen DFC*. Either Do217N-1 W/Nr. 51517 of 5/NJG4, which cr nr Meulan N of Paris. Ofw. Karl Kaiser, pilot WIA, and Uffz. Johannes Nagel, radar op WIA, baled out; Gefr. Sigmund Zinser (AG) KIA. Or Do217E-5 Wrk.Nr. 5558 6N+EP of 6./KG100, crash place u/k. Fw. Heinz Fernau

Date	Type Serial Sqn Enemy A/c details	Pilot-Navigator/Radar Op
20/21.4.44	II 169 Sqn Bf110 Ruhr	(pilot); Hptm. Willi Scholl (observer); Uffz. Josef Bach (WOp); Ofw. Fritz Wagner (Flt.Eng) all MIA.
22/23.4.44	II W4085 169 Sqn Bf110 Bonn area	F/L G. D. Cremer-F/O B. C. Farrell.
22/23.4.44	II W4076 169 Sqn Bf110 Cologne	F/L R. G. Woodman-F/O P. Kemmis.
23/24.4.44	II HJ712 'R' 141 Sqn Fw190 Flensburg	P/O W. H. Miller-P/O F.C. Bone.
23/24.4.44	XVII HK355 125 Sqn Ju88A-14 4m S Melksham	F/L G. J. Rice-P/O R. S. Mallett.
23/24.4.44	XVII HK299 125 Sqn off SW Coast.	W/C E. G. Barwell DFC-F/L D. A. Haigh.
23/24.4.44	XVII HK301 125 Sqn off SW Coast.	
23/24.4.44	XVII HK286 'A' 456 Ju88 in sea, nr Swanage	W/C K. M. Hampshire DSO RAAF-F/L T. Condon.
25/26.4.44	XVII 'B' 85 Sqn Me410 S Selsey Bill	F/L B. Burbridge-F/L F. S. Skelton.
25/26.4.44	XVII HK299 125 Sqn Do217at Sea.	
25/26.4.44	XVII HK353 456 Sqn Ju88 S Selsey	F/L K. A. Roediger RAAF-F/L R. J. H. F. Dobson.
26.4.44	VI 515 Sqn UEA Gilze a/f	S/L H. B. Martin-F/O Smith.
26.4.44	VI 515 Sqn UEA Le Culot a/f	W/O T. S. Ecclestone-F/Sgt J. H. Shimmon.
26.4.44	VI 515 Sqn UEA Brussels Evere	W/O T. S. Ecclestone-F/Sgt J. H. Shimmon.
26/27.4.44	II W4078 239 Sqn Bf110 Essen	F/O W. R. Breithaupt-F/O J. A. Kennedy.
26/27.4.44	XVII HK286 'A' 456 Sqn Ju88 at Sea.	
26/27.4.44	XVII HK297 'V' 456 Sqn Ju88 at Sea.	
26/27.4.44	XVII HK264 456 Sqn Ju88 at Sea.	
26/27.4.44	XVII HK346 'D' 125 Sqn Ju188 S St Catherines Pt	W/C J. G. Topham DFC*-F/L H. W. Berridge DFC.
27/28.4.44	II W4076 169 Sqn Bf110 SE of Strasbourg	P/O P. L Johnson-P/O M. Hopkins.
27/28.4.44	II 239 Sqn Bf110/Ju88 Montzon-Aulnoye	F/O R. Depper-F/O G. C. Follis.

27/28.4.44	II DD622 239 Sqn Bf110 Montzon-Aulnoye	S/L N. E. Reeves DSO DFC-W/O A. A. O'Leary DFC** DFM.
27/28.4.44	VI 605 Sqn UEA (Prob) Couron	F/O R. E. Lelong RNZAF-P/O J. A. McLaren.
27/28.4.44	VI 418 Sqn UEA Toul /Croix de Metz	S/L H. D. Cleveland RCAF-F/Sgt F. Day DFM.
28/29.4.44	XVII HK346 'D' 125 Sqn Ju88 off Cherbourg	W/C J. G. Topham DFC*-F/L H. W. Berridge DFC.
28/29.4.44	XVII HK286 'A' 456 Sqn Do217(Prob) (86m off Curmington).	W/C K. M. Hampshire DSO RAAF-F/L T. Condon
29.4.44	VI 22 'H' 613 Fw190 NW Poitiers	W/C J. R. D. Braham DSO* DFC**-F/L W. J. Gregory DFC.
29/30.4.44	XII 'O' 406 Sqn 2 x Do217 off Plymouth	W/C D. J. Williams DFC RCAF-F/O Kirkpatrick DFM.
2.5.44	VI 'X' 418 Sqn Ju86P (+4 on ground) Griefswald	F/O C. C. Scherf RAAF.
2/3.5.44	VI 418 Sqn 4x Fw190 SW Saarbourg	S/L R. A. Kipp DFC RCAF-F/L P. Huletsky RCAF.
4.5.44	XIII MM446 'Q' 151 Sqn 4 x He111 Dijon area	W/C G. H. Goodman-F/O W.F. Thomas.
6/7.5.44	VI 605 Sqn Me210 St Dizier airfield	W/C N. J. Starr DFC.
7.5.44	VI 'G' 21 Sqn Ju188 Roskilde, 30m N Copenhagen	W/C J. R. D. Braham DSO* DFC**-F/L D. Walsh DFC.
8/9.5.44	II DD709 169 Sqn Bf110 Braine-le-Comte	S/L R. G. Woodman-F/O P. Kemmis. Bf110 of I./NJG4 crewed by Lt. Wolfgang Martsaller and his radar operator/air gunner who had taken off from Florennes at 03.00 hrs shot down Lancaster ND587 of 405 Squadron before their combat with Woodman. The Bf110 belly-landed in a field. Marstaller was KIA in a crash at St. Trond aerodrome in August 1944.
8.5.44	VI 605 Sqn Ju88 Creilsham	F/O R. E. Lelong RNZAF-P/O J. A. McLaren.
10/11.5.44	II W4078 239 Sqn Bf110 Near Courtrai	F/O V. Bridges DFC-F/Sgt D. G. Webb DFM. Bf110 3C+F1 W/Nr 740179 of I./NJG4.which cr at Ellezelles, Belgium. Oblt. Heinrich Schulenberg, pilot, and Ofw. Hermann Meyer, radar operator, bailed out near

Date	Type Serial Sqn Enemy A/c details	Pilot-Navigator/Radar Op
		Flobeq. Meyer was wounded and badly concussed and spent three weeks in hospital and four more weeks at home.
11/12.5.44	II HJ726 'Z' 141 Sqn Ju88 N of Amiens	F/L H. E. White DFC*-F/L M. S. Allen DFC*.
11/12.5.44	II DZ240 'H' 141 Sqn Ju88 SW of Brussels	F/L L. J. G. LeBoutte-F/O R. S. Mallett. Ju88 of 6./NJG2. Wilhelm Simonsohn, radar op & air gunner all baled out. A/c cr. Brussels.
12.5.44	VI NS885 'B' 21 Sqn Fw190 Herning, 10m WSW Aalborg	W/C J. R. D. Braham DSO* DFC*-F/L W. J. Gregory DFC.
12/13.5.44	II W4078 239 Sqn Bf110 Hasselt-Louvain	F/O W. R. Breithaupt-F/O J. A. Kennedy DFM.
12/13.5.44	II W4092 239 Sqn Ju88 Belgium	F/O V. Bridges DFC-F/Sgt D. G. Webb DFM. Ju88C-6 W/Nr 750922 D5+ of 5./NJG3 cr at Hoogcruts nr. Maastricht. Uffz. Josef Polzer, Ogefr. Hans Klünder, radar op, KIA. Gefr. Hans Becker (AG) WIA.
14.5.44	VI 418 Sqn He111 Nancy-Croix Metz	F/L C. M. Jasper-F/L O. A. J. Martin.
14/15.5.44	XVII HK325 125 Sqn Ju88 off Cherbourg.	
14/15.5.44	XVII HK318 125 Sqn Me410 N of Portland Bill.	
14/15.5.44	III 'D' 406 Sqn Ju88 20m SE Portland	W/C R. C. Fumerton DFC*.
14/15.5.44	XVII HK246 456 Sqn Ju188A2 Cr. Larkhill, Wilts	F/O A. S. McEvoy-F/O M. N. Austin.
14/15.5.44	XIII MM551 'X' 488 Sqn Ju188A2 (Henstridge, Somerset)	F/L J. A. S. Hall-F/O J.P W. Cairns
14/15.5.44	XIII HK381 488 Sqn Ju88 at Sea Do217K1 Cr. nr Yeovilton	F/O R. W. Jeffs-F/O E. Spedding. F/O R. W. Jeffs-F/O E. Spedding.
14/15.5.44	XIII HK527 604 Do217 at Sea	F/L J. C. Surman-P/O C. E. Weston.
14/15.5.44	XIII 264 Sqn Ju188 nr Alton	F/L C. M. Ramsay DFC-F/O J. A. Edgar DFM (KIA).

14/15.5.44	VI 418 Sqn He177 Mont de Marson a/f	S/L R. A. Kipp DFC RCAF-F/L P. Huletsky RCAF.
15/16.5.44	XIII 264 Sqn Me410 Over the Channel	S/L P. B. Elwell-F/O F. Ferguson.
15/16.5.44	XIII MM526 604 Ju188 SW Isle of Wight	W/C M. H. Constable-Maxwell DFC.
15/16.5.44	II DZ478? 169 Sqn Bf110/2 x Ju88 Cuxhaven area	P/O W. H. Miller-P/O F.C. Bone.
15/16.5.44	XVII HK297 456 Sqn Ju884-4 Medstead	F/O D. W. Arnold-F/O J. B. Stickley.
16.5.44	VI 418 Sqn He111 Kiel Bay area	S/L H. D. Cleveland RCAF-F/Sgt F. Day DFM (KIA).
16.5.44	VI 'T' 418 Sqn He111/Fw190/ He177/Hs 123/Ju86P	S/L C. C. Scherf DFC* RAAF.
19/20.5.44	VI 605 Sqn He219 Florennes	W/C N. J. Starr DFC-P/O J. Irvine.
22/23.5.44	XVII HK316 125 Sqn Ju188 S St Catherine's Pt	F/O K. T. A. O'Sullivan.
22/23.5.44	XVII HK252 125 Sqn Ju88 nr Southampton.	
22/23.5.44	XVII HK286 'A' 456 Sqn Ju88 S Isle of Wight	W/C K. M. Hampshire DSO DFC RAAF-F/L T. Condon.
22/23.5.44	XVII HK353 'M' 456 Sqn Ju88 nr Southampton.	
22/23.5.44	II DZ309 239 Sqn Bf110 Dortmund	F/L D. L. Hughes-F/O R. H. Perks.
22/23.5.44	II 169 Sqn Bf110 Groningen area	W/C N. B. R. Bromley OBE-F/L P. Truscott. Bf110G-4 W/Nr 720050 D5+ of 3.NJG3 cr at Hoogeveen S of Groningen. Fw. Franz Müllebner (FF), Uffz. Alfons Josten (radar op); Gefr. Karl Rademacher (AG) all WIA. & bailed out.
24/25.5.44	II DZ265 239 Sqn Bf110 Aachen	F/L D. J. Raby DFC-F/Sgt S. J. Flint DFM.
24/25.5.44	II DZ309 239 Sqn Bf110 Aachen	F/L D. L. Hughes-F/O R. H. Perks. Bf110G-4 Wrk Nr 730106 2Z+AR of 7./NJG6 poss shot down by either of these two crews at 02.30 hrs in forest between Zweifall & Mulartshuette SE of Aachen. Oblt. Helmut Schulte (FF) baled out, Uffz. Georg Sandvoss (radar op) KIA, Uffz. Hans Fischer (AG) baled out. Bfl10G-4 W/Nr. 720387 2Z+HR of 7./NJG6, poss

Date	Type Serial Sqn Enemy A/c details	Pilot-Navigator/Radar Op
		shot down by Raby/Flint or Hughes/Perks, cr at 02.35 hrs at the Wesertalsperre near Dipen, S of Aachen. Crew: Uffz. Oskar Voelkel (pilot); Uffz. Karl Hautzenberger (radar op); Uffz. Guenter Boehxne (AG) all baled out.
24/25.5.44	II DZ297 239 Sqn Ju88 15m ESE of Bonn	F/O W. R. Breithaupt-F/O J. A. Kennedy.
24/25.5.44	XVII HK345 219 Sqn Ju88 (Prob)	F/O D. T. Hull (55m E Orfordness).
27.5.44	XVII HK346 456 Sqn Me410 nr Cherbourg.	
27/28.5.44	II DD622 239 Sqn Bf110F Aachen	S/L N. E. Reeves DSO DFC-P/O A. A. O'Leary DFC** DFM. Bfll0F W/Nr. 140032 G9+CR of 7./NJG1 cr at Spannum in Eriesland Province/Neth. at 01.15 hrs. Uffz. Joachim Tank (pilot), slightly wounded; Uffz. Günther Schroeder (radar op), KIA; Uffz. Heinz Elwers (AG), KIA.
27/28.5.44	II HJ941 'X' 141 Sqn Bf109 W of Aachen	F/L H. E. White DFC*-F/L M. S. Allen DFC*.
28.5.44	XIII HK462 'E' 410 Sqn Ju88 nr Lille.	
28.5.44	VI 605 Sqn Ju52 off Sylt	F/L Welch-F/L L. Page DFM.
28/29.5.44	XVII HK257 25 Sqn Me410 50m off Cromer	W/C C. M. Wight-Boycott DSO-F/L D. W. Reid (Me410 Hornisse 9K+KP, of KG51, flown by Fw. Dietrich (KIA) and Uffz. Schaknies (KIA).
29.5.44	XVII HK286'A' 456 Sqn Me410	
31.5/1.6.44	II DZ297 239 Sqn Bf110 Near Trappes	F/O V. Bridges DFC-F/Sgt D.C. Webb DFM.
31.5/1.6.44	II DZ256 'U' 239 Sqn Bf110 West of Paris	F/L D. Welfare DFC*-F/O D. B. Bellis DFC*.
1/2.6.44	II DZ265 239 Sqn Bf110 Northern France	F/L T. L. Wright-P/O L. Ambery.
1/2.6.44	XIX 'K' 85 Sqn Ju88 (Prob) Ipswich	F/L B. A. Burbridge DFC-F/L F. S. Skelton DFC.
3/4.6.44	XVII HK248 219 Sqn He219 Dutch Islands	F/O D. T. Hull.

198

Date	Claim	Crew
5/6.6.44	VI 605 Sqn Me410 7m SE Evreux a/f	F/O R. E. Lelong RNZAF-P/O J. A. McLaren.
5/6.6.44	XIII 409 Sqn Ju88 (Prob) S Coast	F/O Pearce-F/O Moore.
5/6.6.44	II DD789 239 Sqn Ju88 off Frisians	F/O W. R. Breithaupt-F/O J. A. Kennedy. Ju88 G-1 W/Nr. 710454 of 5./NJG3, cr 20 kms N of Spiekeroog. Uffz. Willi Hammerschmitt (pilot), KIA; Uffz. Friedrich Becker (radar op) KIA; Fw. Johannes Kuhrt (AG) KIA.
5/6.6.44	II DZ256 'U' 239 Sqn Bf110 North of Aachen	F/E D. Welfare DFC*-F/O D. B. Bellis DFC*. Poss Bf110 W/Nr. 440272 G9+NS of 8./NJG1 shot down at great height, cr at 00.54 hrs on Northern beach of Schiermonnikoog. Uffz. Adolf Stuermer (pilot, KIA; Uffz. Ludwig Serwein (Radar Op MIA); Gefr. Otto Morath (AG, KIA).
6/7.6.44	XIII 29 Sqn Ju52/3m & UEA over Coulommiers	F/L Allison-F/O Stanton.
6/7.6.44	XVII HK286 'A' 456 Sqn He177 3m S Barfleur?	W/C K. M. Hampshire DSO DFC RAAF-F/L T. Condon.
6/7.6.44	VI 605 Sqn Ju88 Orleans-Bricy a/f	F/L E. L. Williams DFC*-F/O S. Hatsell.
6/7.6.44	VI HR155 'X' 418 Sqn Ju52/3m N Coulommiers a/f	F/L D. A. MacFadyen DFC RCAF-F/L Wright.
7/8.6.44	XVII HK319 219 Sqn Me410 10m E Harwich	F/O D. T. Hull.
7/8.6.44	XVII HK248 219 Sqn Ju88 15m ESE Harwich	W/C P L. Burke AFC*.
7/8.6.44	XVII HK290 'J' 456 Sqn 2 x He177 off Normandy coast	S/L B. Howard -F/O J. R. Ross.
7/8.6.44	XVII HK302 456 Sqn He177 off Normandy	P/O Hodgen.
7/8.6.44	XIII29 Sqn Ju188 + Ju88 S of Paris	F/L Barry-S/L Porter.
7/8.6.44	XIII 29 Sqn UEA Dreux	F/O F. E. Pringle-P/O W. Eaton.
7/8.63.44	XVII HK354 25 Sqn Me410 nr Happisburgh	F/L D. H. Greaves DFC-F/O T. M. Robbins DFC.
8/9.6.44	XIII MM500 604 Sqn Bf110 NE of Laval	F/L J. C. I. Hooper DFC-F/O Hubbard DFM.
8/9.6.44	II DD741 169 Sqn Do217 Paris area	W/C N. B. B. Bromley OBE-F/L P. V. Truscott. Poss Do217K-3 W/Nr. 4742 6N+OR of Stab III./KG100

Date	Type Serial Sqn Enemy A/c details	Pilot-Navigator/Radar Op
8/9.6.44	II DD303 'E' 141 Sqn UEA Rennes	claimed in Paris area but crash-place u/k. Oblt. Oskar Schmidtke (pilot); Uffz. Karl Schneider (Observer); Uffz. Helmuth Klinski (WOp); Uffz. Werner Konzett (Flt.Eng), all MIA.
8/9.6.44	XIII 29 Sqn Ju88	F/O A. C. Gallacher DFC-W/O G. McLean DFC.
8/9.6.44	XIII 29 Sqn Ju88	F/O Wigglesworth-Sgt Blomfield.
9/10.6.44	XII MK4G3 29 Sqn Ju88 8m S Beachhead	F/L R. C. Pargeter-F/L R. L. Fell.
9/10.6.44	XIII 29 Sqn Jul88	Lt Price .
9/10.6.44	XVII HK353 'M' 456 Sqn He177 off Cap Levy	S/L R. B. Cowper DFC RAAF-F/L W. Watson.
	Do217 off Cap de la Hague	S/L R. B. Cowper DFC RAAF-F/L W. Watson.
9/10.6.44	XIII MM460 409 Sqn Ju188 40m SE Le Havre	S/L R. S. Jephson-F/O C. D. Sibbett.
9/10.6.44	XIII 410 Sqn Jul88	F/O Snowden-Lt Wilde.
10/11.6.44	XIII 264 Sqn Ju88/Fwl90 *(Prob)*	F/L J. H. Corre.
10/11.6.44	XIII MM453 409 Sqn Ju188	F/O Fullerton-F/O Castellan.
10/11.6.44	XIII 409 Sqn 2 x Ju88	P/O Preece-F/O Beaumont.
10/11.6.44	XVII HK249 'B' 456 Sqn Hel77 *(Prob)* 40m S Brighton	S/L G. E. Howitt DFC-F/L G. Irving DFC.
10/11.6.44	XIII MM547 409 Sqn Fw190	F/Sgt S. H. J. Elliott-F/L R. A. Miller.
10/11.6.44	VI 605 Sqn Jul88 SE Coulommiers	F/O R. E. Lelong RNZAF-P/O J. A. McLaren.
10/11.6.44	XIII MM555 409 Sqn Ju188 Over France	F/O K. Livingstone.
10/11.6.44	XIII MM523 409 Sqn Do217E Over France	F/O A. W. Sterrenberg.
11/12.6.44	II DZ256 'U' 239 Sqn Bf110 North of Paris	F/L D. Welfare DFC*-F/O D. B. Bellis DFC*.
11/12.6.44	XIX MM642 'R' 85 Sqn Bf110 10m NE Melum a/f	W/C C. M. Miller DFC**-F/O R.O. Symon.
12/13.6.44	XIII HK512 264 Sqn Ju188 Over beaches	F/L M. M. Davison DFC-F/O AC. Willmott DFC.

200

Date	Aircraft / Squadron	Crew
12/13.6.44	XIII HK475 264 Sqn Ju188 Over beaches	F/L Beverley-F/O Sturley.
12/13.6.44	XVII HK286'A' 456 Sqn Ju88	W/C K. M. Hampshire DFC DSO RAAF-F/L T. Condon.
12/13.6.44	XIX MM630 '5' 157 Sqn Ju188 Foret De Compidgne	F/L J. G. Benson DFC-F/L L. Brandon DFC.
12/13.6.44	XIX 85 Sqn Bf110 Near Paris	F/L M. Phillips-F/L D. Smith.
12/13.6.44	XIII MM526 604 Sqn He177 15m NE Cherbourg	F/L R. A. Miller DFC-P/O P. Catchpole.
12/13.6.44	XIII MM500 604 Sqn Ju88	F/L J. C. I. Hooper DFC-F/O Hubbard DFM.
12/13.6.44	VI 605 Sqn Ju88 (Prob) Chievres airfield	F/L E. L. Williams DFC-F/O S. Hatsell.
12/13.6.44	XIII HK366 'o' 410 Sqn 2 x Do217 over Beachhead	W/O W. Price .
12/13.6.44	XIII HK459 'A' 410 Sqn He177 over Channel	P/O C. Kearney-F/O Bradford.
12/13.6.44	XIII HK466 'J' 410 Sqn Ju88 10m off Le Havre	F/O Snowden-F/O Wilde.
12/13.6.44	XIII MM476 'V' 488 Sqn Ju88 Caen-Bayeux	S/L E. N. Bunting DFC*-F/L C. P. Reed DFC*.
13/14.6.44	XIII HK5G2 264 Sqn He177 over Channel	S/L I. H. Cosby-F/L E. R. Murphy.
13/14.6.44	XIII MM56G 'F' 409 Sqn He177 10m E of Le Havre	W/C J. W. Reid-F/L J. W. Peacock.
13/14.6.44	II DZ254 'P' 169 Sqn Ju88 Near Paris	W/O L. W. Turner-F/Sgt F. Francis.
14/15.6.44	XVII HK282 456 Sqn He177 off Fecamp.	
14/15.6.44	XIII 410 Sqn Ju88	S/L March-F/L Eyolfson.
14/15.6.44	XIII 604 Sqn Fw190 (Prob) Carentan	F/O Wood-F/L Elliott.
14/15.6.44	XIII 604 Sqn He177	F/L F. C. Ellis.
14/15.6.44	VI 418 Sqn He111 5 end Sagnkop Isle	S/L R. A. Kipp DFC RCAF-F/L P. Huletsky RCAF.
14/15.6.44	XIII HK476 'D' 410 Sqn Ju88 (with glider bomb)	F/L Dinsdale-P/O Dunn (over Channel).
14/15.6.44	XVII HK356 'D' 456 Sqn Ju88 at Sea	S/L R. B. Cowper DFC RAAF-F/L W. Watson.
14/15.6.44	XIII HK5G2 264 Sqn Ju188 (with glider bomb)	F/L Corre-P/O C. A. Bines (off Normandy).
14/15.6.44	XIII MM513 'D' 488 Sqn Ju88 10m SW St Lô	F/O P. F. L. Hall-F/O R. D. Marriott.

Date	Type Serial Sqn Enemy A/c details	Pilot-Navigator/Radar Op
14/16.6.44	VI 418 Sqn Bf110 Avord airfield	S/L. R. Bannock RCAF-F/O R. R. Bruce.
14/15.6.44	II DZ240 'H' 141 Sqn Me410 North of Uille	W/O H. W. Welham-W/O E. J. Hollis.
14/15.6.44	XIX MM671 'C' 157 Sqn Ju88 Near Juvincourt	F/L J. Tweedale -F/O L. I. Cunningham.
14/15.6.44	XIX 'Y' 85 Sqn Ju188 SW Nivelles	F/L B. A. Burbridge DFC-F/L F. S. Skelton DFC. Ju188 flown by Major Wilhelm Herget, *Kommandeur I./NJG4*. By the end of the war 58 of the 73 victories Herget gained were at night.
14/15.6.44	XIX 'J' 85 Sqn Ju88 nr Creil	F/L H. B. Thomas-P/O C. B. Hamilton.
14/15.6.44	XVII HK315 219 Sqn Ju88 Harwich area	F/L M. J. Gloster DFC-F/L J. P. Oswold DFC.
15/16.6.44	XIX'C' 85 Sqn Bf110 St Trond a/f	S/L F. S. Gonsalves-F/L B. Duckett. Bf110 W/Nr. 5664 G9+IZ of 12./143G1, cr 9 kms. W of Tongres (between St. Trond and Maastricht). Uffz. Heinz Baerwolf (pilot, injured, baled out); Uffz. Fischer (WOP/Radar op) baled out. Ogfr. Edmund Kirsch (AG KIA).
15/16.6.44	XIX MM671 'C' 157 Sqn Ju88 Creil-Seauvais	F/L J. O. Mathews-W/O A. Penrose.
15/16.6.44	VI 605 Sqn Bf1100/Fw190 Le Culot	F/L E. L. Williams DFC-F/O S. Hatsell.
16/17.6.44	XIII 410 Sqn Ju88 SE of Valorges	F/O Girvan-Lt Cardwell.
16.6.44	XVII HK344 219 Sqn Me410	
16/17.6.44	XIII 29 Sqn UEA	F/O Crone.
16/17.6.44	XIII 264 Sqn Ju188 or La Haye de Pais	F/L M. M. Davison DFC- F/L A.C. Willmott DFC.
16/17.6.44	II W4076 169 Sqn Ju88 Pas de Calais	F/O W. H. Miller DFC-F/O F. Bone. Poss Ju88 W/Nr. 710590 of 1./NJG2 cr in Pas de Cancale/France. Hptm. Herbert Lorenz (pilot) KIA; Fw. Rudolf Scheuermann (radar op.) KIA; Flg. Harry Huth (AG) KIA.
16/17.6.44	XIII MM476 'V' 488 Sqn Fw190 St Lô	S/L E. N. Bunting DFC*-F/O C. P. Reed DFC*.

Date	Unit / Aircraft / Location	Crew / Notes
17/18.6.44	XIX 85 Sqn Bf110 Eindhoven	F/O P. S. Kendall DFC*-F/L C. R. Hill. Bf110 of NJG1 shot down at 02.30 hrs & cr at Soesterberg airfield. Müller & 2(?) others KIA.
17/18.6.44	II W4G92 239 Sqn Ju88 Near Eindhoven	F/O G. F. Poulton-F/O A. J. Neville. Ju88G-1 W/Nr 710866 R4+NS of 8./NJG2 which crashed at Volkel airfield. Lt. Harald Machleidt (pilot) Uffz. Kurt Marth (radar op) WIA, Gefr. Max Rinnerthaler (AG) KIA.
17/18.6.44	XIII HK466 'J' 410 Sqn Ju188 6m off Le Havre	F/L C. E. Edinger-F/O C. C. Vaessen.
17/18.6.44	XIII MM499 'C' 410 Sqn Ju188 nr Caen	S/L March-F/L Eyolfson.
17/18.6.44	XIII MM439 488 Sqn Fw190 Quinville area	F/O D. N. Robison RNZAF-F/O K. C. Keeping.
17/18.6.44	XIII MM558 'S' 488 Sqn Ju88 30m S Radox Mather	F/L P. F. L. Hall-F/O R. D. Marriott.
17/18.6.44	XVII HK250 219 Sqn Ju88 (Prob) 18m N Ostend	F/L G. R. I. Parker DSM-W/O D. L. Godfrey.
17/18.6.44	XIII 264 Sqn Ju88 Domtront-Argentan	F/L M. M. Davison DFC-F/L A. C. Willmott DFC.
17/18.6.44	XIII HK473 264 Sqn Fw190	F/L I. H. Cosby-F/L E. R. Murphy.
17/18.6.44	XIII 264 Sqn 2 x Ju188 Over Beachhead	F/O P. de L. Brooke-P/O J. Hutchinson.
17/18.6.44	XIII 264 Sqn Ju188	F/O J. C. Duffy-F/Sgt Newhouse.
17/18.6.44	XIII 29 Sqn Ju88	F/Sgt Johnson.
18/19.6.44	XIII HK470 'X' 410 Sqn Ju88 Over Beachhead	F/O Edwards-F/Sgt Georges.
18/19.6.44	XIII MM571 'Y' 410 Sqn Ju88 Vire area	1/Lt A. Harrington USAAF-Sgt D.G. Tongue.
18/19.6.44	XVII HK346 'D' 125 Sqn 2 x Ju88 Beachhead area	W/C J. G. Topham DFC*-F/O H. W. Berridge DFC.
19/20.6.44	XIII 264 Sqn Ju88 Over Channel	S/L F. J. A. Chase-F/O A. P. Watson.
20/21.6.44	XIII MM573 'B' 409 Sqn Ju188 (Prob)	F/L Taylor-W/O Mitchell.
20/21.6.44	XIII 488 Sqn Fw190 S. Falaise	P/O Vlotman-F/Sgt Wood.
20/21.6.44	XIII 29 Sqn Bf110 Coulanniers	F/L Price-S/L Armitage.
20/21.6.44	XIII 29 Sqn Ju188 (Prob) Bourges	F/Sgt Benyon-F/Sgt Pearcy.

Date	Type Serial Sqn Enemy A/c details	Pilot-Navigator/Radar Op
21/22.6.44	II DZ2950 239 Sqn He177 Ruhr	F/O R. Depper-F/O R. G. C. Follis.
21/22.6.44	XIII MM552 604 Sqn Ju88 (Prob) SSE Ventnor IoW	F/L P. V. G. Sandeman-F/O Coates.
21.6.44	VI PZ203 'X' 515 Sqn Bf110F	S/L P. W. Rabone DFC-F/O F. C. H. Johns. Bf110G W/Nr 440076G9+NS of 8./NJG1 which had just taken off from Eelde a/f shot down at 15.19 hrs. Uffz. Herbert Beyer, 21, (pilot), Uffz. Hans Petersmann, 21, (radar op), & Ogfr. Franz Riedel, 20, (AG), all KIA.
22/23.6.44	XIII 488 Sqn Ju188 E.Bayeux	P/O J. McCabe-W/O Riley.
22/23.6.44	XVII HK23 125 Sqn 3 x Ju88 at Sea	F/O W. J. Grey.
22/23.6.44	XVII HK262 125 Sqn 2 x Ju88 at Sea.	
22/23.6.44	XIII MM527 604 Sqn Ju88 NW Le Havre	F/O J. S. Smith-F/O Roberts.
22/23.6.44	XIII 264 Sqn Ju88 N Rouen	F/O J. C. Trigg-F/L Smith.
23/24.6.44	XVII HK257 25 Sqn Ju88 NW Orfordness	W/C C. M. Wight-Boycott DSO-F/O D.W. Reid.
	Ju188F1 Cr. Chillesford	W/C C. M. Wight-Boycott DSO-F/O D.W. Reid.
23/24.6.44	XIII MM554? 409 Sqn Ju188	F/O Vincent-F/L Thorpe.
23/24.6.44	XIII MM554? 409 Sqn Ju188	W/O Kirkwood-W/O Matheson.
23/24.6.44	XIX 'Y' 85 Sqn Ju88	F/L B. A. Burbridge DFC-F/L F. S. Skelton DFC.
23/24.6.44	XIII HK500 'T' 410 Sqn Ju88 15m NW Beachhead	W/O Jones-W/O Gregory.
23/24.6.44	XIII 264 Sqn 2 x Fw19011 (Prob)	S/L P. B. Elwell-F/O F. Ferguson.
24.6.44	XVII HK262 125 Sqn Ju88 Isle de St Marcouf.	
24.6.44	XVII HK310 125 Sqn Ju88 W of Le Havre.	
24/25.6.44	II DD759 'R' 239 Sqn Ju88 Paris-Amiens	F/L D. Welfare DFC*-F/O D. B. Bellis DFC*.
24/25.6.44	XIII MM466 488 Sqn Me410 20m SW Bayeux	F/L G. E. Jameson DFC RNZAF-F/O A. N. Crookes.
24/25.6.44	XVII HK355 125 Sqn Ju88 W St Marcouf	W/C E. G. Barwell DFC-F/L D. A. Haigh.

204

Date	Aircraft	Crew / Notes
25.6.44	XVII HK287 125 Sqn Ju88 E Le Havre area.	F/L Steele-F/O Storrs.
25/26.6.44	XIII MM518 409 Sqn Ju188/Do217	F/L C. M. Jasper-F/L O. A. J. Martin.
27.6.44	VI 418 Sqn Ju88 2m N Rostock	S/L G. J. Rice-F/O J. G. Rogerson.
27/28.6.44	II HJ911 'A' 141 Sqn Ju88 Cambrai	W/O H. Welham-W/O E. Hollis. Poss Ju88G-1 W/Nr 710455 of 4./NJG3, cr at Arendonk/Belgium. Uffz. Eügen Wilfert (pilot), KIA; Ogefr. Karl Martin (radar op.), KIA; Gefr. Rudolf Scherbaum (AG), KIA.
27/28.6.44	DZ240 'H' 141 Sqn Ju88 S of Tilburg	
27/28.6.44	II DD759 'R' 239 Sqn Me410 E of Paris	F/L D. Welfare DFC*-F/O D. B. Bellis DFC*.
27/28.6.44	II 239 Sqn Fw 190 Near Brussels	W/C P. M. J. Evans-F/O R.H. Perks DFC.
27/28.6.44	II DD749 239 Sqn Ju88 Near Brussels	F/L D. R. Howard-F/O F. A. W Clay.
27/28.6.44	VI PZ188 'J' 515 Sqn Ju88 Eindhoven	P/O C. W. Chown RCAF-F/Sgt D. G. N. Veitch. Ju88 W/Nr. 300651 B3+LT of 9./NJG54 during landing approach at Welschap (after a minelaying operation in the invasion area) at 02.13 hrs. The Ju88 crashed into a house, killing 3 children and Uffz. Gotthard Seehaber, pilot, Gefr. Kurt Voelker, Ogefr. Walter Oldenbruch & Ogefr. Hermann Patzel.
27/28.6.44	XIII 264 Sqn Ju188 Seine estuary	F/L Turner-F/O T. V. Arden.
28/29.6.44	XIII MM589 409 Sqn Ju188	W/O Kirkwood-W/O Matheson.
28/29.6.44	VI NT150 169 Sqn Bf110 nr Mucke	P/O H. Reed-F/O S. Watts.
28/29.6.44	XIII MM466 488 Sqn Ju88 10m NE Caen	F/L G. E. Jameson DFC RNZAF-F/O A. N. Crookes.
29/30.6.44	XIII 264 Sqn Ju188 Seine Bay	F/O R. Barbour-F/O G. Paine.
30.6.44	VI PZ203 'X' 515 Sqn He111 Jagel/Schleswig	S/L P. W. Rabone-F/O F. C. H. Johns.
30.6.44	VI PZ188 'J' 515 Sqn Ju34	P/O C. W. Chown RCAF-F/Sgt D. G. N. Veitch.
30.6/1.7.44	VI DZ265 239 Sqn Ju88 Le Havre	F/L C. J. Raby DFC-F/Sgt S. J. Flint DFC Probably Ju88

Date	Type Serial Sqn Enemy A/c details	Pilot-Navigator/Radar Op
2/3.7.44	XIII MM526 604 Sqn Ju188 15m W of Le Havre	W/Nr. 711114 of 5./NJG2. cr SE of Dieppe/France. Uffz Erich Pollmer WIA. Other crew details u/k.
2/3.7.44	XIII MM465 604 Sqn Ju88 10m N Ouistreham?	F/L R. A. Miller DFC-P/O P. Catchpole.
2/3.7.44	XIII 488 Sqn Ju188	W/C M. H. Constable-Maxwell DFC-F/L Quintin.
2/3.7.44	XIII MM517 604 Sqn Ju88 15m N of Le Havre	W/O T. G. C. Mackay.
3/4.7.44	XIII MM447 410 Sqn Ju188 NE Raz de la Pierce	S/L D. C. Furse-F/L Downes.
3/4.7.44	XIII MM570 'B' 410 Sqn Ju188/Me410	F/L C. E. Edinger RCAF-F/O C.C. Vaessen.
3/4.7.44	XIII HK479 264 Sqn Ju188	F/L S. B. Huppert-F/O J. S. Christie (a/c FTR).
4.7.44	XVII HK325 125 Sqn Do217 (Poss Ju188) Le Havre.	S/L I. H. Cosby-F/L E. R. Murphy.
4/5.7.44	XVII HK356 'D' 456 Sqn He177 30m S Selsey Bill	
4/5.7.44	XVII HK249 'B' 456 Sqn He177 N of Cherbourg.	S/L R. B. Cowper DFC RAAF-F/L Watson.
4/5.7.44	XVII HK282 456 Sqn He177 In Channel.	
4/5.7.44	XVII HK282 456 Sqn Do217 at Sea.	
4/5.7.44	II DZ298 239 Sqn Bf110 NW Paris	S/L N. E. Reeves DSO DFC-P/O A. A. O'Leary.
4/5.7.44	VI PZ163 'C' 515 Sqn Ju88 Near Coulommiers	W/O R. E. Preston-F/Sgt F. Verity.
4/5.7.44	II DD725 'G' 141 Sqn Me410 Near Orleans	F/L J. D. Peterkin-F/O R. Murphy.
4/5.7.44	II 169 Sqn Bf110 Villeneuve	F/L J.S. Fifield-F/O F. Staziker.
4/5.7.44	XIII 264 Sqn Ju88/Me410 Normandy	F/L C. M. Ramsay DFC-F/L D. J. Donnet DFC.
5.7.44	XVII HK312 'G' 456 Sqn He177 In Channel.	
5/6.7.44	XIII MM552 604 Sqn Me410 15m SW of Caen	W/O J. E. Moore-W/O J. A. Hogg.
5/6.7.44	VI NT121 169 Sqn Ju88 South of Paris	F/O P. G. Bailey-F/O J. O. Murphy. Ju88 W/Nr. 751065 R4+ of 5./NJG2, cr nr Chartres/France. Ofw. Fritz

Date	Claim / Aircraft	Crew
5/6.7.44	XIII 264 Sqn Ju88	Farrherr (pilot) KIA; Gefr. Josef Schmid (Radar op) WIA baled out; Ogefr. Heinz Boehme (AG) KIA.
7/8.7.44	XIII MM504 409 Sqn Ju88	F/O Trigg-F/L G. E. Smith.
7/8.744	II HJ911 'A' 141 Sqn Bf110 NW of Amiens	F/O Pearce-P/O Smith.
		S/L G. J. Rice-F/O J. G. Rogerson. Poss Bf110G-4 W/Nr. 730006 D5+ of 2./NJG3 cr 5 kms. W of Chievres/ Belgium. Pilot u/k, baled out; Gefr.Richard Reiff WIA, baled out; Ogefr. Edmund Hejduck KIA.
7/8.7.44	II DD789 239 Sqn Fw190 Pas de Calais	W/C P. M. J. Evans-F/L T. R. Carpenter.
7/8.7.44	II W4G97 239 Sqn 2 x Bf110 Paris	S/L J. S. Booth DFC*-F/O K. Dear DFC.
7/8.7.44	II DZ2958 239 Sqn Bf110 Near Charleroi	F/L V. Bridges DFC-F/Sgt D. G. Webb DFM.
7/8.7.44	XIII 410 Sqn Me410 nr Paris	S/L March-F/L Eyolfson.
7/8.7.44	XIII 410 Sqn Ju88	F/L S. B. Huppert-F/O J. S. Christie.
7/8.7.44	XIII 29 Sqn UEA	F/O Bennett-W/O Gordon.
8/9.7.44	XIII MM465 604 Sqn Ju88 10m W Le Havre	W/C M. H. Constable-Maxwell DFC
	Do217 (Prob) S Bank Seine.	
9/10.7.44	XIII 264 Sqn Ju88 25m NE Bayeux	S/L F. J. A. Chase-F/O A. F. Watson.
10.7.44	VI PZ188 'J' 515 Sqn Ju88 Zwishilnahner a/f	F/O R. A. Adams-P/O F. H. Ruffle) shared.
10.7.44	VI PZ420'O' 515 Sqn	F/O D. W. O. Wood-F/O Bruton) ".
10/11.7.44	XIII 264 Sqn Do217 (Prob)	S/L Elwell-F/O Ferguson.
11/12.7.44	XVII 219 Sqn Ju88 20m ENE Rouen	F/O D. T. Tull.
11/12.7.44	XVII HK248 219 Sqn Ju88	W/C P. L. Burke AFC.
12/13.7.44	XIII HK4S1 264 Sqn Ju88 Seine Estuary	F/O R. Barbour-F/O G. Paine.
12/13.7.44	XIX TA401 'D' 157 Sqn Ju88 SE Etampes	F/L J. O. Mathews-W/O A. Penrose.
14.7.44	VI RS993 '1' 515 Sqn Ju34 Stralsund, NE Cer.	F/L A. E. Callard-F/Sgt E. D. Townsley.

Date	Type Serial Sqn Enemy A/c details	Pilot-Navigator/Radar Op
14/15.7.44	XIX 157 Sqn Bf110 20m NE Juvincourt	Lt Sandiford RNVR-Lt Thompson RNVR.
14/15.7.44	VI NT112 'M' 169 Sqn Bf109 Auderbelck	W/O L W. Turner-F/Sgt F. Francis.
14/15.7.44	XVII HK248 219 Sqn Ju188 SW Caen	W/C P. L. Burke AFC.
17/18.7.44	VI 605 Sqn UEA Schwabish Hall	W/C N. J. Starr DFC-P/O J. Irvine.
17/18.7.44	VI 418 Sqn UEA Altenburg a/f	S/L R. Bannock RCAF-F/O R. R. Bruce.
17/18.7.44	XIII 604 Sqn Ju88	F/L G. A. Hayhurst-W/O Gosling.
18/19.7.44	XIII MM512 409 Sqn Do217	F/O McPhail-P/O Smith.
18/19.7.44	XIII MM589 409 Sqn Ju88	W/O Kirkwood-W/O Matheson.
18/19.7.44	XIII 29 Sqn UEA	W/O A. Cresswell.
19.7.44	XXX 219 Sqn Ju188 Over Beachhead.	
20/21.7.44	VI NT113 169 Sqn Bf110G-4 near Courtrai	W/C N. B. R. Bromley OBE-F/L R Truscott DFC. Bf110G-4 Wrk Nr 730218 G9+EZ of 12./NJG1 cr near Moll, Belgium. Ofw. Karl-Heinz Scherfling (25) pilot, a *Ritterkreuztraeger* since 8 April 1944 & who had 33 night victories (k) Fw. Herbert Winkler, the 31 year old air gunner. (k)Fw. Herbert Scholz (25, radar op, baled out seriously injured.
20/21.7.44	VI NT146 169 Sqn Ju88 Homburg area	P/O H. Reed-F/O S. Watts.
20/21.7.44	VI NTl21 169 Sqn Bf110 Courtrai	F/L J. S. Fifield-F/O F. Staziker.
21.7.44	XXX MM731 406 Sqn 2 x Do217	W/C D. J. Williams DFC RCAF.
23/24.7.44	II HJ710 'T' 141 Sqn Ju88 SW of Beauvais	P/O I. D. Gregory-P/O D. H. Stephens. Poss Bf110G-4 W/Nr. 730117 G9+GR of 7./NJG1, shot down by Mosquito NE' at 01.25 hrs., cr 5 kms. N of Deelen a/f.: Lt. Josef Hettlich (pilot); Fw. Johann Treiber (WOp/Radar Op.) both slightly injured & baled out. AG also baled out. Or, Bfl0 W/Nr. 441083 G9+OR of

Date	Aircraft	Details
		III./NJG1 or 7./NJG1, shot down by Mosquito NF' at 01.47 hrs during landing at Leeuwarden a/f, cr at Rijperkerk N of Leeuwarden. Hptm. Siegfried Jandrey (30, pilot KIA); Uffz. Johann Stahl (25, Radar op) (k); Uffz. Anton Herger (24, AG) injured.
23/24.7.44	VI NS997 'G' 169 Sqn Bf110G-4 near Kiel	F/L R. J. Dix-F/O A. J. Salmon. Bf110G-4 W/Nr 730036 G9+ER of 7./NJG1 was shot down at very low level around midnight. The 110 cr near Balk in Friesland Province, Holland. Fw. Heinrich-Karl Lahmann (25, pilot), Uffz. Günther Bouda (21 AG) both baled out. Uffz. Willi Huxsohl (21, radar op) (k).
23/24.7.44	II DZ661 239 Sqn Bf110 Kiel	F/O N. Veale-F/O R. D. Comyn. At 01.25 hours Bf110G-4 730117 G9+GR of 7./NJG1 was shot down N of Deelen airfield. Lt. Josef Hettlich, pilot, Fw. Johann Treiber, radar operator and the air gunner all baled out safely.
23/24.7.44	XIII 29 Sqn Bf110 nr Leeuwarden a/f	F/L A. C. Musgrove-F/O G. Egerton-Hine. 441083 G9+OR of 7./NJG1, which was shot down at 01.47 hours during landing at Leeuwarden airfield and which crashed at Rijperkerk, just to the N of the base. Hptm. Siegfried Jandrey, 30, pilot, and Uffz. Johann Stahl, 25, radar operator, were killed. Uffz. Anton Herger, 24, air gunner, was injured.
24/25.7.44	XIII MM504 409 Sqn Ju88	W/O MacDonald-F/Sgt King.
25/26.7.44	XIII MM587 409 Sqn Ju88	W/C Reid-F/L Peacock.
25/26.7.44	VI RS961 'H' 515 Me410 Knocke, Belgium	S/L H. B. Martin DSO DFC-F/O J. W. Smith.
25/26.7.44	VI PZ178 239 Sqn UEA Laon Pouvron	F/L D. J. Griffiths-F/Sgt S. F. Smith.
25/26.7.44	XVII 219 Sqn Ju88 50 ENE La Havre	F/O D. T. Tull.

Date	Type Serial Sqn Enemy A/c details	Pilot-Navigator/Radar Op
26/27.7.44	XIII HK462 409 Sqn Ju88 Over Caen	S/L Jephson-F/O Roberts (Mos FTR).
26/27.7.44	XIII 29 Sqn Ju188 Melun	F/O F. E. Pringle-F/O Eaton.
26/27.7.44	XIII 604 Sqn Ju88 Granville	F/O J. C. Truscott-F/O Howarth.
28/29.7.44	XIII MM500 604 Sqn Ju88 Lisieux-Bernay	F/L J. P. Meadows-F/O McIlvenny.
28/29.7.44	XIII MM526 604 Sqn Ju88 3m E Bretal	F/L R. A. Miller DFC-P/O P. Catchpole.
28/29.7.44	XIII MM513 'D' 488 Sqn 2 x Ju88 10m NW Vire	F/L R. F. L Hall-F/O R. D.Marriott.
28/29.7.44	XIII MM439 488 Sqn Ju188 10-15m N Mayenne	F/O D. N.Robinson RNZAF-F/L W. T. M.Clarke DFM.
28/29.7.44	II HJ713 'R' 141 2 xJu88 Metz/Neufchateau	F/L H. E. White DFC*-F/L M. S. Allen DFC*.
28/29.7.44	II HJ741 'Y' 141 Sqn Ju88 Metz area	P/O I. D. Gregory-P/O D. H. Stephens. Ju88G-1 W/Nr. 713649 R4+KT of 9./NJG2, possibly shot down by Mosquito of 141 Sqn (White & Allen or Gregory/Stephens), cr 20 kms SSW of Toul, France. Hptm. August Speckmann (pilot), KIA; Ofw. Arthur Boos (radar op) WIA; Ofw. Wilhelm Berg (Flt Eng) KIA; Uffz. Otto Brueggenkamp (AG) KIA.
28/29.7.44	XIII 410 Sqn Ju88 Beachhead	F/L W. A. Dexter-Lt Richardson.
29/30.7.44	XIII MM466 488 Sqn 3 x Ju88 5-6m S Caen	F/L G. E. Jameson DFC RNZAF-F/O A. N. Crookes DFC.
	Do217 5-6m S Lisseaux	
29/30.7.44	XIII 264 Sqn Ju188 (or 88) 15m SE St Lô	S/L F. J. A. Chase-F/O A. F. Watson.
29/30.7.44	XIII MM621 604 Sqn Ju88 30m S of Cherbourg	F/L Miller.
30/31.7.44	XIII MM589 409 Sqn Ju88	W/O Kirkwood.
30/31.7.44	XIII MM501 410 Sqn Ju88	P/O Mackenzie-P/O C. F. A. Bodard.
30/31.7.44	XIII 29 Sqn Ju88 nr Paris	F/O Pringle.
30/31.7.44	XIII 604 Sqn Ju88 SE of Caen	S/L. B. Maitland-Thompson-W/O Pash.

Date	Aircraft / Squadron / Location	Crew
31.7.44	XXX 219 Sqn Ju88	F/O J. Maday-F/O J. R. Walsh.
31.7/1.8.44	XIII 410 Sqn Ju88	F/L P F. L. Hall-F/O R. D. Marriott.
1/2.8.44	XIII MM498 488 Sqn Ju88 10m E of St Lo	S/L J. D. Somerville-F/O G. D. Robinson.
1/2.8.44	.44 XIII MM477 'U' 410 Sqn RCAF Ju188 NE Tessy	F/L F.C. Ellis-F/O P.C. Williams.
1/2.8.44	XIII 604 Sqn Ju188 SE Caen	F/L A. S. Browne-W/O T. F. Taylor.
2/3.8.44	XIII HK532 488 Sqn Do217-4m S of Avranches	W/O T. G. C. Mackay-F/Sgt A. A. Thompson.
2/3.8.44	XIII MM439 488 Sqn Ju188-8m S of Avranches	S/L J. D. Somerville-F/O G. D. Robinson.
2/3.8.44	XIII MM477 'U' 410 Sqn RCAF Do217 6m NW Pontorson	S/L F. J. A. Chase-F/O A. F. Watson.
2/3.8.44	XIII 264 Sqn Ju188 (or 88) 10m W Argentan	F/L B. E. Plumer-F/O V. W. Evans.
2/3.8.44	XIII 410 Sqn Ju188	F/L P. G. K. Williamson DFC RAAF-F/O F. E. Forrest.
3/4.8.44	XXX 219 Sqn 2 xJu188 Seine Estuary	F/L G. E. Jameson DFC RNZAF-F/O A. N. Crookes DFC (Claim 2nd Ju88).
3/4.8.44	XIII MM466 488 Sqn Ju88 8m N St Lo	
3/4.8.44	XIII HK504 488 Sqn Ju88 ENE of Vire.	
3/4.8.44	XIII MM513 488 Sqn Do217 NW of Barnes.	W/O G. S. Patrick-F/Sgt J. J. Concannon.
3/4.8.44	XIII MM502 488 Sqn Do217 W of Angers.	F/L R. J. Foster DFC-F/L M. F. Newton DFC.
3/4.8.44	XIII HK420 488 Sqn Ju88 W Avranches	S/L I. H. Cosby DFC-F/L E. R. Murphy.
3/4.8.44	XIII MM552 604 Sqn Do217 5m S of Granville	F/L Beverley-F/O P. C. Sturling (Mos FTR crew baled out).
3/4.8.44	XIII 'S' 264 Sqn Ju88	
3/4.8.44	XIII 264 Ju88	
3/4.8.44	XIII 604 Sqn Do217 S Granville	F/L R. J. Foster DFC-F/O M. F. Newton.
3/4.8.44	XIII MM554? 409 Sqn Ju188	F/L. E. Spiller-F/O Donaghue.
3/4.8.44	XIII MM508? 'K' 409 Sqn Ju188	W/O MacDonald-W/O Colborne.
3/4.8.44	XIII 410 Sqn Bf110	F/L W. G. Dinsdale-P/O J.E. Dunn.

Date	Type Serial Sqn Enemy A/c details	Pilot-Navigator/Radar Op
4/5.8.44	XIII MM512 409 Sqn Ju188	W/O Joss–W/O Lailey.
4/5.8.44	XIII 409 Sqn Ju88 (*Prob*)	P/O Haley.
4/5.844	XIII MM514 'B' 604 Sqn Ju188 & Ju88 nr Barnes	F/L J. A. M. Haddon–F/O R. J. McIlvenny.
4/5.8.44	XIII MM449 410 Sqn HS 126*	F/L W. G. Dinsdale–P/O J. E. Dunn.
4/5.8.44	XIII MK403 29 Sqn Ju188 Orly airfield	F/L R. C. Pargeter–F/L R. L. Fell.
4/5.8.44	XIII HK504 'M' 488 Sqn Ju88 ENE Vire	W/C R. C. Haine DFC–F/L A. P. Bowman.
4/5.8.44	XIII 488 Sqn Ju188 NE St Lo	F/O A. L. Shaw–F/Sgt L. J. Wyman.
5/6.8.44	XII) MM513 'D' 488 Sqn Do217K-2 20m from Beacon	F/L P. F. L. Hall–F/O R. D. Marriott.
5/6.8.44	XIII 488 Sqn Do217K-2	F/Sgt T. A. Mackan.
5/6.8.44	XIII MM514 604 Sqn Ju188/Ju88 Rennes area	F/L J. A. M. Haddon–F/O R. J. McIlvenny.
6/7.8.44	XIII MM466 488 Sqn Ju88 15m S Avranches	F/L G. E. Jameson DFC RNZAF–F/O A. N. Crookes DFC.
6/7.8.44	XIII HK420 488 Sqn Jul88 SW Avranches	F/L A. E. Browne–W/O T. F. Taylor (+2 UEA flew into ground trying to evade) One of these poss. Hptm. Helmut Bergmann of 8/NJG4 MIA Invasion area.
6/7.8.44	XIII MM500 604 Sqn Ju188	F/O R. M. T. MacDonald–F/Sgt C.G. Baird.
6/7.8.44	XIII MM465 604 Sqn Ju88 S Avranches	W/C F. D. Hughes DFC**–F/L L. Dixon DFC*.
6/7.8.44	XIII MM449 'B' 604 Sqn 2 x Do217 & Bf110	F/L J. C. Surman–P/O C. E. Weston.
6/7.8.44	XXX 219 Sqn Ju188 Argentan area	F/L P. G. K. Williamson DFC RAAF–F/O F. E. Forrest.
6/7.8.44	XIII MM566 'R' 410 Sqn RCAF Ju88 St Hilaire	S/L J. D. Somerville–F/O G. D. Robinson.
6/7.8.44	XIII 410 Sqn Ju88	F/L R. M. Currie–F/O A. N. Rose.(Hptm. Helmut

* Following an investigation it was confirmed that this aircraft was, in fact, Lysander V9748 of 161 Squadron. The pilot, F/O J. P. Alcock, and his passenger were both killed.

Bergmann, St.Kapt 8./NJG4 (36 night victories, Knight's Cross 9.6.44, MIA 6/.8.44 in Bf110G-4 W/Nr 140320 3C+CS from sortie to Invasion Front area Avranches-Mortain, poss shot down by Mosquito NF).

Date	Aircraft / Location	Crew
7/8.8.44	XIII MM555 409 Sqn Ju188	W/O Henke-F/Sgt Emmerson.
7/8.8.44	XIII MM429 604 Sqn 2 x Do217 nr Rennes	F/O J. S. Smith-F/O L. Roberts.
7/8.8.44	XIII HK525 604 Sqn Ju188 S of Nantes	F/O R. M. T. MacDonald-F/L S. H. J. Elliott.
7/8.8.44	XIII MM517 604 Sqn Ju188 E of Falaise	F/L J. R. Cross-W/O H. Smith.
	Ju88 nr Conde	F/L J. R. Cross-W/O H. Smith.
7/8.8.44	XIII HK524 29 Sqn Bf110 Melun, W Orly	F/O W. W. Provan-W/O Nicol.
7/8.8.44	XXX 219 Sqn 2 x Ju188 W Vire	F/L M. J. Gloster DFC-F/L J. F. Oswold DFC.
7/8.8.44	XIII 264 Sqn Ju88	F/L Davidson-F/O Willmott.
8/9.8.44	XIII MM528 'H' 604 Sqn Do217	F/O T. R. Wood-F/O R. Leafe.
8/9.8.44	XXX 219 Sqn 2 x Ju188.	
8/9.8.44	II DZ256 'U' 239 Sqn Fw190 St Quentin	F/L D. Welfare DFC*-F/O .B. Bellis DFC*.
8/9.8.44	II 239 Sqn Bf109 N France	F/L D. J. Raby DFC-F/Sgt S. J. Flint DFM.
8/9.8.44	VI NT156 'Y' 169 Sqn Fw190 E Abbeville	F/L R. G. Woodman-F/L P. Kemmis.
9/10.8.44	XXX 219 Sqn Fw190 E Evereux	F/L M. J. Gloster DFC-F/L J. F. Oswold DFC.
10/11.8.44	XIII 264 Sqn Ju188 Caen	S/L F. J. A. Chase-F/O A. F. Watson.
10/11.8.44	XXX 219 Sqn Ju88 10m SW Le Havre	F/L G. R. I. Parker DSM-W/O D. L. Godfrey.
	Fw190 5m S Le Havre	F/L G. R. I. Parker DSM-W/O D. L. Godfrey.
10/11.8.44	XIII MM504 409 Sqn Fw190	S/L Hatch-F/O Eames.
10/11.8.44	XIII MM523 409 Sqn Do217	F/O Collins-F/O Lee.
10/11.8.44	VI NT176 'H' 169 Sqn Bf109 Over Dijon	F/O W. H. Miller DFC-F/O F. C. Bone.
10/11.8.44	XIII 264 Sqn Ju188	F/O Daker-F/Sgt J.A. Heathcote.

Date	Type Serial Sqn Enemy A/c details	Pilot-Navigator/Radar Op
10/11.8.44	XIII 410 Sqn Ju88	W/C G. A. Hiltz-F/O J. R. Walsh.
11/12.8.44	XXX 219 Sqn Ju88.	
11/12.8.44	XIII HK429 604 Sqn Do217 (Prob)	F/L R. A. Miller DFC-P/O P. Catchpole.
11/12.8.44	XIII MM619 409 Sqn Fw190	W/O Henke-F/Sgt Emmerson.
12/13.8.44	VI NT173 169 Sqn He219 nr Aachen	F/O W. H. Miller DFC-F/O F. C. Bone.
14/15.8.44	XIII MM477 'U' 410 Sqn Ju88 15m W Le Havre	S/L J. D. Somerville-F/O G. D. Robinson.
14/15.8.44	XIII MM491 409 Sqn Ju88	F/O Collins-F/O Lee.
14/15.8.44	XIII MM466 'B' 488 Sqn Ju88 20-30m S of Caen	F/L J. A. S. Hall DFC-F/O J. P. W. Cairns.
15/16.8.44	XXX 219 Sqn Ju88 15m W Le Havre	F/L G. R. I. Parker DSM-W/O D. L. Godfrey.
15/16.8.44	XIII HK377 488 Sqn Ju88 SE of Caen	P/O McCabe-W/O F. Newman.
16/17.8.44	XIII MM590 'H' 409 Sqn Ju188	W/O MacDonald-W/O Colborne.
16/17.8.44	XXX 219 Sqn Ju188 nr Caen	F/L M. J. Gloster DFC-F/L J. F. Oswold DFC.
16/17.8.44	VI HB213 'O' 141 Sqn Bf110 Ringkobing Fjord	W/O E. A. Lampkin-F/Sgt B. J. Wallnutt.
18/19.8.44	XIII MM560 'F' 409 Sqn Ju88/Ju188	S/L Hatch-F/O Eames.
18/19.8.44	XIII MM622 488 Sqn Do217	F/O M. G. Jeffs-F/O Crookes.
19/20.8.44	XIII MM589 409 Sqn Do217	S/L R. Hatton-F/L Rivers.
19/20.8.44	XXX MM744 410 Sqn 2 x Ju88	F/O J. Fullerton-F/O B.E. Gallagher.
20/21.8.44	XIII MM439 488 Sqn Ju188 15m S of Caen	F/L D. N. Robinson RNZAF-W/O W. N. Addison DFC DFM.
26/27.8.44	VI NT146 'T' 169 Sqn Ju88 near Bremen	W/O L. W. Turner-F/Sgt F. Francis. Ju88G-1 W/Nr. 710542 D5+BR of 7./NJG. cr nr Mulsum 42 kms E of Bremen. Lt. Achim Woeste (pilot), KIA; Uffz. Heinz Thippe, WIA, baled out; Gefr. Karl Walkenberger, WIA, baled out; Uffz. Anton Albrecht KIA.

Date	Unit / Aircraft	Crew
27.8.44.44	XIII HK304 25 Sqn Bf109 Northern France.	F/O R. E. Lelong RNZAF-P/O J. A. McLaren.
28/29.8.44	VI 605 Sqn UEA Chievres airfield	F/L D. L. Hughes-F/L R. H. Perks.
29/30.8.44	II W4097 239 Sqn Ju88 near Stettin	F/L I. E. Maclavish-F/O A. M. Grant.
1/2.9.44	XIII 410 Sqn Fw190	W/C R. C. Haine DFC-F/L A. P Bowman.
1/2.9.44	XIII MM566 'A' 488 Sqn Ju188 10-15m W La Havre	W/C F. F. Lambert-F/O R. J. Lake AFC.
6/7.9.44	VI PZ338 'A' 515 Sqn Bf109 Odder, Denmark	S/L B. A. Burbridge DFC-F/L F. S. Skelton DFC.
11/12.9.44	XIX 'Y' 85 Sqn Ju188 Baltic Sea	F/L P. A. Bates-P/O W. G. Cadman.
11/12.9.44	VI HR180 'B' 141 Sqn Bf110 SW of Mannheim	S/L J. G. Benson DFC-F/L L. Brandon DFC.
11/12.9.44	XIX MM630 'E' 157 Sqn 2 x Ju188 Zeeland	F/L P. S. Kendall DFC*-F/L C R. Hill DFC*.
11/12.9.44	XIX 'A' 85 Sqn Bf109G Limburg area	F/O D. T. Hull-F/O P Gowgill.
11/12.9.44	XVII FIU Ju88 10m S Bonn	F/L R. D. Doleman-F/L D.C. Bunch DFC.
12/13.9.44	XIX MM643 'F' 157 Sqn Bf110 Frankfurt	F/O W. R. Breithaupt DFC-F/O J.A. Kennedy DFC.
12/13.9.44	II 239 Sqn Bf110 Ranschhack	F/L W. W. Provan.
12/13.9.44	XIII HK469 29 Sqn Bf110 SE Frankfurt	S/L R. Bannock RCAF-F/O R. R. Bruce.
12/13.9.44	VI 418 Sqn UEA Kitzingen	F/L L Stephenson DFC-F/L G. A. Hall DFC.
12/13.9.44	XXX 219 Sqn Ju88 Dutch border	F/L W. House-F/Sgt R.D. McKinnon. Bf110G-4 W/Nr.440384 G9+EN of 5./NJG1 *which took off* from Dusseldorf A/F at 22.34 hrs cr. at Birresborn in the Eiffel at 23.35 hrs. Oblt. Gottfried Hanneck, pilot, bailed out WIA., Uffz. Thdch Sacher (radar op) KIA; Uffz. Willi Wurschitz (radar op/AG) KIA.
13/14.9.44	XIX 'D' 85 Sqn Bf110 nr Koblenz	
16/17.9.44	XXX MM743 410 Sqn UEA	F/L C. E. Edinger RCAF-F/O CC. Vaessen.
16/17.9.44	XIII FIU UEA Ardorf a/f	F/O E. R. Hedgecoe DFC-F/O N.L. Bamford.
17/18.9.44	XIX 'J' 85 Sqn 2 x Bf110	F/O A. J. Owen-F/O J. S. V. McAllister DFM. Bf110 G-4 W/Nr. 740358 G9+MY of 11./NJG1 cr E of

Date	Type Serial Sqn Enemy A/c details	Pilot-Navigator/Radar Op
23/24.9.44		Arnhem/Holland. Uffz.. Walter Sjuts KIA; Uffz. Herbert Schmidt KIA; Uffz. Ernst Fischer KIA. Bfl10G-4 W/Nr. 740757 G9+GZ of 12./NJG1 cr E of Arnhem/Holland. Uffz. Heinz Gesse KIA; Uffz. Josef Kaschub KIA; Ogefr. Josef Limberg, KIA.
23/24.9.44	XVII FIU Bf110 10m SE Munster	F/O D. T. Tull-F/O P.J. Cowgill DFC.
23/24.9.44	XXX 219 Sqn Bf110 7-10m NE Cologne	S/L W. P Green DFC-F/L D. Oxby DFM*.
24/25.9.44	XIII MM462 'T' 604 Sqn He 219 55m S Nijmegen	F/L R. J. Foster DFC-F/L M.F. Newton DFC. He 219 (I/NJG1?).
25/26.9.44	XIII MM589 409 Sqn He111H22 Over N Sea	W/O Fitchett-F/Sgt Hardy.
25/26.9.44	XVII 125 Sqn He111H22 Over N Sea	F/O Beadle.
26/27.9.44	VI PZ301 'N' 515 Sqn He111 Zellhausen a/f	S/L H. F. Morley-F/Sgt R. A. Fidler.
26/27.9.44	XXX MM743 410 Sqn Ju87 12m N Aachen	1/Lt A. A. Harrington USAAF-P/O D. G. Tongue.
26/27.9.44	XVII HK257 25 Sqn Ju188 40m S Harwich	W/C C. M. Wight-Boycott DSO-F/L D. W. Reid.
27/28.9.44	VI 418 Sqn 2 x Bf108 Barrow airfield/sea	S/L R. Bannock RCAF-F/O R. R. Bruce.
27/28.9.44	XIX 'J' 85 Sqn Ju188 (Prob) SW Kaiserlautern	F/O A. J. Owen-F/O J. S. V. McAllister DFM.
28/29.9.44	XXX 219 Sqn Ju87 over Low Countries	F/L G. R. I. Parker DSM-W/O D. L. Godfrey.
28/29.9.44	XIX 'Y' 85 Sqn Ju188	F/L M. Phillips-F/L D. Smith.
28/29.9.44	XVII HK357 25 Sqn 2 x He111H22 over N Sea	W/C L. J. C. Mitchell-F/L D. L. Cox.
29/30.9.44	XIX 157 Sqn Me410 (Prob) 10m ESE Yarmouth	F/L Vincent-F/O Monoy.
2/3.10.44	VI 605 Sqn Bv138 Jasmunder Bay	F/O R. E. Lelong RNZAF-P/O J.A. McLaren.
2/3.10.44	XXX 219 3 x Ju87 E Nijmegen	S/L W. P Green DFC-F/L D.Oxby DFM**.
5/6.10.44	XVII HK239 25 Sqn He111H-22 over N Sea.	
5/6.10.44	XIII 409 Bf110	S/L S. J. Fulton-F/O AR. Ayton.

Date	Aircraft / Location	Crew
5/6.10.44	XXX MM760 410 Sqn Ju88 16m NE Namur	F/L C. S. Edinger RCAF-F/O C. C. Vaessen.
6/7.10.44	XIII MM560 409 Sqn Bf110 over Peer, Belgium	F/O R. H. Finlayson-F/O J. A. Webster. Bf110 G9+MN of 5./NJG1. Fw. Robert Kock, who was on his 70th operation baled out and was slightly inj. Uffz. Heinz Forster, bordfunker, and Uffz. Ernst Darg, gunner, were both KIA.
6/7.10.44	XIII 409 Sqn Ju88	P/O F. S. Haley-P/O S. J. Fairweather (baled out).
6/7.10.44	XVII HK317 'Y' 456 Sqn Jul88 20m NW of Nijmegen.	F/L G. R. I. Parker DSM-W/O D. L Godfrey.
6/7.10.44	XXX 219 Sqn Bf110 N Arnhem	F/L J. C. E. Atkins-F/O D. R. Mayo.
6/7.10.44	XXX 219 Sqn Ju87	
6/7.10.44	VI NT234 'W' 141 Sqn Ju88 S of Leeuwarden	F/L A. C. Gallacher DFC-P/O D. McLean DFC. Ju88G-1 W/Nr. 710639 D5+EV of 10./NJG3 cr nr Groningen. Oblt. Walter Briegleb (pilot) WIA; Fw. Paul Kowalewski (radar op) KIA; Uffz. Brandt (Flt. Eng) WIA; Uffz. Bräunlich (AG) WIA.
6/7.10.44	XVII HK257 25 Sqn He111H-22 40m S Southwold	F/L A. E. Marshall DFC DFM.
6/7.10.44	XIII 410 Sqn Bf110	F/L Plumer-F/L Hargrove.
7/8.10.44	XIII 410 Sqn Ju188	F/O Fullerton-F/O Gallagher.
7/8.10.44	XIX MM671 'C' 157 Sqn Bf110 W of Neumunster	F/L J. O. Mathews-W/O A. Penrose.
8.10.44	VI PZ181 'E' 515 Sqn Bf109 Eggebek, Denmark	F/L F. T. L'Amie-F/O J. W. Smith.
11.10.44	II DZ256 239 Sqn Seaplane Tristed	
14.10.44	XVII HK245 125 Sqn He 219 nr Duisburg.	F/L D. Welfare DFC*-F/O D. B. Bellis DFC.
14/15.10.44	XIX 'Y' 85 Sqn 2 x Ju88G Gütersloh a/f	S/L B. A. Burbridge DFC*-F/L F. S. Skelton DFC*.
14/15.10.44	VI PZ245 239 Sqn Fw190 Meland	F/L D. R. Howard-F/O F. A. W. Clay.
14/15.10.44	XIX FIU Ju88G W. Kassel	F/O D. T. Tull-F/O P. J.Cowgill DFC.
15/16.10.44	XIX 'D' 85 Sqn Bf110	F/L C. K. Nowell-W/O Randall.

Date	Type Serial Sqn Enemy A/c details	Pilot-Navigator/Radar Op
19/20.10.44	XXX NT250 'Y' 141 Sqn Ju88 SE of Karlsruhe	F/L G. D. Bates-F/O D.W. Field. Poss Ju88G-1 W/Nr. 712312 2Z+EB of I./NJG6, which cr at Vaihirgen/Marksdorf ENE of Pforzheim/Germany. Oblt. Wilhelm Engel (pilot) WIA; radar op safe.
19/20.10.44	VI PZ175 'H' 141 Sqn Ju88 NW of Nuremburg	F/O J. C. Barton-F/Sgt R. A. Kinnear.
19/20.10.44	XIX TA404 'M' 157 Sqn Ju88 nr Mannheim	S/L R. D. Doleman-F/L D. C. Bunch DFC. Poss Ju88G-1 W/Nr. 714510 2Z+CM of 4./NJG6, which cr at Murrhardt, SE of Heilbronn/Germany. Uffz. Georg Haberer (pilot) KIA; Uffz. Ernst Dressel (radar op) KIA.
19/20.10.44	XIX 'Y' 85 Sqn Ju188 Metz	S/L B. A. Burbridge DFC*-F/L F. S. Skelton DFC*.
19/20.10.44	VI PZ275 239 Sqn Bf110 Strasbourg	W/O P. C. Falconer-F/Sgt W. C. Armour.
22/23.10.44	XXX MM792 219 Sqn Ju88 Verviers area	S/L W. P. Green DFC-F/L D.Oxby.
25.10.44	XVII HK310 125 Sqn He111 Over N Sea.	
28/29.10.44	II PZ245 239 Sqn He111 Dummer Lake	F/L D. R. Howard-F/O F. A. W. Clay.
29/30.10.44	XXX MM767 410 Sqn Fw190 nr St Antonis	I/Lt A. A. Harrington USAAF-F/O D. G. Tongue.
29.10.44	VI PZ344 'E' 515 Sqn Fw190+JuW34	F/L P. T. L'Amie-F/O J. W. Smith.
2910.44	VI PZ217 'K' 515 Sqn Bf110	P/O T. A. Groves-F/Sgt R.B. Dockeray.
30/31.10.44	XVII HK240 125 Sqn He111H22 Over N Sea	S/L L. W. G. Gill-F/L D. A. Haigh. He111H22 of 4./KG53. Fw. Warwas & crew KIA.
1/2.11.44	XIX 'R' 85 Sqn Ju88 20m S Mülhouse	F/O A. J. Owen-F/O J. S. V. McAllister.
2/3.11.44	XIII HK469 29 Sqn Bf110 Handorf a/f	F/O W. W. Provan.
4/5.11.44	XXX MM802 151 Sqn Ju87	P/O Oddie-F/L Gibbs.
4/5.11.44	XXX MM820 488 Sqn Bf110	W/O J. W. Marshall-F/O P. P. Prestcott.
4/5.11.44	XIX TA401 'D' 157 Sqn Bf110 Osnabruck	W/C K. H. P. Beauchamp-P/O Monoy.
4/5.11.44	II 239 Sqn Bf110 Bochum	F/O J. N. W. Young-F/O R. H. Siddons.

4/5.11.44	XIX TA401 'D' 85 Sqn Bf110 Bochum	S/L R. G. Woodman-F/O A. F. Witt.
4/5.11.44	XIX 'Y' 85 Sqn Ju88G 30m S Bonn	S/L B. A. Burbridge DSO DFC*-F/O P. S.Skelton DSO. DFC*.
	Ju88 5m SE Bonn	
	Bf110 N of Hangelar	Bf110 of II./NJG1 which crashed into the River Rhine nr Hangelar airfield at 21.50 hrs. Oblt. Ernst Runze, pilot, (k). Ogefr. Karl-Heinz Bendfield, radar operator, and air gunner bailed out.
	Ju88 N of Hangelar	
4/5.11.44	XIX 'B' 85 Sqn Ju88 S E Bielefeld	F/O A. J. Owen-F/O J. S. V. McAllister DFM. 4/5.11.44. B110 of II./NFG1, shot down by Mosquito NF at 19.00 hrs at 20,000 ft. Uffz. Gustav Sario (pilot) injured & baled out; Uffz. Heinrich Conrads (radar op) KIA; Ogefr. Roman Talarowski (AG) KIA. B110G-4 W/Nr. 440648 G9+PS of 8./NJG1 possibly shot down by Mosquito NF, cr at Bersenbrueck, 30 kms N. of Osnabrück / Germany. Fw. Willi Ruge (pilot) WIA, baled out; Uffz. Helmut Kreibohm (Radar op) KIA; Ogefr. Anton Weiss (AG) KIA. B110 W/Nr. 730272 G9+E2 of IV./NJG1 shot down by Mosquito NF SW of Wezel/Germany. Lt. Heinz Rolland (26, pilot, 15 night victories); Fw. Heinz Krüger (25, WOp/Radar Op); Uffz. Karl Berger (22, AG) all KIA.
5/6.11.44	XIX TA389 68 Sqn He111H22 Over N Sea	F/Sgt Neal-F/Sgt Eastwood.
6/7.11.44	XIX 'N' 85 Sqn Ju188	S/L F. S. Gonsalves-F/L B. Duckett.
6/7.11.44	XXX 'Y' 85 Sqn Bf110 S Bonn a/f	F/O B. R. Keele DFC-F/O H. Wright.
6/7.11.44	XIX 'A' 85 Sqn Ju88 (prob)	Capt T. Weisteen RNWAF.
6/7.11.44	XIX TA391 'N' 157 Sqn Ju188 (prob) Osn/Minden	F/O H. P. Kelway-Sgt Bell.
6/7.11.44	XIX TA404 'M' 157 Sqn Bf110 S of Koblenz	S/L R. D. Doleman-F/L D. C. Bunch DFC.

219

Date	Type Serial Sqn Enemy A/c details	Pilot-Navigator/Radar Op
6/7.11.44	II DD789 239 Sqn Ju188 Osnabruck	F/O G. E. Jameson-F/O L. Ambery.
6/7.11.44	XXX MM726 151 Sqn Ju188	F/O Turner-F/O Partridge. 6/7.11.44. Ju88G-6 W.Nr. 620396 R4+KR of *Stab/IV./NJG3*, shot down by Mosquito and cr at Marienburg/Germany. Hptm. Ernst Schneider (pilot) KIA; Ofw. Mittwoch (radar op) baled out; Uffz. Kaase (AG) baled out. Ju88G-6 W/Nr. 620583 R4+TS of 11./NJG3, shot down by a Mosquito NF and cr SW of Paderborn/Germany. Oblt. Josef Förster (pilot), safe; Fw. Werner Moraing (radar op) WIA; Fw. Heinz Wickardt (AG) WIA.
9/10.11.44	VI 605 Sqn 2 x Ju87	F/O R. H. Smart-P/O P. O. Wood.
9/10.11.44	VI He111	F/O Lomas-F/O Fleet.
10/11.11.44	XVII 125 Sqn He111H22 *(Prob)* Over N Sea	F/O G. F. Simcock-F/O N. E. Hoijne.
10/11.11.44	XVII 68 Sqn He111H22 Over N Sea	F/Sgt A. Brooking-P/O Finn.
10/11.11.44	XIX TA402 'F' 157 Sqn Ju88 Frankfurt-Coblenz	S/L J. G. Benson DFC*-F/L L. Brandon DFC.
10/11.11.44	XXX PZ247 169 Sqn Ju188 NE Germany	S/L R.G. Woodman-F/O A. F. Witt.
10/11.11.44	XXX MT492 25 He111H22 70m S Lowestoft	F/O D. H. Greaves DFC-F/O T. M. Robbins DFC.
11/12.11.44	XIX MM671157 Sqn Ju88 *(Prob)* Bonn	F/O J. O. Mathews DFC-W/O A. Penrose. Ju88 W/Nr. 712268 of 1./NJG4, cr nr Giessen/Germany. Pilot and radar op both u/k, baled out. Gefr. Alfred Graefer (AG) KIA.
11/12.11.44	XIX 'B' 85 Sqn Fw190 30m SE Hamburg	F/O A. J. Owen-F/O J. S. V. McAllister DFM.
18/19.11.44	XXX MM813 219 Sqn Ju87	F/O Atkinson-F/O. Mayo.
19.11.44	XVII 456 Sqn He111H22 Over N Sea	F/O D. W. Arnold-P/O J. B. Stickley.
21/22.11.44	XIX 'N' 85 Sqn Bf110 Near Würzburg	S/L B. A. Burbridge DSO DFC*-F/L F. S. Skelton DSO DFC*.

Date	Aircraft / Engagement	Crew / Details
	& Ju88 Over Bonn	1/Lt A. A. Harrington USAAF-F/O D. G. Tongue
25/26.11.44	XXX MM767 410 Sqn 3 x Ju88G Muntz, (Jacberath & N of Hunxe).	
25/26.11.44	XIII HK425 'D' 409 Sqn Ju52 Rheindahlen	F/O R. I. E. Britten RCAF-F/L L. E. Fownes.
25.11.44	XVII HK2980 'J' 456 Sqn He111H22 75m S Lowestoft	F/O F. S. Stevens-W/O W. A. H. Kellett.
29/30.11.44	XIII MM622 409 Sqn 2 x Ju88	W/O S. F. Cole-F/O W. S. Martin.
30.11.44	VI HR242 169 Sqn He177 Liegnitz	W/C H. G. Kelsey DFC*-F/O E. M. Smith DFC DFM.
30/1.11.44	XIX 85 Sqn Ju88	S/L F. S. Gonsalves-F/L B. Duckett.
30/1.11.44	XIX 157 Sqn Ju188 5030N 0920E	F/O R. J. V. Smythe-F/O Waters.
30/1.11.44	XIII 410 Sqn Ju88	F/O Mackenzie-F/O C. F. A. Bodard.
?.11.44	FIU He111H22	S/L W. H. Maguire DFC-F/L W. D. Jones DFC.
2/3.12.44	XIX 'A' 85 Sqn Bf110	Capt T. Weisteen RNWAF Bf110G-4 W/Nr. 180382 of 12./NJG4 took off Bonninghardt at 20.47 hrs, cr at 21.45 hrs nr Lippborg (near Hamm/Germany). Lt. Heinz-Joachim Schlage (pilot) safe. Fiebig KIA & Uffz. Kundmüller KIA.
2/3.12.44	XIX 157 Sqn Ju88 Osnabruck	F/L W. Taylor-F/O Edwards. Poss Ju88 W/Nr. 714819 3C+WL of 3./NJG4, which cr at Rheine. Ofhr. Erhard Pfisterhammer (pilot) WIA; Uffz. Wolfgang Sode (radar op) WIA; AG u/k probably safe.
4.12.44	XXX MM790 219 Sqn Bf110 nr Krefeld	F/O L. Stephenson DFC-F/L G. A. Hall DFC.
4/5.12.44	XXX 'O' 85 Sqn Ju88 (Prob) Detmold a/f	F/O E. R. Hedgecoe DFC-F/O N.E. Bamford.
4/5.12.44	XIX MM671 'C' 157 Sqn Ju88 Dortmund a/f	F/L J. O. Mathews DFC-W/O A. Penrose DFC.
4/5.12.44	XIX 157 Sqn Bf110 Limburg	F/L W. Taylor-F/O Edwards.
4/5.12.44	XXX 'C' 85 Sqn 2 x Bf110 Germesheim	F/L R. T Goucher-F/L C. H. Bulloch.
4/5.12.44	XXX 'B' 85 Sqn Bf110 50m ENE Heilbronn	Capt S. Heglund DFC-F/O R.O. Symon.

Date	Type Serial Sqn Enemy A/c details	Pilot-Navigator/Radar Op
4/5.12.44	XXX 'H' 85 Sqn Ju88 nr Krefeld	F/O A. J. Owen-F/O J. S. V. McAllister DFM. Prob Ju88G-1 W/Nr. 714152 of 6./NJG4 (85 Squadron's 100th victory), which cr nr Krefeld/Germany. Uffz. Wilhelm Schlutter (pilot) WIA; Uffz. Friedrich Heerwagen (radar op) KIA; Gefr. Friedrich Herbeck (AG) KIA.
6/7.12.44	XXX 'O' 85 Sqn Bf110 West of Munster	F/O E. R. Hedgecoe DFC-F/Sgt J. R. Whitham. Poss Bf110G-4 W/Nr. 140078 G9+HZ of 12./NJG1, shot down by Mosquito & cr 10 kms NW of Münster-Handorf/Germany. Hptm. Hans-Heinz Augenstein Knight's Cross 9.6.44 (St.Kpt 12./NJG1, 46 night victories, of which 45 were four-engined RAF bombers) KIA; Fw. Günther Steins (radar op) KIA; Uffz. Kurt Schmidt (AG) WIA, baled out.
6/7.12.44	XIX MM671 'C' 157 Sqn Bf110 Near Limburg Ju88 15m SW Giessen	F/L J. O. Mathews DFC-W/O A. Penrose DFC.
6/7.12.44	XIX TA404 'M' 157 Sqn Bf110 Giessen	S/L R. D. Doleman DFC-F/L D. C. Bunch DFC.
6/7.12.44	XIX MM638 'G' BSDU Bf110 W of Giessen	S/L N. E. Reeves DSO DFC*-F/O Phillips.
12/13.12.44	XIX 'A'? 85 Sqn Ju88	Capt E. P. Fossum-F/O S. A. Hider.
12/13.12.44	XXX 'O' 85 Sqn 2 x Bf110 20m S Hagen/Essen	F/L E. R. Hedgecoe DFC- F/Sgt J. R. Whitham (with FIU).
12/13.12.44	XXX 'Z' 85 Sqn Ju88 Gütersloh a/f Bf110 2m W of Essen.	S/L B. A. Burbridge DSO DFC**-F/L F. S. Skelton DSO DFC**. Ju88G-1 W/Nr. 714530 of 6./NJG4, cr. at Gütersloh airfield. Uffz. Heinrich Brune, pilot, Uffz. Emil Hoftharth, radar op & Uffz. Wolfgang Rautert (AG) all KIA.
17/18.12.44	XIX MM627 'H' 157 Sqn Bf110 5112N 0635E	W/O D. A. Taylor-F/Sgt Radford.

Date	Aircraft / Squadron	Crew / Notes
17/18.12.44	XIX MM653 'L' 157 Sqn Bf110	F/Sgt J. Leigh.
17/18.12.44	XXX 'J' 85 Sqn Bf110 40m from Ülm	F/L R. T. Goucher-F/L C. H. Bullock.
18/19.12.44	XIII MM569 409 Sqn Bf110	P/O Haley-W/O McNaughton.
18/19.12.44	XIII HK415 409 Sqn Ju88	F/O Finlayson-F/O Webster.
18/19.12.44	XIII MM456 'M' 409 Sqn Ju88 Kaiserworth area	W/C J. O. Somerville DFC-F/O G. D. Robinson DFC.
18/19.12.44	XIX MM640 'T' 157 Sqn He 219 Osnabruck area	F/L W. Taylor-F/O J. N. Edwards. Poss He219A-0 W/Nr 190229 G9+GH of I./NJG1. Uffz. Scheuerlein (pilot) baled out, Uffz. Günther Heinze (radar op) KIA. Taylor and Edwards were killed on 22-23 December trying to land at Swannington.
18/19.12.44	XXX MV527 410 Sqn Ju88 S Bonninghardt	F/O G. E. Edinger RGAF-F/O C. C. Vaessen.
18/19.12.44	XXX MV549 85 Sqn Bf110	F/O D. T. Hull (KIA)-F/O P. J. Cowgill DFC (KIA) accidentally rammed Bf110 G9+CC of Stab IV/NJG1, flown by Hptm. Adolf Breves, Fw. Telsnig (radar op) Uffz. Ofers (AG) as the latter was landing at Dusseldorf a/f at 22.30 hrs. Breves managed to land safely but Hull & Cowgill were killed in the crash of their Mosquito.
21/22.12.44	XIX TA401 'D' 157 Sqn Ju88 N of Frankfurt	W/C K. H. P.Beauchamp DSO DFC-F/L Scholefield.
22/23.12.44	XXX MM792 219 Sqn Ju88	W/C W. P. Green DSO DFC-F/O D. Oxby DFM*.
22/23.12.44	XXX 'B' 85 Sqn 2 x Ju88+Bf110 Saarbrücken area	F/O A. J. Owen-F/O J. S. V. McAllister DFM. Ju88 W/Nr. 621441 2Z+HK of 2./NJG6 cr at Larxistuhl/Germany. Ofw. Max Hausser (pilot) KIA; Ofw. Fritz Steube (radar op) KIA; Fw. Ernst Beisswenger (AG) WIA. Ju88G-6 W/Nr. 621436 2Z+DC of II./NJG6 cr at Lebach, N of Saarbrucken/Germany. Uffz. Werner Karau, aircrew function unknown, KIA; 2 others safe?
22/23.12.44	XXX 'P' 85 Sqn Bf110 Koblenz-Gütersloh	S/L B. Burbridge DSO*DFC*-F/O F. S. Skelton DSO*DFC*.

Date	Type Serial Sqn Enemy A/c details	Pilot-Navigator/Radar Op
22/23.12.44	XIX TA404 'M' 157 Sqn Ju88 5m W Limburg Ju88 (prob)	S/L R. D. Doleman DFC-F/L D.C. Bunch DFC. S/L R. D. Doleman DFC-F/L D.C. Bunch DFC.
23/24.12.44	XXX MM702? 219 Sqn Ju88	F/O W. B. Allison-W/O Mills.
23/24.12.44	XXX NT297? 219 Sqn Ju88	F/O R. L. Young-F/O N. C. Fazan.
23/24.12.44	XXX MM706 219 Sqn Ju88 S Huy	S/L W. P. Green DSO DFC-F/L D. Oxby.
23/24.12.44	XXX NT263 488 Sqn Ju188	W/C R. G. Watts-F/O I. C. Skudder.
23/24.12.44	XXX MM822 488 Sqn Ju88/188 10m W Maeseyck	F/L K. W. Stewart-F/O H. E. Brumby.
23/24.12.44	XXX MT570 'P' 488 Sqn Me410 US Sector	F/L J. A. S. Hall DFC-F/O J. P. W. Cairns DFC.
23/24.12.44	XVII HK247 125 Sqn He111H22 Over N Sea	F/L R. W. Leggett-F/O E. J. Midlane. He111H22 of 7./KG53 Legion Kondor Cr. Holland. Four crew KIA. 1 gunner survived.
23/24.12.44	XVII 68 Sqn He111H-22 Over N Sea	F/Sgt Bullus-F/O Edwards.
23/24.12.44	XIII MM461 409 Sqn Ju188	F/L McPhail-F/O Donaghue.
23/24.12.44	XXX 157 Sqn Ju88 Near Koblenz	F/L R. J. V. Smythe-F/O Waters.
23/24.12.44	XIX 'N' 85 Sqn Bf110 Mannheim-Mainz	F/L G. C. Chapman-F/L J. Stockley.
23/24.12.44	XIII 410 Sqn 2 xJu88	F/O Mackenzie-F/O C. F. A.Bodard.
24/25.12.44	XIII MM462 'T' 604 Sqn He 219.	
24/25.12.44	XXX MM698 219 Sqn Ju188 12m S Eindhoven Ju188 34m E Arnhem	F/L G. R. I. Parker DFC DSM-W/O D. L Godfrey DFC DFM.
24/25.12.44	XXX MM790 219 Sqn Bf110 near Hasselsweiler	F/L L. Stephenson DFC-F/L G. A. Hall DFC.
24/25.12.44	XXX 410 Sqn Ju87	S/L Maclavish-F/O Grant.
24/25.12.44	XXX MV527 410 Sqn Ju87 Wassemberg area	F/L C. E. Edinger DFC RCAF-F/O .C. Vaessen DFC.
24/25.12.44	XXX 410 Sqn Ju88	F/O J. A. Watt-F/L Collis.

Date	Aircraft / Unit	Crew / Details
24/25.12.44	XIX MM671 'C' 157 Sqn Ju88G 3m SW Cologne	F/L J. O. Mathews-W/O A. Penrose.
24/25.12.44	XIX TA404 'M' 157 Sqn 2 x Bf110 Cologne/Duisburg	S/L R. D. Doleman DFC-F/L D. C. Bunch DFC. Bf110G-4 G9+CT W/Nr 740162 of 9./NJG1 flown by Hptm. Heinz Strüning, *Ritterkreuz mit Eichenlab* (Knight's Cross with Oak Leaves) and 56 night victories in *NJG1* & *NJG2* cr at Bergisch Gladbach *Bordfunker* and *Bordschütze* bailed out safely. Strüning hit the tail of his Bf110 and was killed. 2nd Bf110 was G9+GR of 7./NJG1 which crashed nr. Soppenrade at 19.22 hrs. Pilot and Bordfunker survived. Gfr. Wilhelm Ruffleth inj.
24/25.12.44	XXX MM693 406 Sqn Ju88 nr Paderborn	W/C R. Bannock DFC* RCAF-F/L R. R. Bruce DFC.
24/25.12.44	XIX MM676 'W' 157 Sqn Bf110 5038N 0752E	S/L J. G. Benson DFC*-F/L L. Brandon DFC*.
24/25.12.44	XXX 'A' 85 Sqn Bf110 20m N Frankfurt	Capt S. Heglund DFC-F/O B. C. Symon.
25/26.12.44	XXX MM706 219 Sqn Bf110	F/L E. A. Campbell-W/O G. Lawrence.
26/27.12.44	XXX MM792 219 Sqn Ju87 S Huy	S/L W. P. Green DSO DFC-F/L D. Oxby DFM**.
26/27.12.44	XXX 488 Sqn Ju188 (Prob)	F/L H. D. C. Webbe-F/O I. Watson DFC.
27/28.12.44	XXX 410 Sqn Ju88	F/L Dinsdale-F/O Dunn.
27/28.12.44	XIII MM466 G' 409 Sqn 2 x Ju88G Kaltenkirchen	F/O R. I. E. Britten RCAF-F/L L. E. Fownes.
30/31.12.44	XIII MM560 'F' 409 Sqn Ju88G	S/L Hatton-F/O Rivers.
31.12.44	XIX TA389 68 Sqn He111 Over N Sea.	
31.12/1.1.45	XIII MM569 'J' 604 Sqn 2 x Ju87.	
31.12/1.1.45	VI RS518 'L' 515 Sqn Ju88 Lovns Bredning	S/L C. V. Bennett DFC-F/L R. A. Smith. Ju88 of 4./NJG2. Oblt. August Gyory (k). Enemy spun in and dropped into Lim Fijord.
31.12/1.1.45	XIX MT491 'E' 169 Sqn He219 Cologne area	F/L A. P. Mellows-F/L S. L. Drew (att 85 Sqn) He219A-2 W/Nr. 290194 G9+KL of 3./NJG1, cr at Schleiden, 50

Date	Type Serial Sqn Enemy A/c details	Pilot-Navigator/Radar Op
31.12/1.1.45	XIX 'R' 169 Sqn He219	kms SW of Cologne. Oblt. Heinz Oloff (pilot) WIA, baled out; Fw. Helmut Fischer (radar op) WIA, baled out.
31.12/1.1.45	VI RS507 'C' 239 Sqn Ju88 Alhorn area	F/L L. F. Endersby (att 85 Sqn).
31.12/1.1.45	XXX 410 Sqn Ju188 nr Antwerp	S/L J. Tweedale-F/O L. I. Cunningham.
31.12/1.1.45	XXX 410 Sqn Ju880	S/L Currie-F/L Rose.
31.12/1.1.45	XXX 219 Sqn 2 x Ju188	F/L Dexter-F/O Tongue.
1/2.1.45	XXX MM790 219 Sqn Bf110	S/L J. P. Meadows-F/L H. M. Friend.
1/2.1.45	XIII HK529 604 Sqn He219 Munchen Gladbach	F/L F. T. Reynolds-F/O F. A. van den Heuvel.
1/2.1.45	XIII HK526 'U' 604 Sqn 3 x Ju88	S/L D. C. Furse-F/L J. H. Downes.
1/2.1.45	XXX 'R' 85 Sqn Ju188 10m N of Münster	F/L R. J. Foster DFC-F/L M. F. Newton DFC.
	Ju88G 10m E of Dortmund	F/L R. T. Goucher-F/L C. H. Bulloch. 2nd enemy was Ju88G-6. W/Nr 621364 2Z+CP of 5./NJG6 which cr. at Dortmund killing Oblt. Hans Steffen, pilot, Uffz. Josef Knon, Uffz. Helmut Uttler and Uffz. Frierich Krebber.
1/2.1.45	XXX 85 Sqn Ju88	F/O L. J. York.
2/3.1.45	XXX 'N' 169 Sqn Ju188 nr Frankfurt	F/L R. G. Woodman-F/O Simpkins (85 Sqn).
2/3.1.45	XIX TA393 'C' 157 Sqn Ju88 3m W Stuttgart	F/L J. O. Mathews DFC-W/O A. Penrose DFC.
2/3.1.45	XXX 'X' 85 Sqn Ju88 15m SW Ludwigshafen	S/L B. A. Burbridge DSO DFC* F/L F. S. Skelton DSO DFC*.
4.1.45	XIII MM563 604 Sqn Ju88 W Hostmar	F/O P. W. Nicholas-F/O W.M.G. Irvine.
5/6.1.45	XXX 'B' 85 Sqn Bf110 25m N Münster	Capt S. Heglund DFC-F/O R.O. Symon.
5/6.1.45	XIX TA394 'A' 157 Sqn He 219 S Hanover	S/L J. G. Benson DFC*-F/L L. Brandon DFC*. He219A-0 W/Nr. 190188 G9-CK of 2./NJG1 cr 5 kms S

226

Date	Aircraft / Claim	Crew
		of Wesendorf/Germany. Ofw. Josef Stroelein (pilot) KIA; Uffz.. Kenne (radar op) baled out safely.
5/6.1.45	VI RS881 'C' 515 Sqn Ju88 Jagel a/f	F/L A. S. Briggs-F/O Rodwell. Poss Ju88 W/Nr. 620513 R4+CD of *III./NJG2* which cr in Denmark (at Jagel airfield?) Oblt. Bruno Heilig (pilot) KIA; Uffz. Günther Kulas (radar op) KIA; Gefr. Johann Goliasch (Flt. Eng) KIA; Ogefr. Horst Jauernig (AG) KIA.
5/6.1.45	XXX NT283 'Y' 406 Sqn He111 Josum a/f	W/C R. Bannock DFC* RCAF-F/L R. R. Bruce DFC.
6.1.45	XVII HK296 68 Sqn He111H22 Over N Sea	W/O A. Brooking-P/O Finn (FTR).
6.1.45	XXX 488 Sqn Bf110 Holland	F/L F. A. Campbell-W/O G. H. Lawrence.
7.1.45	XXX MM792 219 Sqn 2 x Ju87.	W/C P. O. Hughes DFC*-F/O Dixon.
13/14.1.45	XIII MM459 604 Sqn Ju188 Rotterdam area	F/L K. D. Vaughan-F/L R. D. McKinnon.
14/15.1.45	XXX 'Y' 85 Sqn Ju188 Frankfurt	F/L B. Brearley-F/O J. Sheldon.
14/15.1.45	VI HR294 'T' 141 Sqn UEA Juterborg	F/L T. Smith-F/O Cockayne.
16/17.1.45	VI RS507 'C' 239 Sqn Bf109 Fassberg	F/L K. D. Vaughan-F/Sgt R. D. McKinnon. Poss Ju88G-1 W/Nr. 710818 D5+EP of *Stab/NJG3* which cr 3 kms SE of Friedberg (N of Frankfurt). Ofw. Johann Fels (pilot) KIA; Uffz. Richard Zimmer (radar op) KIA; Gefr. Werner Hecht (AG) KIA.
16/17.1.45	XXX 'Y' 85 Sqn He219 Ruhr	F/L D. H. Young-F/O J. J. Sanderson.
16/17.1.45	VI HR200 'E' 141 Sqn Bf110 Magdeburg	F/O R. C. Brady-F/L M. K. Webster.
16/17.1.45	VI HR213 'G' 141 Sqn Bf110 SW Magdeburg	F/L A. Mackinnon-F/O Waddell.
16/17.1.45	XIX TA446 'Q' 157 Sqn Ju188 Fritzler	F/L P. G. K. Williamson DFC RAAF-F/O F. E. Forrest.
17/18.1.45	XXX MM696 219 Sqn Ju88 10m E Aachen	F/L G. R. I. Parker DFC DSM-W/O D. L. Godfrey DFC DFM.
22/23.1.45	XXX MM703 219 Sqn 2 x Ju87	P/O M. G. Kent-P/O Simpson.
23/24.1.45	XIII MM466 'G' 409 Sqn Ju88 Over Scheldt	

Date	Type Serial Sqn Enemy A/c details	Pilot-Navigator/Radar Op
23/24.1.45	XIII MM456 'M' 409 Sqn Ju188E-1 3m W Dienst	W/C J. D. Somerville DFC-P/O A.C. Hardy (Ju188E-1 A3+QD W/N 260452 of Kommando Olga crewed by FF (pilot) Ogfr. Heinz Hauck, Observer Gfr. Kurt Wuttge, Uffz. Max Grossman (BF) & Fw. Heinrich Hoppe (dispatcher) shot down after dropping 2 Leute (trusted people) in Holland. All crew POW.
26.1.45	VI FIU Bf109	F/L E. L. Williams .
26.1.45	VI FIU Bf109	F/L P. S. Crompton.
1/2.2.45	XIX 157 Sqn Bf110 (Prob) Oberlom	S/L RyalI-P/O Mulroy.
1/2.2.45	XXX NT309 'C' 239 Sqn Bf110 Mannheim	W/C W. F. Gibb DSO DFC-F/O R. C. Kendall DFC. BfllOG-4 W/Nr.730262 G9+CN of 5./NJG1, probably shot down by Mosquito of 157 or 239 Sqn, belly-landed 2km W of Kettershausen. Oblt. Gottfried Hanneck (pilot) WIA.; Fw. Pean (radio/radar op), baled out safely; Uffz. Gloeckner (AG) baled out safely.
1/2.2.45	XXX NT252 169 Sqn Bf110 Stuttgart	F/L A. P. Mellows DFC-F/L S. L. Drew DFC. Prob Bf110 W/Nr. 730370 2Z+EL of 3./NJG6 which cr 25 kms S of Stuttgart. Oblt. Willy Rathmann (pilot) KIA; Fw. Erich Berndt (radar op) KIA; Uffz. Alfred Obry (AG) KIA.
1/2.2.45	XXX MM792 219 Sqn Ju88 2m SW Rheydt	W/C W. P Green DSO DFC-F/L D. Oxby DFC DFM*.
2/3.2.45	XXX MV548 'Z' 85 Sqn Ju88	W/C W. K. Davison.
2/3.2.45	VI RS575 'V' 515 Sqn Ju88 Vechta	W/C H. C. Kelsey-F/L E. M. Smith.
3/4.2.45	XXX 219 Sqn Ju88	P/O M. G. Kent-P/O Simpson.
3/4.2.45	XXX 410 Sqn He 219	F/L B. E. Plumer DFC-F/L Hargrave.
7/8.2.45	XXX NT330 239 Sqn Ju188 Ruhr	F/L A. J. Holderness-F/L W. Rowley DFC. Poss Ju88G-6

Date	Aircraft / Squadron	Details
7/8.2.45	XXX NT361 'N' 239 Sqn Bf110 Ruhr	W/Nr. u/k R4+UB of 9./*NJG5* which cr at Stirnberg/Detmold/Germany. Uffz. Richard Rückert (pilot) KIA; Uffz. Hans Meiller (radar op) KIA; Uffz. Herbert Hoffmann (AG) KIA.
		F/L D. A. D. Cather DFM-F/Sgt L. J. S. Spicer DFM. Bf110G-4 W/Nr. 730322 G9+HR of 7./*NJG1* cr W of Soest (Ruhr). Fw. Heinz Amsberg (pilot) KIA; Uffz. Matthias Dengs (radar op) KIA; Gefr. Karl Kopperberg (AG) WIA, baled out.
13/14.2.45	XIX MM684 'H' BSDU 2 x Bf110 Frankfurt area	F/L D. R. Howard DFC-F/L F. A. W. Clay DFC. Bf110 W/Nr. 480164 C9+ of 5./*NJG5* cr nr Bodenbach (Frankfurt area). Fw. Heinrich Schmidt (pilot) KIA; Uffz. Erich Wohlan (radar op) KIA; Uffz. Adam Zunker (AG) KIA.
14/15.2.45	XXX MV532 'S' 85 Sqn Ju88 Schwabish Hall a/f	F/L F. D. Win RNZAF-F/O T. P Ryan RNZAF.
20/21.2.45	XXX NT361 'N' 239 Sqn Fw190 Worms	W/C W. F. Gibb DSO DFC-F/O R. C. Kendall DFC.
21/22.2.45	XXX NT263 488 Sqn Ju88 Groenlo	F/L K. W. Stewart-F/O H. E. Brumby.
21/22.2.45	XXX NT325 'N' 406 Sqn Bf110 E Stormede a/f	F/L D. A. MacFadyen DFC RCAF.
24/25.2.45	XXX MM792 219 Sqn Ju87	W/C W. P. Green DSO DFC-F/O D. Oxby DFC DFM**.
24/25.2.45	VI 605 Sqn 2 x Fw190 Ludwigslust a/f	F/O R. E. Lelong DFC RNZAF-P/O J. A. McLaren DFC.
28.2.45	XXX NT325 'N' 406 Sqn UEA (*Prob*) Hailfingen	S/L D. A. MacFadyen DFC RCAF.
3/4.3.45	XXX NT368 68 Sqn Ju188 at Sea	F/L D. B. Wills.
3/4.3.45	XXX NT381 'J' Ju188 at sea	F/L R. B. Miles.
3/4.3.45	XXX NT415 125 Sqn Ju188 at Sea	W/C Griffiths.
5/6.3.45	XXX NT361 'N' 239 Sqn 2xJu88 Chemnitz/Nuremberg	W/C W. F. Gibb DSO DFC-F/O R. C. Kendall DFC. Ju88G-6 W/Nr. 622319 C9+GA of *Stab/NJG5* flown by

Date	Type Serial Sqn Enemy A/c details	Pilot-Navigator/Radar Op
		Obstlt Walter Borchers KIA (*Kommodore NJG5*, (59 victories -16 by day, 43 by night) Knight's Cross 29.10.44 KIA; Lt. Friedrich Reul (radar op) KIA (cr nr Altenburg 25 kms NW of Chemnitz in Thuringia). Ju88G-6 W/Nr. 622318 C9+NL of 3./NJG5 cr nr Chemnitz. Uffz. H. Dorminger (FF), Uffz. Max Bartsch (BF), Ogfr. Franz Wohlschlögel (BMF); Uffz. Friedrich Rullmann (BS) all MIA.
5/6.3.45	XXX NT325 'N' 406 Sqn Ju88G Gerolzhofen	F/L D. A. MacFadyen DFC RCAF.
7/8.3.45	VI 'S' 23 Sqn Fw190 Stendahl	F/O E. L. Heath-F/Sgt Thompson.
8/9.3.45	XXX MV555 85 Sqn Ju188	F/L I. A. Dobie-W/O A. R. Grimstone.
12/13.3.45	XXX 410 Sqn Ju88 (*Prob*) Dunkirk area	F/L J. W. Welford-F/O R. H. Phillips.
14/15.3.45	VI HR213 'G' 141 Sqn UEA Lachen, Germany	F/O (2/Lt) R. D. S Gregor-F/Sgt P. S. Baker.
14/15.3.45	XIX TA397 'R' 157 Sqn Ju88G Lutzkendorf	S/L R. D. Doleman DSO DFC-F/L D. C. Bunch DFC.
15/16.3.45	XXX NT309 85 Sqn Ju88 Hanover area	Capt E. P. Fossum-F/O S. A. Hider.
15/16.3.45	XIX TA393 'C' 157 Sqn Ju88 20m S Würzburg	F/L J. O. Mathews DFC-W/O A. Penrose DFC.
16/17.3.45	XXX NT330 239 Sqn Ju188 Nuremberg	S/L D. L Hughes DFC-F/L R. H. Perks DFC. Pilot Maj Werner Hoffmann?.
18/19.3.45	XXX NT364 'K' 157 Sqn Ju88 Hanau	W/O D. Taylor-F/Sgt Radtord.
18/19.3.4	XXX NT271 'M' 239 Sqn He219 Witten	W/C W. F. Gibb DSO DFC-F/O R. C. Kendall DFC. Prob He219 of NJG1 Hptm. Baake (pilot & *Kommandeur I./NJG1*) safe; Uffz. Bettaque (radar op) safe.
18/19.3.45	XXX MV548 'Z' 85 Sqn Bf110	F/L F. D. Win RNZAF-F/O T. P. Ryan RNZAF.
20/21.3.45	XXX NT450 125 Sqn Ju188 at Sea	F/L Kennedy .
20/21.3.45	XXX NT324 'T' 85 Sqn Bf110+He 219V-14	F/L G. C. Chapman-F/Sgt Stockley. Poss He 219V-14

Date	Aircraft	Crew
21/22.3.45	XIII MM466 'G' 604 Sqn Bf110 Dhunn area.	W/Nr. 190014 of 3./NJG1. Oblt. Heinz Oloff (pilot & St.Kpt 3./NJG1); radar op u/k.
21/22.3.45	XIII 409 Sqn Bf110	F/O R. I. E. Britten DFC RCAF-F/O L. E. Fownes DFC.
21/22.3.45	XXX 488 Sqn Bf110	F/O K. Fleming-F/O K. L. Nagle.
23/24.3.45	XXX 219 Sqn Fw 190	F/O Atkins-F/O Mayo.
24/25.3.45	VI 605 Sqn Ju88 Erfurt	F/L A. D. Wagner DFC-F/L E. T. Orringe.
24/25.3.45	XIII 604 Sqn Bf109 Haltern	F/L L. J. Leppard-F/L Houghton.
24/25.3.45	XXX 410 Sqn Bf110	F/L G. R. Leask-F/L J. W. Rolf.
24/25.3.45	XXX 410 Sqn Ju88G	S/L Maclavish-F/O Grant.
25/26.3.45	XIII MM513 'J' 409 Ju88 Dortmund area	F/O R. I. E. Britten DFC RCAF-F/O L. E. Fownes DFC.
25/26.3.45	XIII 264 Sqn Ju88 25m NNE Wesel	F/L C. M. Ramsay DFC-F/L D. J. Donnet DFC.
25/26.3.45	XIII 264 Sqn Ju88 (Prob)	F/O A. Recina-F/Sgt R. A. W. Smith.
25/26.3.45	XXX 219 Sqn 2 x Bf110	F/L Ruffley-F/O Fagan.
26/27.3.45	XIII MM497 604 Sqn Ju88	F/O T. R. Wood-F/O R. Leafe.
26/27.3.45	XXX NT263 488 Sqn Bf110 8m NW Bocholt	F/L K. W. Stewart-F/O H. E. Brumby.
26/27.3.45	XXX NT314 'P' 488 Sqn Ju88 20m N Emmerich	F/L J. A. S. Hall DFC-P/O Taylor (Mos Cr landed).
26/27.3.45	XXX 219 Sqn Ju188	F/O Reed-F/O Bricker.
26/27.3.45	XXX 410 Sqn Bf110	F/L B. E. Plumer DFC-F/L Bradford.
27/28.3.45	XXX 219 Sqn He177	F/O Reed-P/O Bricker.
30/31.3.45	45 XIII 264 Sqn Fw190 SE Münster	W/C E. S. Smith AFC-F/L P. C. O'Neil-Dunne.
3.4.45	XXX 239 Sqn Ju188	F/L D. L. Hughes-F/L R. H. Perks.
4/5.4.45	XXX NT540 'C' BSDU Bf109 W Magdeburg	S/L R. G. Woodman-F/L Neville .
4/5.4.45	XXX 'C' 85 Sqn Ju188 Nr Magdeburg	F/L C. W. Turner-F/Sgt G. Honeyman.

Date	Type Serial Sqn Enemy A/c details	Pilot-Navigator/Radar Op
7/8.4.45	XXX 'Q' 85 Sqn Fw 190NW Mobiis	W/C K. Davison DFC-F/L D. C. Bunch DFC (85/157 Sqns).
7/8.4.45	XXX NT263 488 Sqn UEA 20m SE Osnabrück	F/L K. W. Stewart-F/O H. E. Brumby.
8/9.4.45	XXX NT494 'N' 85 Sqn Ju88 20m W Lutzendort	F/L H. B. Thomas DFC-F/O C. B. Hamilton.
9/10.4.45	VI RS575 'V' 515 Sqn Ju188 SE Hamburg	W/C H C. Kelsey DFC*-F/L E. M. Smith DFC DFM.
9/10.4.45	XXX 219 Sqn He177 Ruhr	F/O Lang-F/O Fagan.
10/11.4.45	XXX 239 Sqn He111	W/C P. O. Falconer-F/Sgt W. G. Armour.
10/11.4.45	XXX MM744 410 Sqn Ju188 Damme area	F/L R. D. Schultz DFC-F/O J. S. Christie DFC.
11/12.4.45	XXX FIDS Ju88 20m NNW Berlin	F/L F. R. L. Mellersh DFC* (Dest 39-42 V-1s 20.6.44-23 Sqn.9.44 with 96 Sqn).
13/14.4.45	XXX N1334 'S' 85 Sqn He219 Kiel	F/L K. D. Vaughan-F/L R. D. McKinnon.
14/15.4.45	XXX 239 Sqn Ju88 Potsdam	S/L D. J. Raby DFC-F/O S. J. Flint DFM.
15/16.4.45	VI PZ398 515 Sqn Ju52/3M Nr Schleissheim	P/O L. G. Holland-F/Sgt R. Young.
17/18.4.45	XXX MV557 55 Ju88 Munich area	W/C K. Davison DFC.
19/20.4.45	XIX 276 'B' BSDU Ju88 S Denmark	F/L D. R. Howard DFC-F/L F. A. W. Clay DFC.
20/21.4.45	XIII MM521 264 Sqn Ju88 20m W Berlin	F/O P. N. Lee-F/O R. Thomas.
21/22.4.45	XIII 264 Sqn 2 x Ju290 20m W Berlin	F/O J. Daber-W/O J. A. Heathcote.
21/22.4.45	XIII 264 Sqn Ju188	W/O A. S. Davies-F/Sgt C. T. Fisher.
21/22.4.45	XXX 488 Sqn Ju52	P/O G. S. Patrick-W/O J. J. Concannon.
21/22.4.45	XXX MV527 410 Sqn 2 x Ju188 Ferrbellen area	F/L R. D. Schultz DFC-F/O J. S. Christie.
21/22.4.45	XIII 264 Sqn Ju88 (Prob) 35m NW Berlin	F/O C. M. Ramsay DFC-F/L D. J. Donnet DFC.
21/22.4.45	XIII 264 Sqn He111	F/O W. A. Craig-F/O A. L. Tauwhare.
21.4.45	VI 23 Sqn Jul88	W/O East-F/Sgt Eames.

22/23.4.45	XIII 264 Sqn Ju88G 20M W Berlin	F/L C. M. Ramsay DFC-F/L D. J. Donnet DFC.
23/24.4.45	XIII 264 Sqn He111 Between Elbe-Berlin	F/O W. H. Foster-F/O F. H. Dagger.
23/24.4.45	XXX NT512 488 Sqn Ju52.	
23/24.4.45	XXX NT327 488 Sqn Ju88.	
23/24.4.45	XIII HK506 'H' 409 Sqn 2 x Ju52	F/O J. H. Skelly-P/O P. J. Linn.
23/24.4.45	XIII HK429 'D' 409 Sqn 2 x Ju87/Fw 190	F/O E. E. Hermansen-F/L D. J. T. Hamm.
23/24.4.45	XIII MM588 'T' 409 Sqn Ju52	P/O J. Leslie-P/O C. M. Turgood.
23/24.4.45	XXX NV548 'Z' 406 Sqn Ju88 Witstock	W/C R. Bannock DFC* RCAF-F/L R. R. Bruce DFC.
24/25.4.45	XIII MM517 'S' 409 Sqn Ju29	W/C R. F. Hatton-F/L R. N. Rivers.
24/25.4.45	XIII 409 Sqn Ju52	P/O L. E. Fitchett-P/O A. C. Hardy (Mos cr. land/Basel).
24/25.4.45	VI 605 Sqn Ju88 Neuburg a/f	F/L A. D. Wagner DFC*-F/O E. T. "Pip" Orringe DFC.
24/25.4.45	XXX 488 Sqn Ju52	S/L F. W. Davison-F/L E. Hickmore.
24.4.45	XXX 29 Sqn Me262a	W/O Dallinson .
24/25.4	VI RS575 'V' 515 Sqn Do217 6m N Libeznice Do217 Prague, Czech	W/C H. C. Kelsey DFC*-F/L E. M. Smith DFC DFM. W/C H. C. Kelsey DFC*-F/L E. M. Smith DFC DFM.
25/26.4.45	XIII HK466 264 Sqn Fw190 W Berlin	P/O J. Hutton-P/O H. E. Burraston.
25/26.4.45	XXX NT527 488 Sqn Fw189	F/O J. W. Marshall-P/O P. F. Prescott.
2/3.5.45	VI 'K' 605 Sqn Fw190 Lecke, Denmark	F/O B. Williams DFC-W/O S. Hardy.

Appendix Two

MOSQUITO FIGHTER/FIGHTER-BOMBER SQUADRONS 5 JUNE 1944.

Squadron	Station	Model	Command
25	Coltishall	VI/XVII	ADGB.
96	West Mailing	XIII	ADGB.
125	Hurn	XVII	ADGB.
151	Predannack	XIII	ADGB.
307	Church Fenton	II/XII	ADGB.
4	Gatwick	XVI/Spitfire XI	2nd TAF.
21	Gravesend	VI	2nd TAF.
29	West Mailing	XIII	2nd TAF.
107	Lasham	VI	2nd TAF.
219	Bradwell Bay	XVII	2nd TAF.
264	Hartford bridge	XIII	2nd TAF.
305	Lasham	VI	2nd TAF.
605	Manston	VI	2nd TAF.
613	Lasham	VI	2nd TAF.
604	Hurn	XII/XIII	2nd TAF.
23	Little Snoring	VI	100 Group.
85	Swannington	XII	100 Group.
169	Gt Massingham	II	100 Group.
140	Northolt	II	100 Group.
141	West Raynham	II	100 Group.
157	Swannington	II/XIX	100 Group.
192	Foulsham	FB IV/Wellington X	100 Group.
239	West Raynham	II	100 Group.
515	Little Snoring	VI	100 Group.
1692 Flt	Gt Massingham	NF II	100 Group.

Index

239